The Financial "Fix"

Exposing:
The Regulator's Ponzi Protection Scheme
The Rigged Financial Industry
The Financial Predator Next Door

By David Levine

Table of Contents

Dedicated To:

My family: your love and support saved me. Kathy: I love you – always have, always will. Please re-read that. Allyson and Stephanie: you inspire me and make every day worth living. Live, laugh, and love – fearlessly. I love you for always and forever.

My mother and father: you did something right. VGB. VGP. Michael and Peter: look what I've done now...I love you both.

The Steinbergs & Matells: always there, no matter what. Love you all.

My team (you know who you are): my gratitude and appreciation.

My detractors (you know who you are): it's on!

Investors everywhere: get connected; be protected.

Foreword
by Bruce Kelly

David Levine is a rarity in the securities industry – an insider once with a notorious firm who wants to tell his side of a story in order to protect investors. His revelations about the rise and fall of the infamous GunnAllen Financial brokerage will arm investors with behind-the-scenes knowledge of firms that financial advisers work with and how to spot danger signs in the adviser/firm relationship.

Bruce Kelly
Senior Columnist, *InvestmentNews*

Introduction: FINRA's Ponzi Protection Scheme

I'm writing this because I'm angry. Time and time again, investors get screwed. The financial services Industry turns investors into victims. Investor protection is compromised via a system that's bought and paid for by the "Industry" – at the expense of investors.

By "Industry," I refer to many of the regulators, brokerage firms, investment advisors, banks, insurance companies, mutual funds and other financial services firms. This Industry has created an unfair system that's deliberately rigged against you. The "fix" is in: whether you invest in stocks, bonds, funds, or insurance products, this Industry has stacked the deck, loaded the dice, rigged the game, and worse.

Gambling and sporting events are considered "fixed" when an outcome is manipulated, when victory's assured for one at the expense of another. Investing is no different. The Industry has secretly rigged the system so it can easily and unfairly take your money. I know this because I've worked in the "Industry" for over 20 years. I'm angry because I know how investors get screwed and I've been unable to do anything about it. Until now.

As a former executive at one of the Industry's fastest-growing independent broker-dealers, I will expose exactly how the Industry has been rigged: from its system of oversight and supervision to its rules and regulations, to the products and services it sells. Investors consistently and repeatedly become victims of rogue brokers, unscrupulous advisors, deceitful planners, outright fraud, excessive commissions, high fees, hidden costs, bad investments, and more, because the Industry fails to adequately protect investors.

The Financial "Fix" will share real-life stories that are almost impossible to believe. The stories, however, are real. The client losses and suffering are horrible, and the greed and excess of brokers are unimaginable.

These are not the headline news stories about Bernie Madoff, or hedge fund manager misconduct, or scams glamorized by *The Wolf of Wall Street*. These are real-life stories about local financial advisors who victimized their next door neighbors using mutual funds, insurance products, brokerage, and advisory accounts. These are stories about families in New Jersey that were sold fake bonds to finance a lavish lifestyle and private school for a broker's five kids; blue-collar workers in Michigan who were convinced to take out mortgages to invest in a Ponzi scheme; a California couple that paid $128,840 in commissions and lost $240,381 out of a $428,000 brokerage account; seniors in Florida who now re-use disposable diapers because they lost everything in an insurance scam.

These investors all became victims. They – along with many others – should have been protected. They weren't.

The Industry doesn't discriminate: any investor – at any firm, in any product – can easily become a victim. In *The Financial "Fix,"* I'll reveal exactly how the Industry repeatedly turns investors into victims. In *The Financial "Fix,"* I'll show how and why the Industry consistently fails to adequately protect investors.

Most important, *The Financial "Fix"* will provide solutions that can help protect you from the Industry.

Part 1 of *The Financial "Fix"* chronicles the rise and fall of GunnAllen Financial Inc., which was one of the Industry's fastest-growing independent broker-dealers. It's my first-hand experience with a brokerage firm that was allowed to grow and thrive while investors were harmed. Despite an extensive pattern of misconduct and an overwhelming volume of customer complaints, the Industry did little to detect problems in advance or to protect investors during or after the fact.

The system failed. The firm didn't stop problems like it was supposed to. The regulators didn't stop problems like they were supposed to. I couldn't stop them. Even after multiple significant problems were uncovered, the Industry chose to collect a fine, instead of taking action to properly protect investors.

By the end of this firm's existence, after dozens of repeated warnings and massive systemic failures, hundreds of investors lost millions of dollars. While it could have been prevented, the Industry's conflicted, flawed self-regulatory system enabled these massive losses to occur. The regulators knew there were problems at this firm. The firm knew there were problems with some of its brokers. Investors didn't know. Investors weren't protected. Investors lost millions.

Yet, if you think problems were isolated to this one firm in particular — think again.

Part 2 of *The Financial "Fix"* will show how, across the entire Industry — at virtually every firm, in virtually every type of product — investor losses have been and continue to be massive. I'll name names. I'll provide *real* stories. Product by product, I'll reveal how investors became victims. I'll show how it happened and how it continues to occur. I'll explain how you can protect yourself from the Industry.

After presenting multiple problems with multiple products across multiple firms, you'll see that the Industry's problems are widespread. In the end, you'll be left with certain questions: Where were the regulators? Why aren't investors better protected? Who's *really* watching Wall Street?

These questions bring us to the heart of the problem. The simple answer is that the Industry's system of regulation, oversight, and supervision is inherently flawed and deeply conflicted.

Long ago, the Industry deliberately created systems, rules, and regulations that favor the Industry over investors. It embedded *The Financial "Fix"* within its very core. After the Stock Market Crash of 1929, the US Government created the Securities & Exchange Commission ("SEC"), to restore and maintain the "integrity" of the US financial service system: "When the stock market crashed, in October, 1929, public confidence in the markets plummeted. Investors large and small, as well as the banks who had loaned to them, lost great sums of money in the ensuing Great Depression. There was a consensus that for the economy to recover, the public's faith in the capital markets needed to be restored. Congress held hearings to identify the problems and search for solutions." From www.sec.gov.

Over 75 years ago, Congress tried to find a solution to an Industry gone wild. The recent repeat of the exact same problems – loose credit, excessive borrowing, the issuance of fraudulent securities (mortgage backed-bonds) that fueled a bubble (stock market and housing) that nearly collapsed the US financial services system, proved the efforts of the US Government and the SEC, to restore "...the public's faith in the capital markets..." has failed. Miserably.

Here's why:

After its creation by Congress, the SEC promptly delegated primary regulatory authority over brokerage firms to The Financial Industry Regulatory Authority, or FINRA (formerly known as NASD http://www.finra.org/AboutFINRA/) – a non-profit, non-government organization. That means FINRA is a private organization. I will discuss that issue shortly. The point is that the SEC delegated primary regulatory authority over broker-dealers to FINRA.

This delegation proved so ineffective that, as recently as 2011, the SEC had to sanction (penalize) FINRA, for altering documents and falsifying information it reported back to the SEC. Consequently, the SEC ordered FINRA to improve its internal compliance – over itself. So FINRA, a regulatory authority that has primary responsibility for investor protection, had to be ordered by the SEC to be more compliant over *itself*!

This doesn't build confidence in the Industry's commitment to investor protection. Yet, it gets worse. FINRA is a self-regulatory organization, or "SRO." As the name implies, a "Self-Regulatory Organization" is designed to regulate itself. First, the Industry created various SROs, like FINRA. Next, the Industry appoints executives to manage these SROs. Then the Industry provides the funding for these SROs, via dues, membership fees, etc.

These SROs, with Industry funding, pay their Industry-appointed executives millions in salary. These Industry-funded SROs, with their highly compensated Industry-appointed executives, are then tasked with enforcing the Industry's own rules – on itself. If all this sounds a bit circular, that's because it is. It was designed this way. The Industry created a self-regulatory system so it could monitor itself and act as its own private police force. Now – guess who this private police force protects? The Industry; not investors! Why?

The answer should come as no surprise: it's all about money. The money trail leads to and reveals the conflict that is at the Industry's core: brokers have to sell products to make money; firms depend on brokers to generate revenue; Industry regulators depend on brokers and firms for funding.

This begs several questions: Will regulators who are dependent on the Industry for funding punish Industry firms for wrongdoing? Will regulatory executives who get paid millions punish misconduct by the Industry firms that essentially pay their salaries? Does the Industry *really* protect investors?

The numbers provide the answers:

- In 2010, FINRA – *a non-profit organization, turned a profit* of $54.6 million, and:
  - Paid executives: $12.0 million+
  - Fined firms and brokers: $42.2 million
  - ***Paid harmed investors: $6.2 million***

- In 2011, FINRA
  - Paid Executives: $11.0 million+
  - Fined firms and brokers: $71.9 million
  - ***Paid harmed investors: $19.4 million***

FINRA pays its executives millions, fines firms and brokers tens of millions, yet barely returns *any* money to harmed investors. Where did all the money from the fines go? Not to harmed investors. FINRA *kept it.*

FINRA's numbers tell the story of a failed system of investor protection – and something even worse.

Unfortunately, presenting this next truth may get me in trouble. My attorneys, colleagues, Industry friends and – most important – my family, are very concerned about potential retaliation against me by the Industry, its regulators, or by some other government agency such as the IRS or FTC. I'm not paranoid; just pragmatic.

Nonetheless, I'll take my chances and tell it like it is.

Industry regulation isn't just structurally flawed and financially conflicted. It's borderline criminal conduct. In some ways, FINRA operates like some of the very fraudulent criminal enterprises it claims to prevent. Based on FINRA's own numbers and operations, it looks like FINRA is running a Ponzi *protection* scheme.

A Ponzi scheme occurs when money is raised from new investors to repay money raised from prior investors. FINRA fines firms and brokers for violating rules and for harming investors. Then FINRA keeps the money it raises from fines. *All of it.* At least most Ponzi schemes return *some* of the new money raised to old investors. FINRA doesn't even do that.

While FINRA raises separate funds for harmed investors, the amount of money returned to harmed investors is a fraction of the money FINRA raises for itself through fines. In my opinion, the amount of fines collected and kept by the regulators, versus the amount of funds returned to harmed investors, is practically criminal. It certainly doesn't speak to investor protection.

Even worse, FINRA permits most of the firms and most of the brokers that are fined to remain in business. According to an October, 2013 Wall Street Journal article, there are: "More Than 5,000 Stockbrokers from Expelled Firms Still Selling Securities."

As a result, new investors are often harmed by the same brokers and the same firms that have paid fines and made restitution for harming prior investors. The Industry allows bad brokers to harm new investors, to pay fines for harming old investors. In my opinion, that's a Ponzi Protection Scheme.

In fact, the Industry knowingly allows high risk brokers to continue to harm investors:

Stockbrokers Fail to Disclose Red Flags

WSJ Analysis Shows More Than 1,600 Stockbrokers Have Bankruptcies or Criminal Charges in Their Past That Weren't Reported

By Jean Eaglesham and Rob Barry, March 5, 2014 10:34 p.m. ET

More than 1,600 stockbrokers have bankruptcies or criminal charges in their past that weren't reported to regulators, leaving investors in the dark, a Wall Street Journal analysis shows.

Each should have been promptly disclosed to investors. None was.

These same brokers have also accumulated more disciplinary actions by regulators and complaints from clients, on average, than other brokers, the Journal's analysis of hundreds of thousands of stockbroker records shows.

http://online.wsj.com/news/articles/SB10001424052702304026804579411171593358690

Even when there are red flags and a known probability of causing harm, the Industry fails to adequately protect investors. You simply can't allow a greed-based profit-motivated Industry to supervise itself. Too much money changes hands. There are too many transactions. There are too many conflicts of interest. A self-regulatory system that's funded by the Industry it regulates is doomed to failure. Repeatedly. The fox can't guard the henhouse; the inmates can't run the asylum. Yet they do.

This is why there is little meaningful investor protection today.

Now – I'm not questioning the personal integrity of every individual at FINRA or the SEC. Most Industry employees are good people who want to make a difference. I believe they don't want to see investors become victims. It's the *system* that's flawed. I'm challenging the flawed system that was built long ago and which has become increasingly corrupted over time.

And I'm not just referring to stock brokers or the stock market:

Is the bond market rigged?

By Stephen Gandel, senior editor March 6, 2014: 5:00 AM ET

Big IPO-like spikes, clients being favored over others, and the potential for unfair Wall Street profits. This certainly sounds like another manipulated market.

FORTUNE -- Wall Street may have a new debt problem.

Late last week, Goldman Sachs (**GS**) disclosed that regulators are probing how it allocates and trades bonds. Citigroup (**C**) is reportedly in regulators' crosshairs as well, along with the rest of Wall Street. At issue is how banks decide who gets to buy into bonds when they are initially offered.

http://finance.fortune.cnn.com/2014/03/06/bond-market-rigged/?iid=HP_LN

You see, Financial "Fixes" are everywhere: they're even embedded in the Industry's rules and regulations. For example, Industry regulators actually created a rule that prohibits a firm, advisor, or broker from offering a "guarantee" against losses. Even though many investors *want* a guarantee against a loss, and even though there *are* investments that provide a guarantee against loss, it's against Industry rules to offer you a "guarantee" – see *FINRA Rule* 2150(b) *(Prohibition Against Guarantees* http://finra.complinet.com/en/display/display.html?rbid=2403&record_i d=13336&element_id=8692&highlight=2150#r13336).

Since investing involves risk, the Industry doesn't want to confuse you by offering guarantees. The Industry doesn't think you're smart enough to know that some investments are safe and others are risky. Instead, Industry geniuses determined it would be best to present you with pages upon pages of unintelligible risk disclosures, caveats, terms, conditions, and so forth, and let you – the buyer – beware.

Another example of rigged regulation is an Industry rule that prohibits paying a broker more when they make you money and less when they lose you money. The regulators, in their infinite wisdom (and, allegedly, for your benefit) determined it could create a potential conflict of interest if a broker's compensation were based on performance – see: *FINRA Rule* 2150(c) *(Sharing in Accounts* http://finra.complinet.com/en/display/display.html?rbid=2403&record_i d=13336&element_id=8692&highlight=2150#r13336).

Unlike virtually every other business, in which compensation *is* based on performance, the Industry determined a pay-for-performance arrangement would be unwise between customers and brokers. Yet, for itself, the Industry was all in favor of it. As FINRA states in its annual report, its executive "...compensation philosophy is a pay-for-performance model..." – see FINRA 2012 Year in Review and Annual Financial Report , p. 17 (http://www.finra.org/web/groups/corporate/@corp/@about/@ar/docu ments/corporate/p127312.pdf)

So – while you can't pay your broker based on performance, Industry executives can and do get paid on performance. In fact, some Industry executives even get massive paychecks and enormous severance checks while markets crash, financial services firms fail, and record fraud occurs. Again, while you lose, the Industry gets paid.

These "fixes" consistently create advantages for the Industry at the expense of investors.

Want more proof that the Industry is rigged? Consider the most important rule to successful investing: "buy low and sell high." Now consider the truth about trading stocks: the Industry actually created a system that makes you buy high and sell low – on each and every stock transaction.

 Long ago, the Industry determined it would quote two prices for the exact same stock at the exact same time. There's a bid price, which is the price a buyer is willing to pay, and there's an ask price, which is the price a seller is willing to accept. By communicating bid and ask prices, the Industry allegedly created a fair and efficient marketplace for buyers and sellers to transact. So – how did the Industry rig the system?

After creating two prices for each security, the Industry decided the bid price must *always* be lower than the ask price. Then the Industry created a system that forces you to buy from the Industry at the higher "ask" price and sell to the Industry at the lower "bid" price.

BUY HIGH

$12.00

Investors Buy ← Industry Sells

Investors Sell → Industry Buys

$11.75

SELL LOW

To give you an example, if a stock were quoted with a bid price of $11.75 and an ask price of $12.00, you would pay $12.00 to buy from the Industry. At the exact same moment, if you immediately sold the same stock *back* to the Industry, you would only receive $11.75. To make things worse, not only are you forced to buy high and sell low, but the Industry also keeps the spread between the bid and ask prices. In this example, there's a $0.25-per-share spread. On a 1,000 share trade, this spread could cost you $250 on the buy and another $250 on the sell.

In reality, Investors don't buy and sell stock from each other. Investors must buy from the Industry at a higher price and sell *back* to the Industry at a lower price. The Industry rigged the system by:

1. Creating two prices for most securities
2. Requiring investors to buy from the Industry and sell to the Industry
3. Forcing investors to pay higher prices when they buy and accept lower prices when they sell

In any other business, two different prices for the same item would be a mistake. In any other business, such an unfair system would be considered "rigged." It likely would be illegal. Yet, the Industry created two prices for each security, to rig the system and gain an unfair advantage.

in fact, the Industry makes so much money when you trade, it created bid and ask prices for almost every security: stocks, bonds, ETFs, closed-end funds, options, currencies, and more. It doesn't matter if you make money when *you* trade, the Industry can make money *whenever* you trade. If you think your discount broker is cheap, think again. If you think it's cheap to produce TV commercials and pay for all the advertising done by "discount" brokers, think again. If you think all the "free" trades you get for opening a new "discount" account are free, think again.

Since stocks and bonds were the first investments to reach large numbers of investors, the Industry first designed the two-price bid-ask price system to create an unfair advantage for itself over investors. Subsequently, the Industry has found ways to rig the system against investors in mutual funds, insurance products, annuities, banking products, and too many more to list. It goes on and on. The Industry has an unfair advantage over you.

It's not just ironic that an Industry that's all about making money isn't all about making money for investors. It's this way by *design*. The Industry puts its own interests ahead of yours. The Industry has created regulators, rules, systems, products, and services that help it make money with an unfair advantage over investors. I'm not saying you *can't* make money by investing; it's just that the Industry makes it significantly harder for investors, because the Industry rigged the system, to ensure that it profits *first*.

For investors, it's hard enough to pick a good investment, to buy it at the right price and at the right time and then to know when to sell it, and then to sell it at the right price and at the right time. But – rest assured – through spreads, commissions, or recurring fees, the Industry has built in an unfair advantage to make money whether your investment selection is good or bad, or your timing is right or wrong, or you pick the right or wrong price at which to buy and sell. The "Fix" is definitely in.

But, for investors who lose money, the Industry's unfair advantage becomes most painfully clear. One of the most blatant examples of the Industry using a financial "Fix" to put its interests first is the rigged system of dispute resolution. The Industry has created rules and regulations to manipulate the handling of disputes. Since investing involves risks and, since disputes often arise, Industry regulators determined that disputes should be resolved via a binding arbitration process.

In a master stroke of premeditation, the Industry requires that investors give up their legal rights to sue their financial advisor or their firm. Before you get the privilege of entrusting your hard-earned savings to the Industry, you must *first* agree to settle disputes via this binding arbitration process.

Now – guess who developed the rules and regulations that govern the arbitration process: the Industry against which you have a dispute!

You're investing in an Industry that profits by doing business with you but is supposed to put your interests first. Yet, the record shows this Industry already puts its interests ahead of yours. The Industry created a system that gives it an unfair advantage every time you trade securities. The Industry prohibits offering you guarantees – even if you want them. The Industry prohibits paying for performance – even if you want to. The Industry limits your rights in the event of disputes. So, it should come as no surprise investors keep getting screwed by the Industry.

But, don't feel singled out if you have investment losses. Back in 2007, during the market downturn, FINRA's own portfolio was down by more than $624 million dollars. Historically, FINRA would earn over $100 million per year by investing. This begs a few additional questions. What money and how much money does the non-profit Industry regulator invest for itself? And, how in the world can investors trust a regulator that lost more than $624 million in the market? If the primary Industry regulator can't protect its *own* money – how can it be entrusted to protect yours?

Financial "Fixes" create risk and cause investor losses. There are many risks investors knowingly face: no planning, poor planning, bad markets, bad investments, incorrect timing, low returns, high fees, uninsured loss, underfunded retirement, insufficient income, excessive debt, unsuitable asset allocation, concentrated positions, excessive trading, rogue brokers, unethical firms etc. However, these are risks you can try to avoid.

What you can't avoid is what you don't know; or what's hidden from you. You can't avoid the risks created by a flawed, conflicted, and rigged financial services Industry. You can't avoid *The Financial "Fix,"* if you don't know about it.

You could be the next victim. The criminal could be a local financial advisor, a pious planner, a former military man or a slick caller with a New York accent. From its rules and regulations, to the firms that manufacture products, to the army of brokers, advisors, planners, and agents, the Industry consistently abuses investors. Past performance *does* guarantee one fact: investors keep losing.

Yet – there *is* hope.

In the biblical story of David and Goliath, there was a positive outcome – for David, that is. The financial services Industry is a Goliath. It doesn't matter if you're a large institution, a private client, or an individual "retail" investor. Against the massive size and scale of the Industry, you are David. Make no mistake: if you chose to invest, you've picked a fight with the Industry. Whether you're investing just a little or entrusting your life savings, you're walking into a vastly unfair fight.

You're going up against enormous players who have created the rules, markets, and systems to which you would entrust your money. And you want to profit? Try just to *survive*. Remember Lehman Brothers, Bear Stearns, IndyMac Bank, Washington Mutual, Conseco Insurance, AIG, Wachovia, JP Morgan, Bank of America, Merrill Lynch, Morgan Stanley, Goldman Sachs, etc.? Recently, these firms either failed or needed a bailout. Many of the Industry's own players couldn't survive within the Industry they helped create.

Make no mistake: every time you invest via the Industry, you're taking on Goliath.

Yet, David still managed to defeat Goliath. David didn't win because he was bigger, stronger, or faster. David won because he was *informed*. David knew the only way he could defeat a far bigger and stronger foe was to use a weapon that enabled him to strike from a distance.

With information about his foe, David didn't just even the odds; he gained the advantage. David won because he essentially brought a rifle to a sword fight. David's weapon – the tool that enabled victory – was a slingshot. David was victorious because he had the right tool for his particular job.

So, there *is* hope. The tools do exist to better protect investors. Every year, the Industry spends millions of dollars on supervisory and surveillance systems that can detect problems and protect investors.

Unfortunately, these "tools" are used almost exclusively by the Industry *for* the Industry.

So – I had a simple idea: since I know the problems, I can provide a solution. I could take the Industry's tools and make them available *directly* to individual investors. With these tools, investors can truly see what's really going on with their accounts and their investments. Investors can be forewarned of potential problems – *before* money is lost. Investors can get independent reviews of brokers, advisors, products, strategies, and more. Investors can minimize fees, improve product selection, and receive better information. Investors can also easily monitor accounts and receive alerts when changes occur.

The tools exist to help investors. I'll make those tools available to help protect investors.

It's time to force some changes on the Industry. It's time to let investors see the truth behind the Industry's "fix." It's time to arm investors with some of the Industry's own weapons.

It's time to fix the "fix."

Part 1 is the story behind the rise and fall of GunnAllen Financial, Inc.

Part 2 exposes the Industry's failure to protect investors across all products at all firms.

Why write this now?

I'm writing this because I'm sick and tired of the Industry's lies and cover-ups. For over 20 years, I've worked in the financial services Industry without ever receiving a single customer complaint. As a broker and an advisor, I served my clients well and with integrity. I was the Director of National Sales for one of the Industry's fastest-growing broker-dealers. Most recently, I was the Director of Business Development for both the Broker-Dealer and the Registered Investment Advisor divisions of a publicly traded financial services firm with hundreds of brokers, tens of thousands of clients, and billions of dollars of assets under management.

David Levine

Over my career, I've seen more products and services than most brokers see in a lifetime. I've seen an incredible volume of suitable transactions using appropriate products and services. I've also seen an incredible volume of bad sales practices, excessive fees, bad products, rogue brokers, fraudulent schemes, and more. I've always done my best to protect investors.

Yet, I've been fined and sanctioned by the SEC. I was named in an arbitration (the Industry's version of a lawsuit) that sought $40 million in damages by a former broker who was fired by my old firm for impersonating a client and attempting to "move" client funds.

I helped fire a broker who is now barred from the Industry, who has 40+ customer complaints against him, and who is presently serving a lengthy prison sentence for multiple felony counts of grand theft and abuse of the elderly. Yet, the Industry allowed this broker to continue to prey on investors for years – even after his misconduct was known. Then the Industry allowed this now-barred felon to file an arbitration against me and others for allegedly ruining his career and damaging his name and reputation.

I'm writing this because the Industry enables this nonsense.

Intellectually, I simply can't stand the Industry's hypocrisy. I graduated from an Ivy League school with a degree in Economics. I went on to business school and earned a Master degree in Finance. I know...big deal. All that means is I'm book-smart.

Actually, it means I'm smart enough to know when something doesn't make sense. The Industry's rules, regulations and – most important – its supervisory structure makes absolutely *no* sense. I'm writing this book primarily to expose how the Industry doesn't do enough to protect investors. More important, I'm writing this book to share information that can help investors protect themselves.

I've reached a point in my career where I want to make some changes. Many of us know the definition of insanity is to do the same thing over and over again and expect a different result. I'm done running on the Industry's hamster wheel.

I've worked at some of the largest financial services firms during some of the best and worst economic times. I've worked for a bank and a private bank. I worked for a registered investment advisor that managed billions. I worked in a retail brokerage. I spent the majority of my career working in the fastest growing sector of the Industry – the independent broker-dealer space. I have a lot of experience in a lot of different environments. I'm confident about what I know.

I've seen good and bad markets. I've worked with great brokers and advisors who truly cared for and helped their clients. Then I worked for a firm where some rogue brokers went wild. Clients were destroyed. I couldn't stop it. The firm didn't stop it. The Industry did far too little and waited far too long to stop it. Investors lost millions. The Industry failed to protect investors.

I love the Industry and many of the people who work in it. There are many employees, brokers, advisors, and managers who do the right thing. Unfortunately, I've seen too much. I need to unburden myself. The consequences will be what they will be. I will tell the truth. The public record speaks for itself. Everything I'll expose is known to the regulators. They can try to ruin my career after this; but they'll have to come up with something good, because what's written here is *fact*. Chapter and verse.

The simple truth is that investors want to invest. Many *need* to invest. Most want help. In my experience, investors simply want good advice. They want to work with someone they can trust. They don't hate brokers or advisors. They hate being "told and sold." They hate not being treated honorably or fairly. They want and deserve clear recommendations and good products that can help them achieve their goals.

Unfortunately, I witnessed an Industry that enabled absolutely ruthless animals to charm seniors out of their life savings. I know of a 90-year-old in Florida who has to wash his disposable diapers, because a rogue broker effectively stole every dollar he had. That same broker took over $4.3 million from at least 94 other clients and sold a Ponzi scheme that may have cost other investors everything. The broker lied about the safety of investments to clients. The broker falsified client information to my old firm, to unethically and unlawfully gain approval of unsuitable transactions.

Eventually, after an overwhelming pattern of misconduct was detected, this broker was fired. It shouldn't have taken so long. I couldn't fire this broker. The supervisors who detected the problems weren't authorized to fire the broker. Multiple times, with thick files of evidence, staff tried to fire this broker. Management wouldn't act. Even after presenting a recorded phone call, during which this broker impersonated a client in an attempt to move client funds, the firm's President still tried to keep this broker from getting fired. Eventually, he *was* fired. Finally. His Industry record reflected multiple customer complaints, various acts of misconduct, and his termination for impersonating a client.

Nonetheless, a new firm promptly re-hired him. However, the state of Florida would not approve this broker's license to do business. So, when this broker couldn't get his securities license approved, he submitted business under someone else's name. The broker's new employer figured this out and fired him. *Again*. His new misconduct was reported and he was fined and suspended by FINRA. For his misconduct, dozens of additional customer complaints were filed against this broker. Even more complaints were made – but many were never recorded properly.

Eventually, this broker lost his securities license. He was barred from the securities Industry. But, that wasn't the end. This former broker continued to prey on seniors for years. His new weapon was insurance.

After four more years as a serial financial predator, this same broker was finally arrested by the state of Florida. He was charged with scamming multiple senior citizens out of more than $2 million by fraudulently "selling" insurance products. Convicted, he now resides in a Hillsborough County jail cell.

The Industry allowed this broker to destroy investors for years. This same Industry enabled this former broker to use the Industry's *customer complaint* system to file a $40 million complaint against me and others for allegedly damaging his career by ruining his "good name and reputation."

Screw him. And screw FINRA for allowing this to happen. I'm sick and tired of the Industry's lies and cover-ups.

The truth is that most investments aren't bad. The majority of brokers and advisors aren't evil. There is nothing inherently wrong with commission and fees – as long as they're reasonable. The problem is that investors can't trust that they are being treated fairly, served properly, or charged appropriately. Worst of all, *it doesn't have to be this way.*

The Industry's system is terribly flawed. It's simply broken. Every broker-dealer has spent millions of dollars on systems to detect and prevent broker misconduct. Every firm in the Industry has supervisory systems that review customer accounts for suitability, unnecessary trading, excessive commissions and/or fees, concentrated positions that create risk of loss, illiquid positions, inappropriate investments given a client's stated investment objective, risk tolerance, time horizon, age, – the list goes on.

The problem is that the Industry uses these systems to warn *itself.* Generally, these systems identify problems *after* the fact. After a problem is detected, the damage is already done. Accordingly, the Industry shifts its focus to damage control, instead of proactive investor protection. Instead of actually protecting investors from monetary losses, the Industry tries to protect itself from reputation risk.

I'm living proof.

I mentioned that I was fined and sanctioned by the SEC. I present to you the details. Now – mind you – I have to be careful about what I say or write, because the SEC made me agree I would never deny their allegations. They've already tried to silence me, once. Not this time!

When my former firm was going out of business, there were thousands of mutual fund and variable annuity account holders who didn't have a broker providing any services for three months or more. Since there was no broker providing service, and since the firm was going out of business, these customers were at risk of being "abandoned" when the firm closed. Since I was knowledgeable about mutual funds and variable annuities, I asked the firm's President if I could offer to provide services to these clients.

I was told that if I paid the cost of a mailer to notify these clients that the firm was going out of business, I could include an offer to provide services. This would relieve the firm of the cost of a mailer, provide clients with a required notice, and enable me to offer to provide services. It was a win-win-win situation.

Or – so we all thought.

I asked our Chief Compliance Officer to check with the SEC. I was told that the SEC advised us to deal directly with FINRA, since FINRA was the firm's primary regulator. We consulted FINRA's published guidance on the matter. Broker-dealers had closed before. FINRA had provided guidance for this very situation. For regulators who are notorious for providing vague guidance, in this situation, there was perfectly clear guidance as to what needed to be done:

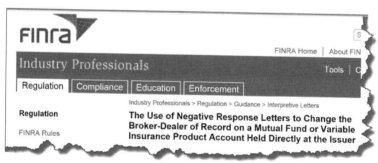

http://www.finra.org/Industry/Regulation/Guidance/InterpretiveLetters/
p012109

With letters signed and paperwork drawn up, a securely transmitted file was created and stored on a password-protected laptop. The deal was sealed. I resigned from the firm in April, 2010. I joined a new firm in May of 2010. I waited until the old firm filed for bankruptcy. I waited until the old firm filed to withdraw its broker-dealer status with FINRA. The firm had no brokers; it was no longer operating; it no longer had any selling and/or servicing agreements with any vendors. It was no longer providing any client services. All remaining accounts had been abandoned. This was in Mid-May of 2010.

In June, as agreed and approved by the old firm's President, notices went out regarding the firm's closing. The notice followed FINRA's guidance as to content. Shortly after the letters went out, the SEC stepped in and launched an investigation. I testified under oath for hours. I provided all the emails, documents, signed authorization, and more. I provided the SEC with FINRA's guidance. The record reflects considerable time and effort was spent attempting to comply with FINRA's guidance and firm policies.

The SEC didn't seem to care. Certain staff in a particular division of the SEC determined that I, along with several other executives – one of whom wasn't even with the firm at the time – had allegedly violated certain provisions of consumer privacy law. According to the SEC, I "willfully aided, abetted, and caused non-public consumer financial information" to be shared with a third party.

At first, I was shocked. After the SEC staff provided an explanation, I was outraged.

According to the SEC, when I was affiliated with the firm, it was ok for me to have the data. However, once I resigned, I became a third party. Even though I was clearly still myself, according to the SEC, I had technically become a non-affiliated third party. Consequently, when I shared the data I already had with my non-affiliated self, I caused a data breach. According to the SEC, I shared data with myself after I had become a third party from myself.

I'm not making this up. There was nothing funny about this.

That was the SEC's "legal" position. I was charged with violating the law. I was threatened with a $50,000 fine or years of costly litigation, during which I wouldn't be allowed to work.

Ultimately, I settled the matter with a $20,000 payment to the SEC. My record will forever reflect this regulatory action against me. It was a first in the Industry. The regulators were charging me and several other big bad evil broker-dealer executives with a privacy law breach to show concerned consumers how serious this matter was. Even though there was not one complaint against me.

The regulators even issued a press release, to tout their successful protection of investors. Then the most amazing thing happened: after the SEC's press release, my phone rang off the hook with calls from firms wanting to hire me – for my account list!

Only in the Industry.

Now, I'm not for a second minimizing the importance of protecting consumer information...but seriously? While Madoff, Stamford, Nadal and others ripped off billions of dollars, the SEC went after me for a list that was given to me – under FINRA's guidance. At my prior firm, hundreds of customers lost millions of dollars over multiple years. Real money. Never to be recovered. Yet, there was not one customer complaint against me concerning privacy. There was not one customer complaint against me for causing investment losses.

In my opinion, my own case highlights the Industry's hypocritical approach to "damage" control, instead of investor protection. I'm certain many investors who lost real money would gladly share their non-public financial information with either me or my third party self, if either one of us could help them get their money back. Yet, without one single customer complaint against me, I was fined by the SEC.

Now – guess who kept the money for the alleged harm I caused? The SEC. Not one cent was returned to any "harmed" investors. In addition, taxpayers footed the bill to pay for this whole "investigation."

So, while I don't deny the SEC's allegations, I do think this whole process was complete bullshit. I also think the regulators are hypocrites. I think they attacked me, but covered up their own failings.

My experience at my prior firm further proves this point. The firm grew too fast. It hired many brokers with multiple customer complaints and known prior regulatory problems. The firm lacked adequate systems, management, and capital to properly supervise those brokers. All of this was known.

Yet, instead of shutting down the firm, the regulators chose to collect fines for themselves. Instead of stopping bad brokers from causing investor losses while the firm was alive, the regulators fined me – after the fact. Instead of repaying money to any harmed investor, FINRA and the SEC kept the money from fines. Investors were left with losses and claims against a closed, bankrupt firm.

The regulators do more to protect themselves than they do to protect investors. Want more proof?

Consider asking the SEC or FINRA about a robbery in 2006 at FINRA's Boca Raton office, when about ten laptop computers were stolen. Among other data, these computers contained non-public financial information for thousands of customers. Social security numbers, dates of birth, account numbers, etc. FINRA covered it up. The SEC did nothing about it. Zero accountability.

Top Financial Regulator Confirms Data Theft
FINRA, formerly known as The National Association of Securities Dealers, has confirmed a burglary in its local offices resulting in the theft of 10 laptop computers. Though the burglary occurred on February 25, 2006, the regulator made no public mention of the breach until confronted with a Police Report on June 30th – over four months later. Boca Raton, FL (PRWEB) July 6, 2006...

http://www.prweb.com/releases/2006/07/prweb408169.htm

The Industry *sucks* at protecting investors. While hundreds of investors keep losing millions to rogue brokers, SEC officials chose to pursue me in their mission to "protect investors." I respectfully suggest the SEC work a little harder to detect and prevent *real* losses and actual scandals such as ENRON, Madoff, Countrywide Mortgage, AIG, MF Global, JP Morgan, LIBOR, etc.

Perhaps the SEC staff was simply too busy surfing porn to perform their job properly:

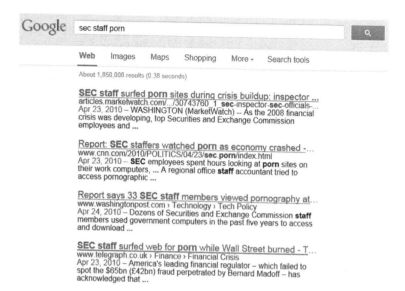

Not only do SEC employees get to watch tons 'o porn on the job, they don't even get fired when they do!

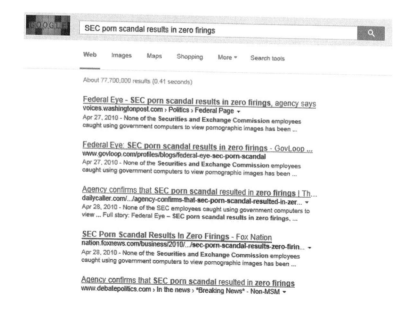

Once again – zero accountability.

So – why didn't I fight the SEC's allegations? Why did I settle? The answer is simple: short of the IRS, the SEC is one of the most powerful government agencies. The SEC accused me of wrongdoing. Unlike every other legal situation, in which you're innocent until proven guilty, the SEC and FINRA work backwards.

Once accused, I had to *prove* my innocence. To do that, it would take years and cost hundreds of thousands of dollars to plead my case before a civil judge who is employed and paid by the same employer as my accusers, the same employer that created the SEC: the government.

I felt like I was being extorted. The regulators have the power to levy fines as if they were impromptu taxes. I was charged and it would cost a fortune to prove my innocence. I settled because, financially, I couldn't win. The fix was in; the process was rigged. I became a victim of the Industry. I would have had to fight the Industry *and* the government, which played by different rules than you or me or any other investor.

If you think I'm even the slightest bit a conspiracy theorist, consider the following: the U.S. Congress (which created the SEC) was until recently *exempt* from the laws that prohibit insider trading. Up until July, 2012, members of Congress were permitted to trade stocks based on non-public (inside) information without any restrictions. Government officials – who could approve billion-dollar deals involving international trade, corporate subsidies, healthcare spending, and more – could freely trade on this information.

There would be fines and jail time if you or I traded on inside information. Yet, members of Congress could legally trade on inside information – and they did. According to *60 Minutes*, several members of Congress allegedly used confidential information to invest and profit. In fact, in 2004, a paper published in the Journal of Financial and Quantitative Analysis showed that U.S. senators who traded stocks – allegedly with inside information – beat the market by 12% per year.

After this was exposed, Congress finally banned insider trading for members. This ban just passed in July, 2012.

Yes – I'm pissed off. You should be, too. The Industry is rigged. It plays by different rules than you and me. It has an unfair advantage over investors. It fails to adequately protect investors. But, as I said before and will again, it doesn't have to be this way.

I'll show you how to protect yourself from the Industry. I've pretty much seen it all. So – I've taken all the information and tools the Industry uses to protect itself and made them available directly to investors. You can avoid rogue brokers, bad investments, unsuitable recommendations, concentrated positions, excessive transactions, high fees, hidden charges, and more loss-causing issues.

I may have settled with the SEC, but it's now time to settle the score with the Industry.

That's why I'm writing this book.

I welcome any calls with questions: (561) 350-3737.

PART 1: GunnAllen Financial, Inc

Member FINRA | SIPC

4/1997 – 4/2010

R.I.P

1997: THE OPENING BELL: GunnAllen Financial is born

The United States stock market started one of its longest and most spectacular advances – known as a bull market run – from about 1983 to 2007. There were brief declines, such as the crash of 1987 and the dot-com bust of 2000–2002, but these declines merely paved the way for greater advances.

GunnAllen was born and raised in these go-go days. Named after its founders – Donald J. **Gunn** and Richard **Allen** Frueh (pronounced "free") – the two business partners at first debated calling their firm GunnFrueh or FruehGunn, but wisely selected a different name.

Accordingly, GunnAllen was born, opening its doors early 1997 – just as the best part of the first major market advance would begin. As stock pickers, there was virtually no better time to recommend stocks to investors. Just about anyone could recommend any stock and it would go up. This wasn't a brain game – it was a brawn game. In this rapidly rising market, anyone could be right, so hiring more brokers and pitching more stocks was a formula for success. GunnAllen's timing was phenomenal.

Until it wasn't.

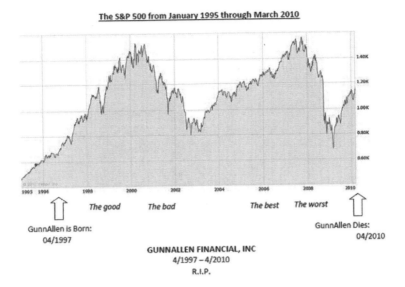

The S&P 500 from January 1995 through March 2010

The good — The bad — The best — The worst

GunnAllen is Born:
04/1997

GunnAllen Dies:
04/2010

GUNNALLEN FINANCIAL, INC
4/1997 – 4/2010
R.I.P.

GunnAllen was an independent broker-dealer. Unlike a traditional "wirehouse," such as Merrill Lynch or Morgan Stanley, where brokers are employees, GunnAllen's brokers were independent contractors. The primary difference is simple economics. At a "wirehouse," a broker generally gets paid about 40% of the commissions they generate and the firm generally covers all operating expenses such as rent, computers, and support staff. At an independent firm like GunnAllen, the broker could get paid up to 90% or more of the commissions they generate; however, the broker has to pay all their own expenses, such as rent, staff, and computers.

Over the past 20 years, the Industry underwent tremendous changes. The Industry experienced the rapid growth of discount brokerage firms and the creation of an entire independent financial services marketplace that includes: financial planners, registered investment advisors, and independent brokers.

In the past, if you wanted to invest, there was Merrill Lynch, Morgan Stanley, Smith Barney, etc. Today, most of these firms have merged and/or combined with banks. However, they now face competition from discount brokerage firms such as Schwab, Fidelity, and TD Ameritrade –

and also from broker-dealers that have independent contractors, such as Ameriprise, LPL Financial, Raymond James, and others.

MANAGED ASSETS BY BROKER-DEALER

COMPANY	MANAGED ASSETS FOR 2Q'10*	CHANGE FROM Q1'10
Morgan Stanley Smith Barney	$386 billion	-4%
BofA-Merrill Lynch	$312 billion	-5%
Wells Fargo	$197 billion	-5%
UBS	$162 billion	-5%
Schwab	$95 billion	-4%
Fidelity	$90 billion	-2%
Ameriprise	$83 billion	-3%
LPL Financial	$79 billion	-3%
Raymond James	$45 billion	-8%
Edward Jones	$39 billion	9%

Source: Money Management Institute, Dover Financial Research

*Defined as investment solutions delivered via a platform or through other advisor programs as of 6/30/10.

While there are economic differences between a Wall Street wirehouse and an independent broker-dealer, the rules and regulations are the same. These rules are predominantly created by the Securities and Exchange Commission ("SEC") and by the Financial Industry Regulatory Authority ("FINRA" formerly the NASD). In addition, GunnAllen was also an SEC Registered Investment Advisor and a General Insurance Agency.

In total, GunnAllen was regulated by the SEC and FINRA, subject to federal and state securities laws, federal and state laws for investment advisors, and federal and state laws for insurance agencies.

With all these rules and regulations, and with all these "responsible authorities" governing its business, it's hard to imagine how *any* individual investor could get hurt. You might think bad things can't happen to investors in one of the most highly-regulated industries in the world.

You would be horribly wrong.

In GunnAllen's early days, the company set out with a noble vision: to be a firm for brokers run by brokers. That sounds good – if you assume brokers know how to run a business in one of the most highly-regulated industries in the world.

GunnAllen's timing was perfect. The market was going up rapidly. Clients and brokers were making tons of money. It was almost *too* easy. Except – running a brokerage firm in an Industry full of rules and regulations is anything *but* easy. Especially during a period of unprecedented market growth, followed by the "dot com implosion," followed by another growth cycle, followed by the near collapse of the US financial system. Even if the firm had done everything right, external events and the market's extraordinary volatility created unprecedented risks. This was a challenging environment, even for the most skilled managers.

For others, it was fatal.

In 2005, I was hired by GunnAllen to help build out the firm's investment advisory services. I was tasked with creating a platform that would enable GunnAllen's brokers to offer high quality products and services to clients for fees, instead of commissions. Over the next five years, my role and responsibilities grew considerably. I became an Executive Vice President and the Director of National Sales. I attended senior management meetings. Many of the firm's divisions reported to me, including: mutual funds, insurance products, investment advisory services, retirement plans, and others. While I was part of management, I was one voice among many. No matter how loud I was, my voice was often unheard, ignored, or undermined.

Things were simply going too well.

As we all know, what goes up, must come down. GunnAllen went up too quickly and fell even faster. At its peak, GunnAllen had about 1,000 brokers in almost every state serving almost 70,000 brokerage and advisory accounts with more than $5 billion in total customer assets under management.

In 2007, GunnAllen's total revenues peaked at around $151 million. That same year (2007), GunnAllen's top broker was exposed as having been involved in a Ponzi scheme. While this broker's involvement in the Ponzi scheme started long before he was affiliated with GunnAllen, the Ponzi scheme unraveled while the broker worked at GunnAllen and the blame fell on the firm. It was flooded with customer complaints and regulatory inquiries from the SEC, FINRA, and from multiple states.

Then the market crashed. In 2008, the S&P 500 declined by more than 37%. It was the beginning of the end. By 2009, customer complaints and legal fees were climbing rapidly. Revenue was falling faster. To cap it off, in the summer of 2009, a high yielding oil and gas investment program out of Texas was also exposed as a Ponzi scheme. GunnAllen, along with approximately 60 other broker-dealers, unwittingly placed clients' money in a scam.

From GunnAllen alone, almost $40 million of investor's money was likely lost. The firm faced a new wave of customer complaints, legal bills, and liabilities.

By 2009, GunnAllen's revenues had dropped – from over $150 million to around $100 million. While that might still seem like a lot, it wasn't. GunnAllen paid out almost 90% of every dollar of revenue to its brokers. The firm's fixed costs and operating expenses were higher than its revenues in almost every year. At the same time revenues were dramatically declining, expenses dramatically increased. In 2009, GunnAllen spent almost $8 million on legal fees alone. It was a total disaster.

In addition to millions in debt owed to bondholders that financed the firm's rapid growth, the firm's liabilities from customer complaints and broker misconduct exceeded $50 million. There was no cash flow left to invest in better supervisory systems or to improve operations or to repay client losses.

In December of 2009, GunnAllen's primary investor and controlling shareholder resigned from the Board. GunnAllen's financial backers had determined that the firm's legal costs and mounting liabilities were unsustainable.

It was the last straw.

In March of 2010, in the overwhelming face of the obvious, GunnAllen's primary regulator finally stepped in and determined that the firm lacked sufficient capital to continue operations. GunnAllen was, effectively, shuttered. Not for mismanagement. Not for harming investors. The regulators essentially closed GunnAllen due to an "accounting" problem.

That almost says it all. When the firm had the ability to pay massive fines to FINRA, it was allowed to remain in business. Without the ability to pay fines or to cover customer complaints, the firm wasn't permitted to continue operations.

By April of 2010, the brokers had all left and gone to work for other broker-dealers. The firm had virtually no revenues and virtually no assets.

In May of 2010, GunnAllen filed for bankruptcy. By filing for bankruptcy protection, all customer complaints were put on hold. It didn't matter when the loss occurred, or how much was lost, or why the loss happened.

For investors who lost money, there was little hope of any meaningful recovery. It was over.

For me, this was how it began...

The Beginning: A Call from GunnAllen

In mid-2003, I moved my family to south Florida. Prior to moving, I'd worked at an independent broker-dealer in New York City. This firm was comprised predominately of insurance agents, financial planners, and financial advisors. There were some stock brokers, but not many.

I helped build that firm's investment advisory (fee-based asset management) platform. The advisors gathered a very significant amount of assets in a relatively short period of time.

The firm had been around for about 20 years, prior to my joining. I came in toward the end. In this case, the end was a good thing. The founder sold the firm for a great price to New England Financial – a division of MetLife. The buyer was one of the largest financial services firms in the Industry. It was a good, clean transaction all around. The large amount of assets on the platform I helped create added significantly to the value of the firm. Fee-based assets generate steady recurring revenue, which is very desirable for *any* business. It's particularly desirable in the volatile securities business.

After the acquisition, there was considerable management turnover. I was asked to stay on by the new firm. Between New England Financial, MetLife, and my old firm, there were at least five (5) separate broker-dealers. There were constant conference calls to eliminate overlap and to integrate staff, platforms, and products. My firm had built a great platform and the other broker-dealers wanted to use it.

I became a man in demand.

After months of seemingly endless conference calls, I became stifled by the bureaucracy. Before this, I'd been in charge of a division at a very entrepreneurial firm. I was authorized and empowered by the prior firm's owner. I would present my ideas, back them up with detailed financials, and get authorization to execute a plan. I'd frequently report my results and, through performance, I'd earned the right to run a division. Where I loved my job before, I quickly become bored as a division manager at a very large insurance company. So – I resigned.

Over the next few years, I developed a business helping transactional firms add investment advisory services to their platforms. The more hardcore the transactional firm was, the greater the challenge, but also the greater the opportunity. Transactional brokers had the most to gain, since they generally managed only 10% of their client's speculative money, whereas fee-based advisors generally managed 90% of their client's serious money. Moreover, traditional commission-based brokerage firms were under attack. Clients were leaving large firms and moving accounts to discount brokers and local fee-based advisors. My "field" was booming.

In addition, I'd also started up my own institutional cash management business. I was practicing what I preached. I offered high quality institutional money market products to institutions. I could provide clients with safety, liquidity, and a higher yield than they were earning elsewhere. In return, I would earn a fee for adding value. Fortunately, that business was sufficient to support me and my family. I could run it from anywhere, so we decided to move to Florida.

Like any New York transplant in Florida, we spent the first year going to Disney. A *lot*. My young daughters loved it. We would go during the week, since it was less crowded. It was on the drive back from one of our trips that I got the call.

"David? My name is Rick Frueh. I own a brokerage firm in Tampa called GunnAllen Financial. I was given your name and number and told you were the man who could help me build an investment advisory platform. Is this a good time to talk?"

I explained that I was in the car with my family, so we arranged a call for the next day.

We spoke the next day and, two days later, I was in Tampa. Richard Allen Frueh – Rick – was charming. He was very interested in my background and experience. He introduced me to his staff, in what was a typical overcrowded high-energy independent-broker dealer environment. Employees were running around processing business. The firm was growing rapidly and they had no internal expertise to do what I did. I was taken to lunch and then to dinner. By the end of dinner, we had a deal. I became a consultant to GunnAllen Financial.

Since I lived in south Florida, I agreed to commute to Tampa once a month and to provide weekly progress reports. I submitted a plan to build the firm's investment advisory platform inside of six months.

The distance, my lack of familiarity with the firm's brokers at the time, and my limited access to information about what was going on at the Tampa headquarters were all a blessing. From a distance, and after checking around, I was told GunnAllen was a little "rough," but was rapidly growing and had a lot of potential.

To me, GunnAllen's potential for good or bad had yet to be determined.

Good from Far; Far from Good

I've compiled some information to give you some perspective about GunnAllen. Below is a record, from FINRA's BrokerCheck®, of the number of recorded customer complaints against certain wirehouse and independent broker-dealers, through July 2012. In the Industry, a formal customer complaint is referred to as an arbitration. According to FINRA's BrokerCheck®, GunnAllen had 13 reported customer complaints, as of July 2012.

	ARBITRATIONS *(complaints)*
Merrill Lynch	985
UBS	386
Schwab	246
Raymond James Assoc	134
Ameriprise	70
Morgan Stanley	44
LPL	42
GunnAllen	13

Mind you, in 2005, I was looking at different numbers with a vastly different perception of the firm than I have now. Anyway, based on the above statistics, GunnAllen's 13 reported arbitrations didn't look that bad, when compared to other firms. So, while I'd heard the firm was a little "rough," the numbers appeared to tell a different story. In 2005, GunnAllen was one of the fastest-growing, brightest stars in the independent broker-dealer Industry.

Fast forward to today, after my firsthand experience with GunnAllen, and I can present a vastly different perspective. I've added each firm's total assets under management next to its number of arbitrations. Ranked by assets under management, GunnAllen is *still* at the bottom of the list.

	ARBITRATIONS (complaints)	ASSETS UNDER MANAGEMENT
Merrill Lynch	985	$2,200,000,000,000
UBS	386	$620,000,000,000
Schwab	246	$1,500,000,000,000
Raymond James Assoc	134	$370,000,000,000
Ameriprise	70	$248,000,000,000
Morgan Stanley	44	$305,000,000,000
LPL	42	$464,000,000,000
GunnAllen	13	$5,000,000,000

Compared to these other firms, GunnAllen *still* doesn't look too bad.

Yet, as they say, the devil is in the details. In order to *accurately* compare GunnAllen to these other firms, I adjusted the number of customer complaints in proportion to each firm's assets under management.

For example, at the time of this report, Merrill Lynch managed 440 times more assets than GunnAllen. Accordingly, if you multiply GunnAllen's number of customer complaints by 440, you would get a number that represented the average number of complaints per assets under management. By this method, if GunnAllen managed the same amount of assets as Merrill Lynch, then GunnAllen could have had over 5,720 complaints, as compared to Merrill's 985.

Based on its assets under management, GunnAllen generated significantly more complaints than *any* of these other firms.

FIRM	Firm's ARBITRATIONS (complaints)	GunnAllen's ARBITRATIONS (adjusted by assets)	Firm's ASSETS UNDER MANAGEMENT
Merrill Lynch	985	5,720	$2,200,000,000,000
UBS	386	1,612	$620,000,000,000
Schwab	246	3,900	$1,500,000,000,000
Raymond James Assoc	134	962	$370,000,000,000
Ameriprise	70	645	$248,000,000,000
Morgan Stanley	44	793	$305,000,000,000
LPL	42	1,206	$464,000,000,000
GunnAllen	13	13	$5,000,000,000

By this measure, against any other firm above, GunnAllen rises to the top of the list. Unfortunately, earning the top spot on a list of customer complaints is the worst spot on the worst list for any firm.

What's even more noteworthy is that GunnAllen achieved this extraordinary volume of complaints in a very short timeframe. While Merrill has been around since 1914 – or almost 100 years – GunnAllen was only around since 1995, or just about 15 years.

From afar, GunnAllen looked good. I would soon learn GunnAllen was far from good.

Safety tip 1: Any investor can look up any broker and any firm. FINRA and the SEC each maintain public sites that provide information about every broker and advisor's licensing status, employment history, and disciplinary history in the Industry:

FINRA BrokerCheck® – Research Brokers, Brokerage Firms, Investment Adviser Representatives and Investment Adviser Firms
(http://www.finra.org/Investors/ToolsCalculators/BrokerCheck/)

SEC Investment Advisor Search
(http://www.adviserinfo.sec.gov/IAPD/Content/Search/iapd_Search.aspx)

No Press like Bad Press: The Mob on Wall Street

Bad press about GunnAllen started early. It just took a while to catch up.

Way back in December of 1996, *BusinessWeek* ran a cover story titled, "The Mob on Wall Street." That story provided some of the best information to this day about the association of mobsters with broker-dealers and the methods they use to make money — especially with penny stocks, market making, and IPOs. The story revealed how corrupt people were taking advantage of the Industry's flawed systems.

The *BusinessWeek* story never mentioned GunnAllen. It did mention a brokerage firm called Sovereign Equity Management Corp., which was at the center of the "Mob on Wall Street" case in the U.S. District Court for the Middle District of Florida.

Unfortunately, in 2004, with the growth of the Internet, a blogger at www.siliconinvestor.com made a connection between the *BusinessWeek* story and GunnAllen. Focusing on the investment banking and trading activities regarding the stock of a company called Matrixx, the blogger revealed the following connection:

> Matrixx and GunnAllen have ties that go back to March 1997, when an investment banking agreement between Matrixx, then known as Gum Tech, and Sovereign Equity Management Corp., was transferred to PG&G Management Group. In December 1997, PG&G changed its name to GunnAllen Management. The name change was requested by GunnAllen Financial, according to Florida corporate records. About the same time that Gum Tech began its investment banking relationship with GunnAllen, a number of employees who worked at Sovereign transferred to GunnAllen.

Several – including Richard Frueh, GunnAllen's chief executive officer, Gunn, its president and Alex Rivera, its head trader – still work at GunnAllen. Sovereign was shuttered by securities regulators in November, 1997, for failing to pay a fine for previous misconduct. GunnAllen continues to use the same telephone number that Sovereign used and the firm's headquarters in Tampa, Fla. also occupies old Sovereign offices in that town.

Gunn said that the "seven or eight" Sovereign employees that left the firm to form GunnAllen were "independent" and had nothing to do with what happened at Sovereign.

"We are not Sovereign or have anything to do with Sovereign," he ["Gunn"] said. Documents obtained by Dow Jones Newswire, showed that Gum Tech entered in a banking advising agreement with Sovereign in November 1996. Under that deal, Gum Tech agreed to compensate Sovereign in cash and options to buy 100,000 shares. Those options were distributed to Gunn, Frueh and another Sovereign employee in March 1997.

While evidence of the mob's infiltration of Wall Street is clear, I never believed that the founders of GunnAllen had mob ties. What they had was incredibly bad luck.

GunnAllen's founders had been brokers at a firm that was mentioned in the *BusinessWeek* story. They were not management. They simply ran their own branch. They already left the allegedly mobbed-up firm by the time the story went public. But the damage was done.

It was hard enough to gain credibility as a broker-dealer in the state of Florida. Boca Raton was the Mecca of penny stock deals, which is synonymous with fraud. Tampa was primarily a military base and a college town. By adding the populations of Tampa, St. Petersburg, and Clearwater, you maybe have a top ten US "City." Yet, with no public transportation system and a sprawling geography, Tampa was fairly isolated. That isolation, however, didn't apply to media coverage or regulatory scrutiny.

Despite having severed all ties to the alleged mob-affiliated firm, GunnAllen's founders were considered by some to be guilty by association. Although they changed firms, GunnAllen stayed in the same building, used the same phone numbers, and owned and traded one of the same stocks as the former allegedly "mobbed-up" firm.

The particular stock featured in the blog happened to be down more than 50% from the time they bought it for clients at the prior – and alleged mob-connected – firm. Now, one might ask why GunnAllen continued to own a huge position in a stock that was down by more than 50%. The answer in the Industry is always simple: money.

In this instance, it takes some explaining to reveal just how *much* money.

First, GunnAllen was a market maker in this particular stock. As a market maker, GunnAllen could use the Industry's two-price bid/ask system to make money via the spread between the higher "ask" price paid by buyers and the lower "bid" price received by sellers. As a market maker, GunnAllen was always making money between purchases and sales.

The stock happened to be a low-priced thinly-traded stock. As the *BusinessWeek* story pointed out, with low-priced (penny) stocks and thinly-traded (low volume) stocks, there can be a significant spread between the bid and ask prices. For example, in an extreme case, a stock could have an "ask" price of $4.00, which is paid by buyers, and a "bid" price of $0.50, which is received by sellers. If a market maker has a buyer and seller at the same time, the market maker can execute a trade between the buyer and seller and make $3.50 per share – without risk.

For more information about bulletin board stocks, click here: OTC Bulletin Board (http://en.wikipedia.org/wiki/OTC_Bulletin_Board).

In the case of Matrixx/Gum Tech, GunnAllen brokers had raised money for the company, which is normal for a firm with an investment banking department. GunnAllen was a market maker in the firm's stock, which also is normal for a firm that makes markets in stocks. It appears that

GunnAllen did accumulate and control a sizable position in the firm's tradable stock. This gave GunnAllen's market makers the ability to profit from trading in the stock.

In addition, every time a GunnAllen broker recommended a purchase or sale of the company's stock, the broker would also charge a commission. GunnAllen also earned a portion of the broker's commission.

In addition, most independent broker-dealers charge their brokers a flat ticket charge for each executed trade. The ticket charge is another revenue source, above and beyond the broker's commission. GunnAllen earned money from ticket charges every time a broker executed a trade.

On top of the commission to the client and the ticket-charge to the broker, many firms also charge a postage and handling fee. The postage and handling fee is a separate charge, imposed each and every time there is a transaction in a client's account.

In total, GunnAllen stood to earn money on each and every trade as follows:

1. a market making spread
2. a commission
3. a ticket charge
4. a postage and handling fee

The Industry made it perfectly legal for a firm like GunnAllen to make money at least four different ways on every stock trade in this particular security.

So, while I respectfully submit that GunnAllen and its principals didn't have mob ties, as the blogger's connection might imply, they were still interested in making a profit.

Yet – for some – four different ways of making money *still* wasn't enough.

Safety tip 2: Know the fees to buy and sell securities. Also know the ongoing internal fees charged by the investments you own, i.e. ETFs, mutual funds, insurance, annuities, etc.

The cost of *all* services, whether for an individual stock trade or for general advice, should be clearly provided – in writing – for each transaction. The ongoing (or internal) fees for each investment should also be clear, so you understand the annual cost of ownership.

Any investment recommendation should be made with a thesis – or a rationale – as to:

- why the investment makes sense in general,
- why it makes sense in particular, for you as a investor,
- why it make sense to buy something now, and
- when it would make sense to sell it.

In short, clear understandable reasons should be provided for each and every transaction. Clients should ask for a written investment policy statement. All investments should be made according to an overall plan that's clear and measurable.

SCAM ALERT 1: BROKERS – Churning, Burning, & Converting

Churning, or excessive activity, is a fraudulent practice whereby a broker engages in trading for the purpose of generating commissions for themselves at the customer's expense and in disregard of the customer's investment objectives. While it's theoretically possible for a broker to make money for an investor, even while churning the client's account, it's practically impossible. Even if, by some miracle, the stocks picked by the broker went up, the massive amount of commissions and trading costs could consume any profits. In fact, if there were gains, the broker would sell, to "take a profit." If there were losses, the broker would also sell to "minimize the loss."

Churning is bad. Excessive commissions are bad. Losses are bad. Churning an account to generate excessive commissions with massive losses is *really* bad. Watching a broker churn an account and generate excessive commissions and massive losses and not doing anything about it is as bad as it gets.

The irony is when it's "shocking" or newsworthy that there are consequences for such a failure to protect an investor. Yet, GunnAllen even managed to screw up the consequences of its own misconduct:

The Leading Information Source for Financial Advisers

Boilerplate pact foils GunnAllen

By Bruce Kelly | May, 1, 2006 - 12:01 am EST

NEW YORK - In a legal blunder, GunnAllen Financial Inc. of Tampa, Fla., last month lost a $1.8 million federal court case that most likely never had to go to trial.

Judges and juries almost never hear securities cases against broker-dealers brought by disgruntled clients. That's because the standard contract that clients sign when opening a brokerage account requires them to submit to arbitration with NASD of Washington or the New York Stock Exchange, the industry's self-regulatory organizations.

But a California attorney intent on taking his client's case against GunnAllen to trial got his way because of the language in a boilerplate contract.

The attorney, Lawrence Padway, tried to submit his client's arbitration claim to the NYSE in March 2005, alleging that his client, Royal Yates, had been charged excessive fees and that his account had been churned by GunnAllen-affiliated representative Curtis Williams, who had Mr. Yates' account from February until April 2004.

- -

According to court papers, Mr. Yates opened the account in February 2004 with cash and securities totaling $428,000. By May of that year, his losses included commissions of $128,840 and trading losses of $240,381, according to a joint pretrial statement.

In the above case, the investor lost over $128,000 or 30% of his account value to commissions. In addition, the investor *also* lost more than $240,000 or 50% of his account value to losses. A $428,000 account lost more than $368,000 to commissions and losses.

The net result of churning is that the client loses money while the broker makes money. *Every time.* While it's more work for a broker to actually show up each day to churn an account than it is to simply rob a bank, it's just as illegal. Churning is basically stealing. The broker is essentially taking money from the client by converting the client's cash into a commission. The money leaves the client's account and winds up in the broker's pocket.

In reality, this doesn't have to happen; but the Industry's flawed system enables it to occur. While every brokerage firm has supervisory systems that detect excessive trading, excessive commissions, and excessive losses, it's still up to the firm to stop the misconduct. While FINRA provides general guidelines, it's left up to each firm to set specific policies and make their own determination as to how much trading, commissions, and/or losses are considered "excessive." Unless the Industry first identifies the problems and then does something about it, investors are at risk.

In this case, GunnAllen *did* identify a problem with churning. Unfortunately, the problem was detected long after the fact. Even worse, the firm did little to stop it. Months after the problem was detected, the broker continued to churn the account and the customer's losses continued to increase. The firm didn't stop it quickly enough. The regulators didn't get involved until after the customer filed a complaint. By then, it was way too late.

The result was very costly for the investor. It also appeared it was going to be very costly to GunnAllen.

This case was notable because it wound up in court – instead of Industry arbitration – due to a technical error. Despite the initial legal victory for the client, GunnAllen was also able to use the legal system. GunnAllen filed a successful appeal, in which the punitive damages were significantly reduced. However, since the broker left the firm and, since GunnAllen ultimately filed for bankruptcy, I don't know if the client ever recovered any money.

In part 2, I'll discuss the very low probability of recovering losses. For GunnAllen clients who lost money, there was *no* recovery once the firm closed. There were no assets, no insurance – no recourse. The money investors lost was long gone.

Safety tip 3: **Monitor Account Activity and Check Your Balances Regularly!**

For every transaction, an investor should receive a confirmation. Confirmations should provide specific details, such as the date, time, price, capacity in which the broker or advisor acted in providing services, and the type of order placed or received.

For every account, an investor should receive a monthly statement (quarterly, if there's no activity). Every statement should list the starting value and the ending value. The change in value for the period should be clear and prominently displayed. There should also be a list of all holdings — by category and details — regarding all transactions during the period.

A broker/advisor can act in one of two capacities:

- As a **principal**, a broker may charge a mark-up on a purchase or a mark-down on a sale. A mark-up or mark-down effectively adds the broker's commission into the price of the transaction and affects the actual price paid on a buy (higher) or received on a sell (lower).

- As an **agent**, the broker's commission is fully disclosed as a separate charge. The price for the purchase or sale of a security is separate from any commissions, fees, or charges imposed by the broker.

The clarity and quality of the disclosure of your fees, commissions, charges, etc., is generally better when the broker acts as agent.

There are generally two types of orders:

- A *solicited* trade, which means the broker called and explicitly recommended buying or selling a specific security at a specific price for a specific reason for a specific fee.

- An *un-solicited* trade, which means you called the broker and requested a transaction.

The responsibility and liability on the broker is higher for solicited trades. Solicited trades provide greater investor protection, should there be any disputes down the road.

Dishonorable Mention: Rogue Broker Misconduct

Not to be outdone by traditional forms of misconduct, such as churning, another GunnAllen broker actually threatened a public company executive in an attempt to extort inside information. Once again, it involved a small cap company (low-priced stock) with low volume (thinly-traded) that a broker hoped to manipulate through illegal information and tactics:

News Release

FOR RELEASE: Tuesday, April 18, 2006
CONTACTS: Nancy Condon (202)728-8379, Herb Perone (202)728-8464

NASD Hearing Panel Suspends, Fines Former GunnAllen Broker for Threatening Public Company Washington, DC – An NASD hearing panel has suspended former stockbroker Shawn Aaron for two years and fined him $50,000 for threatening and intimidating Optelecom-NKF, Inc. (OPTC), a Nasdaq SmallCap company, while he was registered with GunnAllen Financial, Inc., of Tampa, FL. NASD had charged that Aaron engaged in a scheme to defraud and extort OPTC by threatening to drive down the price of its stock from $13 to $6 per share unless it provided him with confidential business information.

The hearing panel found that Aaron purchased 5,180 shares of OPTC for his own account and another 134,540 shares for 54 of his customers in early April 2004. By mid-April, Aaron and his clients together held 139,720 shares. or about 4% of OPTC's outstanding shares. on April 16, 2004, Aaron left a voicemail with OPTC's Chairman and CEO stating that he owned 10% of the company's stock and that he wanted to talk to him about taking the stock to "the next level."

On April 19, 2004, Aaron talked to OPTC's investor liaison consultant. Aaron again claimed that he owned 10% of the company, or about 300,000 shares. Aaron asked OPTC's investor liaison consultant for reasons to keep buying OPTC. Otherwise, Aaron stated, he "could drive the stock down to six bucks if I dumped 300,000 shares on the market, unless you have institutions lined up." Aaron boasted that he was GunnAllen's top producer and claimed to have a special relationship with its president, with whom he shared his "best ideas" about promoting stocks. Aaron also claimed he was instrumental in increasing the stock prices of at least two other publicly traded companies.

http://www.finra.org/Newsroom/NewsReleases/2006/P016373

The NASD (now known as FINRA) determined that GunnAllen broker Shawn Aaron attempted to extort a public company by threatening to drive down the price of its stock if officials didn't provide him with confidential information. The company, instead, contacted regulators.

While this broker's misconduct occurred in 2004, no action was taken for more than two years – almost to the day. GunnAllen was not charged in the matter – and yet, during that entire time, this broker continued to work and GunnAllen continued to grow and expand.

2004: One of the Best Investments Ever

As I began developing GunnAllen's wealth management platform, its founders had been working on the firm's best investment ever. It wasn't a stock, or a bond, or a mutual fund. It wasn't an investment GunnAllen sold to its customers. It was a real estate deal – for the firm, by the firm.

As GunnAllen hired more brokers, the firm outgrew its original location. When another local firm over-expanded and filed for bankruptcy, GunnAllen placed a lowball bid for their unfinished-but-beautiful new office building.

In March, 2004, GunnAllen purchased a five-story 118,000 square-foot office building at 5002 W. Waters Ave., in Tampa, from Tropical Sportswear International Corp. The fully furnished building featured a five-story atrium with fiber-optic lights depicting stars in the night sky. There were outdoor balconies, a two hundred-seat auditorium with a fully raised stage and multi-colored lights, plus a cafeteria and a fitness center.

GunnAllen paid $9.5 million – approximately $80 per square foot – which was about half of the original cost. It was a steal. Even so, GunnAllen's parent company borrowed money to finance the purchase.

The firm proudly issued a press release, to celebrate its growth and success:

GunnAllen Financial Purchases New Headquarters to Accommodate its Tremendous Growth.
http://www.businesswire.com/cgi-bin/mmg.cgi?eid=4604265

TAMPA, Fla.—(BUSINESS WIRE)—March 30, 2004

In 2002, GunnAllen Financial set out to be more than just another securities brokerage and trading company. Today marks the crowning achievement in the company's rise to leadership in the Industry with the closing on the new headquarters building located at 5002 West Waters Avenue in Tampa, Florida.

The five-story, 118,000-square-foot headquarters on West Waters Avenue was completed in late 2002, but was never utilized by the previous owner. It includes a 200-seat auditorium available to community groups with a new parking deck and trading floor to be added before GunnAllen Financial relocates to the facility later this year.

GunnAllen Financial has grown to become one of the top fifteen independent brokerage firms in the U.S. and the company's rapid evolution is evident in its revenue growth, national expansion, increase in advisors and the introduction of its new brand identity.

From one location in Tampa in 1996 to 161 locations in 32 states today, GunnAllen Financial has close to doubled in revenue and number of advisors each of the last three years. In January 2002, there were 198 independent brokers at GunnAllen Financial. Today, there are more than 900 independent brokers with a projected increase to 1,250 by the end of 2004.

"We were literally busting at the seams at our current headquarters so the question was not when, but where," stated Richard A. Frueh, Chairman and Chief Executive Officer of GunnAllen Financial. "Our people have worked hard and we are adding advisors and services to support them at a pace that requires a larger headquarters. We are proud of our growth and do not see it slowing down any time soon."

GunnAllen Financial is a full service retail-orientated brokerage firm specializing in the trading and sale of both equity and fixed income securities, including mutual funds. The company currently maintains approximately 100,000 customer accounts representing an estimated $4.8 billion in assets.

In the Tampa Bay area, there are more than 300 employees (corporate and registered representatives). The majority of these will move to the new corporate headquarters this summer from its current location at 1715 N. Westshore Boulevard in Tampa.

In other recent developments, GunnAllen Financial introduced its new branding and identity package in an effort to enhance its efforts in marketing and recruiting in late 2003. On March 3, 2004, GunnAllen Financial converted its main clearing platform from First Clearing Corp. to Pershing, a Bank of New York Company. Pershing is the largest clearing firm in the world and has almost 80% of the independent market.

Gunn Allen Holdings, Inc., a Florida corporation ("GAH"), is a holding company engaged in securities brokerage, securities trading, investment banking, and money management activities through its wholly owned subsidiary GunnAllen Financial, Inc. In addition, GAH has another subsidiary, GAF Insurance Services, Inc., a Florida corporation, which serves as an insurance broker for insurance products offered and sold through GunnAllen Financial.

The building was spectacular. All the executives got massive offices. The CEO and President's offices had huge plasma TVs, private bathrooms with showers, private conference rooms, private kitchenettes, external balconies, etc.

It was nicer than any other independent-broker dealer's headquarters that I'd ever seen. In fact, it was far more spectacular than any of the offices of any of the other broker-dealers with whom I'd ever been employed.

GunnAllen moved into this beautiful new building and into the big leagues. But, while the firm could change its location, it couldn't leave its past behind.

Also On the Move – The Rise of the NASD/FINRA in Florida

Around the same time GunnAllen moved to new offices, the National Association of Securities Dealers ("NASD") – the predecessor to FINRA – also opened a new office in Florida. GunnAllen's largest offices were in New York and Florida. I don't know if it was a coincidence, but FINRA relocated a New York-based executive to run the new Florida office.

In November of 2004, the NASD, now known as FINRA, announce the appointment of Mitchell Atkins as the director of its new Florida district office in Boca Raton.

News Release

FOR RELEASE: Thursday, November 17, 2004
CONTACTS: Nancy Condon 202-728-8379, Herb Perone 202-728-8464

NASD Names Top Officials for New Florida District Office

Washington DC – NASD announced today that Long Island Office Associate Director Mitchell C. Atkins will assume new duties as the Director of NASD's new Florida District Office in January, 2005.

The Florida District Office, located in Boca Raton, will open in the spring of 2005 and will have a permanent staff of more than 40.

"Throughout his career, Mitch has demonstrated exceptional leadership, teamwork and commitment to the work of NASD," said Robert C. Errico, NASD's Executive Vice President for Member Regulation. "Florida has a huge presence in the securities industry – with approximately 280 securities firms now located there, it trails only California and New York in the number of registered representatives and branches. Under Mitch's leadership, our new Florida District Office will make NASD more accessible to Florida's firms and investors, and will make them more accessible to us."

Since October, 2003, Atkins has headed up NASD's Long Island office. Prior to that, he served as Supervisor in the New Orleans District Office. He has been with NASD since 1993.

GunnAllen's broker misconduct had caught the attention of the Industry's primary regulator and watchdog. The chess pieces were now in position.

As GunnAllen grew, so began the rise of what would become one of FINRA's largest offices and one of FINRA's brightest stars. The more GunnAllen paid in fines, the higher Mitchell Atkins was promoted at FINRA.

With all the retirees, customer complaints, and outright securities fraud occurring in Florida, Mitch Atkins would build his career by cracking down on bad brokers and bad firms. He was a man with a mission. He was a zealot. He generated a massive amount of revenue for FINRA with fines and fees.

It didn't take him long to get started on GunnAllen; it simply took too him too long to finish. GunnAllen may have survived for so long by paying massive fines to FINRA. There might also have been another reason GunnAllen survived so long.

It might have had something to do with Mitch Atkin's past.

FINRA Pays a Visit: GunnAllen will pay a price

With rumors of mob ties, customer complaints, and allegations of churning and extortion, FINRA decided to examine GunnAllen.

Each year, FINRA's staff would show up at GunnAllen's home office, to conduct an audit. The objectives of the regulatory audits, generally, were to determine if the firm:

1. complied with all applicable Industry rules and regulations, and
2. established adequate compliance policies and supervisory procedures to properly manage its operations and supervise its brokers

New firms, in general, and fast-growing firms, in particular, face restrictions on growth – precisely because the regulators want to ensure these firms have adequate capital, systems, policies, procedures, and management to operate in a compliant manner.

By every measure, GunnAllen blew through any reasonable rate of growth. In just three years, the firm grew from around 200 brokers to around 1,000. This violated FINRA's rules that essentially governed growth. Every brokerage firm must apply for regulatory approval **_prior_** to any material change in operations. A material change would include growing the number of brokers above certain limits. Other criteria that also require obtaining regulatory approval, in advance, include expanding into new states, adding business lines, opening more branches, and so forth.

GunnAllen had a limit on the number of branches it was permitted to open in Florida. The firm required regulatory approval to increase its number of branches. So, GunnAllen found *another* way to achieve its goal. I call it the "branch shell game."

Just as every broker-dealer must be registered with FINRA, each branch of a broker-dealer also must be registered with FINRA. Every broker within each branch also must be registered with FINRA. There must be a clear hierarchy that shows where a broker is registered and how the broker is supervised. It's a simple chain-of-command structure that should allow for better monitoring and supervision. This system works well – except when you play the branch shell game and start recycling branch numbers.

When a branch closes, the branch number should be retired. All the activity, accounts, trades, etc. for that branch should have a start date and an end date, consistent with the branch's opening and closing dates.

Since regulators imposed limits on the number of branches GunnAllen could open, and since increasing the limit on branches required regulatory approval, GunnAllen's management determined there was an easier way to open new branches: re-use old branch numbers. Like a shell game of "now you see it, now you don't," branches were opened and closed all the time in different places. It may not sound like a big deal, unless it's:

1) against the rules, and

2) you get caught

Using an old branch number circumvents the regulatory requirement that a firm must first register a new branch, prior to conducting any business.

When FINRA came to audit GunnAllen, one of the first things they noticed was the branch shell game. It wasn't the first time a fast growing broker-dealer tried this trick. FINRA asked for account statements and transaction reports for specific branches. When branch numbers are re-used, the records for multiple branches wind up getting merged. It didn't take long for FINRA to ask such questions as:

- Why did a closed branch conduct business in five different locations across the state?
- How is new business being conducted in a closed branch?

When regulators notice that a firm is playing fast and loose with fundamental, basic, and simple rules, it sets a bad tone. In addition, GunnAllen's bad press, allegations of mob ties, and egregious misconduct by a couple of brokers didn't help.

The firm was squarely in the regulator's crosshairs.

When FINRA's examiners showed up in 2004, the firm underwent its most extensive audit ever. The findings would not be good.

GunnAllen's life had really just begun. Now, it was about to fight for its survival.

SCAM ALERT 2: TRADERS – Front Running

The first of what would be multiple strikes against GunnAllen hit soon after FINRA's audit. A prior regulatory review of the firm's market making and trading operations identified a troubling pattern.

Imagine if 91% or more of your stock trades were profitable. You'd be the most successful and fabulously wealthy trader of all time. Alternatively, you could be the head trader of a broker-dealer that traded *ahead* of large orders, keeps profitable trades for himself, and gives losing trades to investors.

This is exactly what GunnAllen's head trader got caught doing. The following text is an actual excerpt from FINRA's findings:

I. Alexis J. Rivera's Trade Allocation Scheme

GunnAllen Financial, Inc., acting through Alexis J. Rivera, its former head trader, engaged in a violative trade allocation. or "cherry picking." scheme during the period from January 2002 through December 2003.

During the relevant period, certain registered representatives of the firm aggregated retail customers' day trading orders and comunicated an opening transaction to Rivera by telephone or instant messaging. Rivera, knowing by experience that the representatives generally engaged in day trading and that an opening transaction would be followed the same day by a closing transaction, would work the order in a fum proprietary account, sometimes allocating a first profitable trade to his wife's personal account. For example, on October 8, 2003, at 11:47:22, Rivera received an order to short sell 10,000 shares of Linear Technology Corporation common stock (LLTC) and executed the trade at a price of 39.40. At 11:47:43, Rivera covered the short position at a price of39.335 for a profit of $650 and allocated the trades to his wife's account. Later the same day, at 14:24:33, Rivera again sold short 10,000 shares of LLTC at a price of3 9.32 and then covered the position between 15:09:28 and 15:45:45 at an average price of 40.14. He allocated those trades and the resulting loss of $8,200 to the accounts of the customers whose orders comprised tbe 10,000 share block order.

During the relevant period, Rivera effected 446 buy and 446 sell transactions in his wife's account, most of which were handled in substantially the manner described above. Of these transactions, 91 percent were profitable, earning his wife $270,194.

In addition, by virtue of this conduct, the firm, acting through Rivera, at times did not give the affected customers best execution when it delayed execution of customer orders, allowing Rivera's wife to take trading profits, and subsequently executed trades for the customers at prices less favorable than the prevailing inter-dealer price at the time of receipt of the customers' orders.

FINRA found that, in 2002 and 2003, GunnAllen's head trader used customer orders to trade for his own benefit. He took profitable stock trades and put them into his wife's account and booked losing trades into GunnAllen customer accounts. Rivera allegedly made over $270,000 in illegal profits doing this.

In short, Rivera's profits should have gone to investors. Specifically, the GunnAllen clients who placed trades that Rivera "hijacked" should have made these profits. Instead, Rivera personally gained at the investors' expense.

The trade allocation scheme violated FINRA rules and the federal securities laws' anti-fraud provisions. For this misconduct, GunnAllen's ex-head trader was suspended in 2004. He was fired from GunnAllen in 2005. It took until 2006 before he was barred from the securities Industry by FINRA.

Since Rivera was profiting personally and not acting on the firm's behalf, GunnAllen was not charged in the matter. The firm did pay a fine for its failure to detect or prevent this misconduct.

It takes at least four factors to enable the occurrence of this type of misconduct:

1. a lack of proper supervisory systems;
2. a lack of internal policies and controls;
3. a firm culture that either tolerates or is blind to misconduct;
4. a conflicted Industry that is funded by fines

At the time, the findings of churning, extortion, and front-running were private and confidential. While the problems were uncovered early, it took years for the information to become public. It was all still in the investigation phase. Yet, certain members of GunnAllen's management team knew. The Industry regulators knew.

Unfortunately, investors didn't know.

Ultimately, investors would get screwed several times by the Industry and the regulators. In addition to a failure to detect, prevent, or even warn investors, the Industry failed to make harmed investors whole. Once Rivera's misconduct was identified, FINRA's remedy was not to return the lost profits to harmed investors. There was no restitution. Instead, FINRA charged a fine. FINRA kept the money.

In fact, I don't believe harmed investors were *ever* even informed they'd been victims of fraud. If you think about it, investors lost, GunnAllen paid a fine, and FINRA benefitted by keeping the money.

Safety tip 4: Monitor Your Results

Every brokerage account investor should request, receive, and review a gain/loss statement at least annually, if not quarterly. A gain/loss statement will show the profits or losses in total for the account and for each specific transaction. Realized gains measure actual gains or losses already incurred. Unrealized gains or losses are on paper – but would be realized, if all securities were immediately sold at that time. Every investment advisory client should request, receive and review a quarterly performance report that tracks an account's performance relative to a specific benchmark and against known Industry indexes, such as the S&P 500.

2005: The President's Speech

In 2005, I attended GunnAllen's national conference in Orlando. At the time, I was still a consultant. The CEO had offered me a full-time job and I was invited to attend the conference, at the firm's expense.

GunnAllen's issues with churning, extortion, front-running, etc. had all been uncovered at the time – but nothing was public. In fact, the information was handled very privately and discretely. Within the Industry, multiple investigations were underway. These investigations were strictly confidential between the regulators, GunnAllen's senior management, and GunnAllen's expensive lawyers. Management kept the information and accusations quarantined. At the time, like almost everyone else, I was unaware of the extent and potential severity of the firm's pending regulatory issues.

However, at the conference, it was obvious GunnAllen had a broker "quality" problem. That's a polite way of saying the firm's brokers were less than ideal. Despite frequent reminders regarding a business casual dress code, unshaven brokers were walking around during the day in sweatpants or bathing suits. At night, they were staggering around drunk.

Over the next three days, almost 300 brokers would attend meetings, presentations, and exhibits, and have breakfast, lunch, and dinner with GunnAllen's management, its staff, and Industry vendors.

Brokers' names were recorded at each event they attended. Brokers who were present won awards, such as flat screen TVs. These awards were handed out for attending an event the broker was *supposed* to attend. Through the grapevine, I did hear rumors/complaints that the same brokers won prizes every year and that the executive who handed out the prizes had a house lined wall-to-wall with flat screen TVs. This same executive's garage was allegedly filled with golf balls, DVD players, etc.

Anyway, on the last day of the conference, the firm's Chief Compliance Officer ("CCO") gave a speech. I stood in the back of the auditorium and listened to a speech about the need to have a "magic letter" on file. According to the CCO, who was an attorney and a former SEC employee, every broker should have every customer sign a letter acknowledging that investing was risky, trading was speculative, and that losses could occur. The attorney beamed when he said: "With this letter, you have a 'get out of jail free' card. It's like magic. Hence, I call it the 'magic letter.'"

I looked around in disbelief. I understood what he was saying. I just couldn't believe these words were coming from a Chief Compliance Officer. I'd never heard such a thing before and have not heard anything like it since. I don't expect I ever will.

Fortunately, the firm's President stepped up, took the microphone, and ended this speech a bit earlier than the beaming Chief Compliance Officer expected. With deep emotion and a perfectly sincere delivery, the President simply said: "Listen guys. With all due respect, you should never ever need a 'magic letter.' If you just work hard each day to make your clients money, you never have to worry about anything." He meant what he said. He founded the firm, his name was on the building, and he practiced what he preached. I truly believe to this day that the President cared deeply for his clients.

The President's words, sincerity, and passion won me over. If the firm's President stood up and said the right things, he could be trusted. Right?

I had dipped my toe in the water as a consultant. I would soon be all in as an employee.

Growing Pains – Growth at a Price

In show business, they say, "No press is bad press." In the Industry, the opposite is true: *most* press is bad press. In GunnAllen's case, bad press quickly tarnished GunnAllen's reputation. The firm became the Industry's poster child for its "bad-boy" behavior. However, the bad press was primarily limited to Industry publications. Investors generally didn't read *Registered Representative* or *Investment News*. These publications were read mostly by brokers and advisors. Also by a few regulators.

So, while the bad press didn't increase awareness of GunnAllen's problems among investors, it *did* increase concern with regulators, brokers, and advisors. Consequently, in addition to increased regulatory scrutiny, the bad press started to affect GunnAllen's ability to recruit new brokers. Specifically, GunnAllen's ability to attract high quality brokers was compromised.

Without recruiting, the firm couldn't grow. If the firm was profitable, maintaining and/or improving current operations would have been a perfectly sound business strategy. But, the firm wasn't profitable. It *needed* to grow. The founders had promised others it would grow.

The firm had raised money from investors. To support its rapid growth spurt, GunnAllen had paid brokers a *lot* of money to join the firm. In order to pay brokers large up-front cash bonuses to join the firm, GunnAllen had to raise money from investors. To buy its gorgeous new building, GunnAllen had to raise even *more* money from additional investors. GunnAllen issued stock and borrowed money and promised investors rates of return with high projections of future growth potential.

In any other business, rapid growth like GunnAllen's would have been praised. It's not easy to build a business or recruit brokers or properly administer a firm that doubled, then tripled, then quadrupled in size so quickly. Except – upon closer examination – it was clear GunnAllen took some shortcuts to grow so fast. In particular, the firm hired brokers with questionable backgrounds.

As other "bad" firms went out of business, GunnAllen would swoop in and offer brokers who already had to find a new firm a lot of money to join GunnAllen. Often, GunnAllen would pay large signing bonuses to recruit brokers with multiple customer complaints from firms that were closing. As I would later argue, it made no sense (or cents) to me to throw cash at brokers who were on fire. But, GunnAllen's head of recruiting saw it differently. He was paid to hire – and hire he did.

This raised the question: if you hire "bad" brokers, does it make you a "bad" firm? Opinions were forming. The firm's reputation was at stake. One of the Industry's leading publications summed up GunnAllen's situation perfectly:

Growth at a Price.
Registered Rep.
October 1, 2005

Byline: JOHN CHURCHILL

GunnAllen Financial, in Tampa, Fla., had been in business for six years and had about 200 brokers and $1.2 billion in assets. Its founders, Richard Allen Frueh (pronounced "free") and Jay Gunn, realized they could not put their growth strategy on hold. So, they went into overdrive, recruiting known producers who were willing to take a chance on a new independent firm that offered open architecture and the freedom to run their businesses how they wanted.

Three years later, GunnAllen has 907 reps and $5.8 billion in assets. But along with all that growth, GunnAllen acquired something else—a reputation for hiring a relatively high proportion of reps with heavily marked up U4s, including some who have received criminal complaints. As recently as July, 4.3

percent of GunnAllen reps were under "enhanced supervision," because they had three or more marks on their U4s. According to the NASD, only 0.6 percent of the nation's 660,000 registered persons have three dings; only 10 percent have any.

Nobody is accusing GunnAllen of running a crooked business—indeed, the company says it goes to great lengths to investigate the nature of customer complaints and to eliminate the truly bad eggs. And, today, the firm no longer hires reps with more than three marks, no matter the circumstances, says Frueh. But the number of marked up reps still at the firm—and the notoriety of one of the firm's top producers, who has a whopping 24 hits on his U4—still raises questions. "They've hired a lot of shady brokers," says a recruiter who asks not to be named. "If you're on the cusp of sloppiness, you could have a place at GunnAllen." On the other hand, he says, the firm is not in the same league with the notorious bucket shops.

"All the reputable firms we deal with have a list with the names of other firms to avoid," says the recruiter. "If you've ever worked at one of them—for two months even—they won't hire you. The good news is GunnAllen isn't on that list, yet." But it's precariously close, he says.

A Bum Rap

Chief executive Rick Frueh says that's a bum rap. "Look, the firm hasn't grown because we hire people with U4 blemishes," he says. Sure, more reps with bad marks may get hired at GunnAllen than at Merrill. But that's because GunnAllen is willing to look at how the complaint arose—and not to simply eliminate any applicant who does not have a pristine U4. "Do we look at their past? Yes. But we also look past the marks and examine what is the mark—what's the nature of the complaint?" says Frueh. He says of the last 1,000 interviewees, only 152 have been hired.

The firm says it also keeps a close eye on its hires. Indeed, heightened supervision of reps with multiple U4 dings is not a required practice, but is recommended by the NASD. (Some state securities regulators do require it in certain cases.) The NASD proposed the policy of constant surveillance of trades, transactions and emails of reps with more than three customer complaints in a notice to members two years ago. But while it's voluntary, many firms have chosen to adopt its guidance, according to the NASD. Marc Menchel, NASD Regulation general counsel, says that high numbers of reps under heightened supervision certainly will attract more attention from the regulator, "but it also means the firm is doing the right thing." And, Frueh points out, since July, the firm has decreased the number of reps under heightened supervision by 10—they resigned or were fired—leaving the number under extra scrutiny at 32, or about 3.5 percent of the broker force.

Danny Sarch, a recruiter and founder of Leitner Sarch Consultants in White Plains, N.Y., says the high number of reps with U4 issues is partly a function of size. To grow as quickly as it did, a small firm like GunnAllen had to look at applicants whose U4 dings eliminate them from wirehouse consideration. "The wires won't touch you if you have three or more, so it's an unfortunate circumstance of being a small start-up firm," he says. "They have trouble getting A-player brokers unless they've been tainted somehow."

Frueh came up through the independent-broker ranks in Tampa at Chatfield Dean & Co., where he worked for five years, followed by a brief stint at W.J. Gallagher, and two years as an independent contractor rep at Sovereign Equity Management. (Frueh says he immediately left Sovereign in 1997 after it was revealed that the firm allegedly had ties to a New Jersey crime family.) Frueh says it was experiences like that that made him want to build a better independent firm. Now he thinks the company has reached a size where it can attract better candidates. And, he says, the moment is right to build a major independent network. "I'm confident we can compete with any of the independents," he says adding, that "both clients and reps want unbiased choice," a desire the firm says it can meet.

This year the firm has hired 243 reps and GunnAllen's once tiny southeastern footprint now includes 236 offices in 35 states. And while the average GunnAllen rep is a $145,000 producer with $6.5 million in assets, this year's hires average $235,000 in production, $21 million in assets and 11 years in the industry.

Frueh says the firm's improvements to its infrastructure and ever-expanding wealth management platform, which now includes 165 approved money managers, have made it a lot easier to woo reps from better firms. In earlier days, the ranks were dominated by RIAs and independent reps who were switching firms. Frueh estimates that wirehouse reps account for nearly 50 percent of new hires, while reps from regionals represent nearly 25 percent. In early September, for example, a high-profile Morgan Stanley wealth-management team in Atlanta came over to GunnAllen. Gratus Capital managed over $800 million at Morgan Stanley last year and was ranked 48th on *Barron's* list of Top 100 Brokers in 2004.

A Big Kahuna, In More Ways than One

But a rep with a Morgan pedigree is not always a good one. One of GunnAllen's top producers—and the rep with the most customer complaints—is a former Morgan broker who remains under heightened supervision per a requirement by Indiana state regulators. He is Indianapolis-based Marc Jaffe, 49, who has made headlines in Indiana, the firm's home state of Florida and in national industry publications for his legal tangles. In June, the 14-year veteran was found guilty of misdemeanor intimidation (he was initially charged with felony intimidation) in an Indiana court and sentenced to one year of jail (it was dismissed), and one year of probation, for leaving threatening phone messages on the answering machines of two former partners at Morgan Stanley after the partnership dissolved. Jaffe was fired from Morgan Stanley in October 2004 because of the calls.

Jaffe came to Morgan in 2001 after 10 years at Merrill Lynch, where he'd become one of its stars in relatively little time. (His success at Merrill even put him on the cover of this magazine in September 1999). He resigned from Merrill in 2001 while under internal review for allegedly exercising unauthorized discretion in customer accounts. According to the Central Registration Depository (CRD), Jaffe has had 24 customer complaints in the past five years, 22 of them arising from his tenure at Merrill, and two related to his time at Morgan Stanley. The majority of the complaints allege churning, unsuitable recommendations and unauthorized trading. Bruce Skolnick, one of Jaffe's attorneys, says disgruntled clients that lost money in the tech wreck and bear market brought the great majority of these cases.

Jaffe's grandmother filed one of the complaints. In March 2001, she claimed she lost $1.1 million under her grandson's watch. According to the complaint, she alleged he exercised discretion, mismanaged and churned her account. She was awarded $400,000 by an arbitration panel in September 2002. All told, Merrill has paid $3.78 million to settle arbitrations; Jaffe has paid $179,600 out of his own pocket, according to the CRD.

So why would a company with GunnAllen's ambitions take on such a seeming liability? Why would the company operate with 30 or 40 reps under enhanced supervision? "We'd like that number to be zero, of course," says Richard Nummi, former chief compliance officer at GunnAllen, who is now the firm's corporate counsel. In the case of Jaffe, the size of his book would seem to be a factor in keeping him around. Jaffe would not disclose his assets under management, but says it is significantly more than $300 million (his book's value in 1999 when *Registered Rep.* profiled him).

But Frueh denies that, and says Jaffe was a special exception. "I've known Marc and his family for 20 years," says Frueh of his fellow Tampa native, "and I knew he was a good person," he says. But he also says there was "nothing in Jaffe's file that disturbed us" and points out that the firm has had no problems or complaints regarding Jaffe since he arrived. The fact that he was able to bring the majority of his book from Morgan Stanley, executives say, is further evidence that he is not a problem broker.

Jaffe, in defense of his record, says the timing of his exit from Merrill—when the market was unraveling—didn't make for a happy goodbye from the firm. "A lot of people wanted to keep my business," says Jaffe. While he declined to elaborate, published reports have said Merrill encouraged clients to file complaints against him when he left—a claim Merrill has vehemently denied. "Marc Jaffe is not a bad broker," says Jaffe. "I'm very passionate about what I do and I work harder than anybody for my clients. But when someone decides to go after you, there's a pile-on effect."

Nummi and Frueh say the company can take on Jaffe and others that would be considered problem brokers elsewhere because GunnAllen has invested an inordinate amount of money and personnel in compliance and supervision. "We watch all of our reps—every email, every trade, every bit of their activity is under surveillance," he says. "We can see everything they do." In other words, no matter what a rep has done in the past (whether it was nefarious or just careless), he or she is unlikely to get away with doing it again.

According to Frueh, the firm spent $4 million last year on "hard compliance costs," including the installation of FrontBridge, an email archiving and monitoring software package, compliance examinations and new personnel. All GunnAllen branches are subject to surprise examinations annually, and some receive more than one visit, says Nummi. "We want to know our reps like they know their clients," Frueh says. Exams typically take 36 hours and include picking through 35 percent to 40 percent of client files opened in the last year, checking for anything out of the ordinary or inappropriate, he says. The firm also employs 48 compliance personnel, which is nearly three times as many as at Commonwealth Financial, which has 1,028 reps, and equal to the number at Securities America, a much larger firm with 1,613 reps.

So far however, the beefed up surveillance and compliance system is not foolproof. Take the case of Shawn Aaron. The Tampa-based rep joined GunnAllen in 2000 and this June was charged by the NASD with attempting to extort and intimidate Nasdaq SmallCap company Optelecom. Aaron, who was let go by the firm in August, has contested the charges and is awaiting his hearing. The NASD is seeking to have Aaron permanently barred from the industry.

Nummi and Frueh say Aaron, who has "faithfully served his clients for 10 years," will be welcomed back at the firm if he is found innocent of the charges. While he had no customer complaints when he was hired, Aaron had been prohibited from selling securities for 25 years in the state of Massachusetts in 1998. Aaron, and several fellow reps at Brauer & Associates (including another future GunnAllen rep) in St. Petersberg, Fla., settled the charges that they sold unregistered securities in the state by withdrawing their Massachusetts registrations.

One prominent New York securities attorney, who wished not to be identified, says the bottom line is that there will always be good reps working at bad firms and bad reps working at good firms. "But if GunnAllen is the latter of those cases, and I think it is, and the firm is sincerely trying to make good on a checkered past, only hiring high-quality people, *and* it can demonstrate that to the NASD, it should be given a chance."

Cleaning House

Some very recent and significant additions and subtractions at the firm would suggest the firm has decided it's time to clean house. National sales manager Dave McCoy, who was hired in 2002 as the chief operating officer, was fired in August for what Frueh says was "behavior unbecoming an officer." (Executives Frueh and Nummi would not comment any further in regard to McCoy because the firm has filed a civil suit against him in Florida seeking the return of a promissory note and his share of the firm's stock. According to that complaint McCoy was fired for engaging in "extremely inappropriate conduct, which was potentially unlawful and certainly placed the firm at risk.")

According to a report in *Investment News*, McCoy was instrumental in the firm's rapid growth, and helped bring in many of reps "with blemishes on their records." The *Investment News* report also noted that 65 reps were "axed," including 10 of those under "heightened supervision."

Frueh says "axed" is an inaccurate characterization, and that the pruning took place over a few months and that a majority of the reps resigned or were dismissed primarily for low production. "It was all part of the normal evaluation process of our reps," he says. "A guy producing $60,000 or $80,000 per year—is he worth the risk when you can replace him with a guy producing $150,000 to $300,000 per year?" Frueh says the firm is weighing risk versus reward with all its reps as it strives to move upmarket and bring aboard higher caliber reps. Meanwhile, the firm has also made some recent key *additions* at the top, including Declan O'Beirne, hired in July as the new CFO; and, Marc Ellis, a respected industry attorney, who was hired in August as chief compliance officer, taking over for Rick Nummi, who became corporate counsel.

Frueh doesn't like the house-cleaning analogy, but he accepts the positive associations. "The 'old' GunnAllen and the 'new' GunnAllen—if you wanted to look at it like that, yeah OK, that's more accurate," he says. "Our core values have always been there, but given what's occurred, it makes sense for us to raise the bar. And keep raising it."

GunnAllen had grown too fast. Whether you hire "good" brokers or "bad" brokers, you still have to supervise them. This required certain systems. If you're going to take a calculated risk and hire "bad" brokers, then you better have really good supervisory systems to watch them extra carefully. If not, you deserve what you get. Right?

Wrong. The Industry has rules intended to slow growth. The rules are designed to make sure a firm has all the capital, systems, policies, procedures, and appropriate management in place to support future growth. Without a proper foundation, even the best-built house will ultimately collapse.

GunnAllen was a ticking time bomb. Without proper systems, the firm had *no* way of properly supervising all the brokers it had hired. Supervisory systems should have come first; broker growth second. GunnAllen's founders knew this. Industry regulators knew this.

While the regulators did nothing, at least GunnAllen's founders scrambled to play catch-up. They tried to back-fill a foundation under the house they'd already built. The firm started investing in supervisory systems it should have had from day one. The firm claimed it was changing its hiring practices. The firm made additions to management.

The article's title, "Growth at a Price," raised another question: what price would GunnAllen pay for its incredibly fast growth?

The answer would come soon enough.

An Employee and a Manager

Around the time the *Registered Rep* article came out, I was offered a full-time job at GunnAllen. I wasn't simply going to be an employee; I was hired to manage several divisions. All the employees within those divisions would report to me. I was responsible for the firms' mutual fund and retirement plan divisions, and its registered investment advisor and insurance agency. I would also handle media – especially after the *Registered Rep* article.

Two major areas specifically excluded from my responsibility/control were investment banking and stock and bond trading for commissions. The founders had staff in place to handle those lines of the business. I'd been a vocal opponent to much of the misconduct I believed was occurring in those areas of the firm. Consequently, management kept me away.

In fact, management didn't just keep me away from those business areas. Like other managers, I was isolated from key meetings, information, and reports. By compartmentalization, management limited access to information about regulatory inquiries, customer complaints, supervisory reports, risk reports, legal actions, and so forth. Only certain individuals had access. Even during meetings, information was limited. Everything was strictly confidential and sharing information was strongly discouraged or prohibited.

In any event, I was offered an executive office on the fifth floor. Instead, I chose to stay on the fourth floor, where my staff was located. I wanted to stay out of the executive politics and do my job. I wanted to be with the employees who were doing their jobs and interacting with brokers. I believed in communicating and sharing information with my staff.

I was given a large corner office with a private bathroom. There was enough room for a conference table in my office. There were also two beautiful dark wood bookcases in which I placed pictures of my family. There was a TV and a refrigerator and a VCR. I had my own secretary who sat outside my office, to answer my phone.

It was excessive.

As part of my job, I was asked to attend Tuesday morning manager meetings. These meetings started at 8:30 am sharp, in the firm's massive auditorium. Rick, the CEO – and Jay Gunn, the President – arranged tables and chairs into a more intimate horseshoe. They would sit at the top of the shoe, and then "go around the horn," with each department manager providing a status update.

Since I lived in south Florida, I commuted to Tampa and would only make the meeting about twice a month. That was more than enough.

Business Development, or recruiting, would generally start off the meeting. The President's brother-in-law ran Business Development. The presentation typically went something like: "This week we have three groups coming in from Atlanta, New York, and Boston. These groups represent over $5 million in gross production with customer assets of more than $25,000,000. Last month, we had a total of 12 groups with $15 million in production and $50,000,000 in assets. Year-to-date, we've had a recruiting pipeline with $126 million in production and over $400,000,000 in potential assets under management."

Rick and/or Jay Gunn would proudly exclaim: "Great job!" or "That's fantastic!" or "Excellent!"

Most attendees would nod in appreciation of how much business these recruiters were bringing into the firm. Business Development's Tuesday morning numbers were always very high. Each week, they got higher.

Transitions and Operations followed Business Development. These departments were run by the President's sister. It was a family affair.

Transitions handled the transfer of accounts from recruits that joined the firm. Over time, a clear pattern emerged. There was a vast difference between what Business Development projected would come over and what Transitions actually processed. The new brokers who got all this money to join the firm never seemed to bring over more than a *fraction* of the accounts or assets they claimed they controlled.

It seemed like no one noticed the huge gap between Business Development's promises and actual results. This equation was critical for a very simple reason. If a broker didn't bring over assets and accounts, then they couldn't generate the business they were hired to generate. If you paid them up-front money for a certain amount of business, and the broker couldn't deliver that business, you were going to lose money.

I don't think anyone kept track of the figures discussed in prior meetings or reconciled the promises to the results. Week after week, I wondered why such a small number of the expected recruits actually joined the firm. Even more troubling was the fact that, when brokers *did* join the firm, only a fraction of the assets the brokers claimed to manage actually transferred to GunnAllen. Clearly, something *had* to be wrong with the numbers.

The question was: whose numbers were wrong? Was it the recruits, or Business Development, or Transitions? I was pretty sure I knew the answer.

Operations would present the number of new accounts that were opened last week, month-to-date, and year-to-date. The answer was in *these* numbers. If new brokers joined the firm and they weren't opening client accounts and transferring in assets, the numbers told the story.

Except – no one wanted to deal with the *real* numbers. Or the obvious facts those numbers told. It was like a dysfunctional family get-together. There was a *lot* of conversation about nothing.

At GunnAllen, it wasn't *just* a family affair; it was also a pep rally. Rick would tell a good motivational story and Jay Gunn would remind everyone to treat our brokers with respect, since they paid our salaries.

Week after week, this would go on and on. Nothing but good news and more growth to report. There seemed to be an unspoken rule to not discuss *any* problems. Problems were only to be discussed in private.

Silly me, I actually thought management was *supposed* to discuss and solve problems.

I always sat on the side, away from the horseshoe. I kept to myself. I let my employees provide their own updates. One day, Rick called out to me and asked if there was anything I wanted to discuss. I was lost in thought, so I paused and looked around at the expectant faces.

An idea hit me. It was time to discuss a problem. I decided to break the unspoken rule. This was a chance to change the pattern.

"Yes Rick, I'm glad you asked," I said. "I have a problem I'd like to discuss." An uneasy tension started to creep into the room. "In my office, I had two bookcases. When I arrived this morning, I noticed there was only one. While I don't mind anyone going into my office, I would like to get my other bookcase back. Does anyone have any idea what could possibly have happened to my bookcase?"

There was a moment of silence and, fortunately, a few laughs, too. Finally, the head of Business Development spoke up: "Actually, we had a new recruit join the firm and we needed a bookcase for his office."

Of all the bookcases in all the offices in the entire 118,000-square-foot building, he *had* to take mine. This wasn't about a bookcase. He wanted to send a message. I was a new employee – he considered himself to be a founder of the firm. He was telling me that guys like me came and went. To him, I was interchangeable, like furniture. He could take what was mine whenever he wanted.

I got his message and delivered one right back: "No problem," I said. Then, I added: "Make sure you replace it. Next time, ask me first. In fact, if you want anything from anyone in any of my departments, ask me first. Before you make any promises to any potential recruits about any products handled by my departments, check with me first. Your job is to recruit. Stick to that. I'll handle financial products and services, so I can maintain the integrity and profitability of my department. Going forward, do not take things that are not yours to take and do not give away things that aren't yours to give. I'm glad we cleared this up. That's all from me, Rick. Thank you."

There was silence. No one could believe I just spoke to the President's brother-in-law like that. To me, it was simply time to start a long-overdue process of change. It wasn't that big a deal.

But it was. It was also a little bit personal. This guy said anything to anyone and did anything he wanted. He promised recruits the world, promised inflated numbers to management, and always got away with it. In my opinion, he was ground zero for many of GunnAllen's problems.

I knew before I asked the question that he took my bookcase. I wanted to send a public message. My message to him was that, while I was around, if something was in "my" part of the business – even just a bookcase – he needed to ask me for permission. His unilateral decisions *had* to stop.

Although he never got me a new bookcase, within a short while, he had to get himself a new job.

Landing a Whale

2005 ended with some good news. The firm had just landed a whale.

Frank Bluestein was every recruiter's fantasy. He was a multi-million dollar producer with over $100 million in assets under management. He'd been with his last firm for the past six years, which implied stability. Frank's prior firm was well-regarded in the financial planner/investment advisor community. Frank didn't have any significant customer complaints, nor did he have any negative regulatory history.

Frank himself was widely regarded as one of the top planners in the business. Any broker-dealer executive who attended industry trade shows or conventions was likely to hear Frank speak or see Frank win some award. Frank was a production machine. He was also very smart and very charming.

Frank had been in GunnAllen's recruiting pipeline for years. His first go around ended poorly. GunnAllen's prior national sales manager wined and dined Frank and took him to a club. Then, according to Frank, the sales manager went home with some girls and left Frank alone at the club. Frank was *not* impressed.

I started talking to Frank by phone. We never actually met until after he joined GunnAllen. We discussed products and services and business strategies. Frank knew more details about most products than almost any other broker I'd met – before or after. He was also knowledgeable about planning strategies. It appeared Frank really knew how to best use products to maximize client benefits.

It also turns out Frank was great at selling a Ponzi scheme. Unfortunately, we wouldn't learn that until it was too late.

While Frank was at GunnAllen, his production and performance were outstanding. He was the highest-producing broker with the most assets under management. He picked stocks, sold insurance, and managed investment advisory accounts for a fee. He did it all.

I remember reviewing quarterly performance reports for Frank's managed accounts. These were fee-based advisory accounts. Frank had discretion, meaning he could buy and sell stocks without having to consult with his clients. There were no commission charges in these accounts, just a quarterly fee, based on the assets he managed. Each quarter, I would get a disc with performance reports for the entire firm's managed accounts. Each performance report had a chart that showed the change in an account's value. The line went up for positive performance and down for negative performance. I scrolled through report after report, watching the line barely wiggle up or down.

Suddenly, I came across a bunch of accounts where the line jumped up sharply. These accounts were *killing* it. This advisor was making his clients a fortune. It was – of course – Frank Bluestein. I called him and he simply said, "Why do you think I charge so much? To lose my clients money? Listen kid, I'm the best fucking manager there is."

In hindsight, there were warning signs. After Frank agreed to join the firm, GunnAllen sent teams of employees to help transition his business. GunnAllen's staff would help Frank's staff fill out account opening forms and account transfer paperwork. GunnAllen employees took turns living for a week at a time in Michigan, to help transition Frank's business.

Multiple teams, over multiple weeks, kept going back and forth to Michigan. The problem was getting the correct information necessary to transfer Frank's clients. There were almost 2,000 clients and a *lot* of information was required, to complete transfer paperwork properly. The problem was that the volume of missing information was overwhelming. The explanation for the missing information was simple: it just came at a very steep price.

It turned out Frank had been selling scam investments in a Ponzi scheme out of a separate office in the multi-story building he owned. While most of Frank's clients owned legitimate investments, such as mutual funds and annuities, many also owned illegitimate Ponzi scheme "investments." In order to hide his illegal activity, many forms and, sometimes, entire client files were hidden. In hindsight, I now understand. Frank's transition was such a mess because his files were deliberately sanitized.

This is clear now. Back then, my phone would ring and Frank would literally scream: "I'm not fucking kidding. You better get some competent people to clean up this fucking mess. I've never seen such a fucked-up transition. I'm gonna' sue all you motherfuckers for tricking me into joining your shitty firm."

Frank yelled. People jumped. I kind of laughed. His cursing was funny. Our transition teams were excellent. I thought the man was a little crazy and just blowing off steam. Changing firms and transferring accounts could interrupt business for 2 to 3 months. His production was approximately $200,000 per month. He was looking at a $500,000 hit to income. His bills didn't stop; his staff and rent had to be paid.

Frank yelled and screamed to the point that we pulled our staff and paid for him to transition his own accounts. A shrewd move, indeed. Had we not bent over backwards for the whale, we might have uncovered the Ponzi scheme. Instead, we paid *extra* money to bring over a broker who almost single-handedly killed the firm.

However, at the time, we just landed a whale. If GunnAllen, despite its bad reputation, could recruit a top broker like Frank Bluestein, then the firm could *really* go places. I was about to go on a ride that would make the nastiest roller coaster look boring. Little did I know I was going to be dressed up and used like the conductor – with no one on the brakes.

2006: GunnAllen moves to upgrade image

By the middle of 2006, I was given the title of Senior Vice President & Director of National Sales. The prior national sales manager had been fired for "extremely inappropriate conduct." I think he had sex with an employee in his office – but, according to him, it was after hours and on *his* desk, so it shouldn't have counted against him.

Anyway, I still lived in south Florida. I only commuted to Tampa about every other week, for just a few nights. The firm needed a new executive and I was available.

Back in college, I majored in both Economics and English. As a bit of a romantic, I confess to loving *Romeo and Juliet*. Among the most famous lines often quoted (incorrectly), Juliet says:

> *What's in a name? That which we call a rose*
> *By any other name would smell as sweet;*

Was Juliet correct in saying something good was good, no matter what the name; conversely, was a firm with bad brokers a bad firm, no matter what the image?

InvestmentNews
The Leading News Source for Financial Advisers

GunnAllen moves to upgrade image
By **Bruce Kelly**
Jul 24, 2006 @ 12:01 am (Updated 12:00 am) EST

David Levine

NEW YORK – In an effort to pump new life into its growth plan, GunnAllen Financial Inc. plans to launch a recruiting and advertising campaign by fall that focuses on the services it offers to registered representatives and advisers.

The moves come amid recent additions to, and revamping of, the Tampa, Fla.-based firm's roster of executives – including hires from key competitors, such as Wachovia Securities LLC of Richmond, Va.

"We have great programs now, the depth and breadth of our platform," said David Levine, senior vice president and director of national sales for GunnAllen. "The message, the identity of the firm, needs to be redefined and better communicated."

As proof of the firm's added strength, Mr. Levine cited a number of new hires, including last Tuesday's announcement that Christopher Frankel, until recently a top executive with Sterne Agee & Leach Group Inc. of Birmingham, Ala., had been named chief operating officer.

GunnAllen has shown unprecedented growth in the recent past, growing to 900 registered reps last year, from about 200 brokers a few years earlier.

Last summer, the firm said that it was cutting ties with some brokers who had multiple knocks – or "yes" answers – on their compliance records.

Last spring, before it began its purge, the firm had 42 brokers – about 4.5% of its total – under heightened supervision. According to published reports, just 0.6% of Washington-based NASD's 660,000 registered reps last year had three "yes" answers on their form U4s, the uniform registration forms for registered reps.

GunnAllen was No. 20 in the most recent *InvestmentNews* survey of independent-contractor broker-dealers and networks last year, with $135 million in gross revenue. One industry observer applauded the changes at GunnAllen.

"I'm impressed. A firm can absolutely recover from that if they're disciplined, have a clear focus or a message, and a game plan," said Larry Papike, president of Cross-Search, a recruiting firm in Jamul, Calif.

He has recruited for GunnAllen in the past, he said, but hasn't worked with the firm in about a year.

Another recruiter, however, stressed that "time will tell" if the firm can overcome its history.

"I hear that, and my feeling is that actions speak louder than words," said Jonathan Henschen, a brokerage recruiter based in Marine on St. Croix, Minn.

"Time will tell if they change their colors," he said, adding that a clear positive is that the firm is bringing in quality management and improving its quality controls over its recruited reps.

In addition to Mr. Frankel, GunnAllen in June said it had hired as general counsel David Jarvis, a veteran of Wachovia Securities, who also worked with that firm's independent-broker-dealer affiliate, Wachovia Securities Financial Network LLC, which is known as FiNet.

The changes in management are "part of the growth strategy," Mr. Levine said.

"We grew very quickly," he said. "This is putting in a really good management team."

And Mr. Levine pointed to the firm's success in capital markets offerings and its fee-based advisory platform as two strong points.

"There's just a range and a depth that I don't think the Street yet perceives to exist at GunnAllen," he said.

Mr. Levine said that the number of reps under special supervision has been cut in more than half, but he isn't aware of the exact number.

"I think in the past, if we were too cavalier in accepting 'yes' answers, we've become much more strict about it," Mr. Levine said. "But for people who are already with GunnAllen, it's on a case-by-case basis."

The firm has changed its recruiting targets and standards, and so far, that has paid off, Mr. Levine said.

"Right now, our goal is $250,000 in [gross dealer concession] and $25 million in assets, which is substantially higher than it was in the past," he said.

Through last month, the firm had recruited nearly 60 registered reps, with $16 million in production, Mr. Levine said, noting that that was ahead of the firm's per capita goal.

"Our revenues continue to grow, and our profitability has improved," he said.

Brokers pass through two committees when joining GunnAllen, with the first looking at employment and regulatory history, and the second examining their production and business mix.

The process is "unbiased, and it's strict – I would say much more so than it was in the past," Mr. Levine said.

"You strip out their production," he said. "You don't take someone with 'yes' answers because they do over $1 million of gross" dealer concession.

Mr. Levine added that a "yes" answer doesn't disqualify a broker right away, because it sometimes includes information about the rep that isn't related to the financial services industry.

"You have to look at things with a degree of compassion and understanding," he said.

Mr. Levine said that about half of GunnAllen's recruits come from wirehouses, while the other half come from other independent broker-dealers.

"The policy we have is, if the regulators say there's a door open or there's an issue, we're going to close the door," he said.

"We are looking to prove to the regulators that we're ahead of the curve, and I'd like to think that over the past year, we've made significant progress demonstrating that," Mr. Levine said. "It's a greatly evolved GunnAllen Financial."

I believed what I said. I believed GunnAllen could be a great firm.

Could GunnAllen's image be changed? Could the firm be great? I thought so. I was all in.

At that moment, I forgot that both Romeo *and* Juliet died, in the end.

Senior Management

Every Thursday, about 10 to 12 executives who comprised GunnAllen's "executive management team" would gather at 12:00 for a senior business meeting. Along with a free lunch, the firm's key issues would be discussed, debated and – occasionally – decided. These meetings were exclusive, confidential, and by-invite-only. As a consultant, I'd delivered presentations to the senior business group. One day, after becoming an employee, I ran into Rick Frueh in the hallway and he invited me to attend. I had to ask if I was supposed to attend on an ongoing basis. His answer was, "Sure. Why not?"

We all sat around a beautiful long dark cherry wood glass-covered conference table, in high-back plush leather seats, in the fifth floor conference room. There were floor-to-ceiling windows and an outdoor balcony. There was a private bathroom and a kitchen and a fully stocked refrigerator. It was gorgeous.

Rick hosted the senior business meeting. He sat at one end of the table. Jay Gunn sat at the other end of the long table. As the firm's CEO, I thought Rick was an effective leader. He would request updates from each of us, discuss issues, solicit opinions, build consensus, and make executive decisions. At times, when disagreements were fierce or when the consensus was not to Rick's liking, he would make an executive decision to table the conversation. In my opinion, Rick would enable management to make decisions with which he agreed; otherwise, he made executive decisions and communicated them as needed. Everyone knew Rick was the boss.

Jay Gunn was almost always in attendance. He rarely spoke. When he did, he was sincere. At one of the first meetings I attended, Jay Gunn made quite an impression. As a traditional commission-based stock broker, Jay did things the old fashioned way. He would find a stock, research it thoroughly, and build a sizeable position. Jay would have a thesis, or rationale, in support of his stock picks. In particular, Jay liked to find what he called "special situations," or low-priced stocks that were not widely covered by Wall Street. I think he believed he could add more value following stocks that weren't widely held or recommended by others. In my opinion, there might have been a reason these stocks weren't widely held or recommended by others. Nonetheless, Jay cared for his clients and his clients cared for him.

While I liked Rick and interacted with him often, I had virtually no relationship with Jay Gunn. My interaction with him was limited. I'd clashed with his sister, who ran Operations, and with his brother-in-law, who ran Business Development. Jay was always cordial, but distant. Personally, I thought Jay was a good guy. He showed care and concern for his employees and clients. We just never clicked.

In hindsight, I realized I resented Jay He was part of management, yet he was silent. His name was on the building. He had all the opportunity in the world to impact the management of the firm. To me, his voice and his management position were wasted. It was frustrating.

In any event, during one particular senior business meeting, after some important issues were resolved, Rick asked Jay if he had anything to add. Jay thought for a while and then, I could almost see the light bulb go off. He said, "You know, I was thinking. I'm a car guy. Each day, I drive to work. You know – in my car. So, when I'm sitting in traffic, I can't help but notice the car in front of me. Often, a car will have a license plate holder that's customized. It got me thinking. Why don't we create GunnAllen license plate holders? You know, it would be great for branding. We could even sell them online to our brokers."

I looked around and didn't say a word. I'd hoped for something a little more substantial. Whereas, Rick managed day-to-day affairs, I thought just maybe we would finally hear something from Jay about setting specific goals for his firm. Perhaps we could define a mission statement, establish targets for revenues, profitability, broker count, and/or assets under management.

Instead, I was going to have the opportunity to buy a GunnAllen license plate holder.

32 Fucks

The title of this chapter stands for the number of times a broker used the word "fuck" in a voice mail message he left for a senior executive at GunnAllen. This wasn't just any broker – and it wasn't my voicemail.

I'd met this broker for the first and last time at GunnAllen's national conference, in 2005. This particular broker caught my attention for the way he wore his sunglasses. For no apparent reason, the broker always wore sunglasses. Even at night. Not over his eyes – up in his hairline, like a bandana. The sunglasses were big and gold and shiny. I think he thought his style was cool. It wasn't. He looked like a bug.

On the last night of the conference, there was an award ceremony. The awards recognized production – total commissions generated. Top branches and top brokers were called out by name and presented with an award. There was also the obligatory handshake and photo opportunity with Jay Gunn and Rick Frueh. Dinner was served, drinks were flowing and award after award was presented. The crowd cheered more loudly over the course of the night. It was late as the top ten brokers were called up, one by one. The applause got louder. There were whistles, cat calls, and shout-outs.

The big moment finally arrived when the number one top-producing broker would be recognized. This was "The Man"…"The Dude"…"The Killer" who generated the most commissions in the past year; the alpha male among alpha males; the biggest swinging dick in a sea of tremendous dicks. You get the point.

Clearly feeling no pain, Rick stood onstage with the microphone and, like a showman, announced, "And the number one top-producing broker of 2005 is……………SunGlasses! (clearly this was <u>not</u> his *real* name).

"Come on up and get your award, you big stud!"

The crowd went wild. To my surprise, the idiot with the sunglasses jumped up. He made his way onstage, fist-pumping the whole time. He climbed on stage and hugged Jay and Rick. *Big* hugs. *Lots* of love. Then he grabbed the microphone.

To this day, I remember his speech:

"When I was looking to join a firm, I thought about Goldman Sachs or Merrill Lynch. Instead, I joined GunnAllen. That decision changed my life. This firm has enabled me to build a business. I am making more money than I ever thought possible. You can, too. So – fuck Goldman Sachs, fuck Merrill Lynch. We're gonna' take over the *world*."

The crowd went wild. I went home.

So – back to the voicemail message with a "fuck" count of 32.

About a year later, a GunnAllen executive was instructed to call SunGlasses, to discuss multiple problems with significant customer losses, excessive trading, and massive commissions. SunGlasses had one particular account from a high net worth executive with several million in assets. Almost every month, this account had massive losses while SunGlasses generated excessive commissions.

From any standard, by any measurement, this was wrong. To me, it was stealing. Plain and simple robbery. SunGlasses was basically taking client money and converting it into commissions. Yet, each month, the client wired more money into the accounting.

In my opinion, SunGlasses' conduct was unacceptable. It was also bad business. The firm would never make enough money to cover the likely losses we would eventually face if and when the client ever filed a complaint. The misconduct *had* to stop. To some of the other executives, however, this was <u>SunGlasses</u> – the firm's "top producing" broker. According to these other executives, SunGlasses earned the right to be treated with respect.

I agreed that a top broker *should* be treated with respect; however, I pointed out that SunGlasses didn't earn the right to steal, or violate rules, or destroy his clients. Management finally relented and decided

SunGlasses needed to get a call. Management also decided that another executive should make the call, since I'd clearly expressed my opinion – against SunGlasses.

Apparently, SunGlasses didn't appreciate being called out about his excessive commissions. Or the client's massive losses. Or his horrendous performance. SunGlasses thought it was completely inappropriate for *anyone* at GunnAllen to question him about his business. Who the hell did GunnAllen think it was? The fact that the firm was obligated by law to supervise him didn't seem to matter.

So – along with death threats, threats of all different types of beatings – including arm breaking, head smashing, and other promises of violence – SunGlasses left a message in which he used the word "fuck" 32 times.

I heard the message. We counted. 32 "fucks."

Later, at a senior management meeting, I suggested SunGlasses should be fired. In fact, I *insisted*. Despite the voicemail and the threats, the executive in charge of recruiting insisted we *not* fire SunGlasses. As he explained to me, the situation wasn't simply  black or white. I interrupted the speech I was about to receive and said, "This broker is a thug and a thief. This <u>is</u> black and white. Fire him." For emphasis, I added, "Fuck him."

The broker was permitted to resign without any derogatory filings on his record. A copy of his resignation letter is depicted here:

With this resignation letter, the "fuck" count rose to 33.

But, our bad-broker count went down by one.

A small step forward, but a step, nonetheless.

Doubling Down

GunnAllen's new headquarters was such a spectacular building that, in October, 2006 – just a few years after buying it for $9.5 million – GunnAllen sold it for about $23.5 million. That sale generated a profit of about $14 million. The sale was done quietly.

The sale generated more than enough profit to pay off the debts the firm owed to investors. With the profits, GunnAllen could pay off the funds investors loaned to the firm, to fuel its rapid growth. Instead, GunnAllen's founders doubled down. It was decided the money would be used, for even *more* aggressive growth.

GunnAllen was going to form a bank. Then the firm was going to consider clearing its own trades, like the two largest firms in the independent broker-dealer space.

Both initiatives would require considerable capital. Moreover, both banking and clearing involved compliance with even more rules, regulations, and regulatory agencies. GunnAllen would have to apply for regulatory approval and demonstrate suitable capital, systems, and management to gain approval to operate either a bank, a clearing firm, or both.

In my opinion, both initiatives were a long shot. I didn't believe for a minute that GunnAllen would get the required regulatory approval, considering the firm's less-than-stellar reputation in the brokerage business. I counseled management to remain focused on our current business. I strongly advocated getting better at the business we were in, before attempting to operate a new business.

My recommendation was ignored. The founders of GunnAllen had built one of the Industry's fastest-growing broker dealers. Now they were sitting on top of a pile of cash. So – double down they did. Like many US homeowners at the time, GunnAllen mortgaged its future in order to spend in the moment.

Even though the real estate market was hot, it wasn't so hot that GunnAllen's building simply doubled in value in just a few years. One of the reasons GunnAllen received such a high sales price for the building was because GunnAllen agreed to lease the building *back* from the new owners. After the sale, GunnAllen became the sole tenant and paid rent to the new owners. The sale price was largely based on the amount of rent GunnAllen agreed to pay going forward.

With GunnAllen's commitment to pay a very high rent, the buyer could justify paying a very high price for the building.

The only problem was that, while GunnAllen and its founders got an immediate lump sum of cash, the business got stuck with extremely high rent payments. The firm truly did mortgage its future. If the firm couldn't continue to grow, it wouldn't be able to support the massive rental payments to which the founders had agreed.

With their history of growth and with a pile of cash, it must have looked like a good bet at the time. Accordingly, GunnAllen sold the building for a huge profit.

However, the profits from the building didn't go to GunnAllen Financial. They went to Gunn Allen Holdings – the entity that *owned* GunnAllen Financial. To some, this might simply seem like keeping cash in your left pocket versus your right.

The difference is more significant.

While the cash was made available to GunnAllen Financial – the broker-dealer that generated all the revenue and the only operating entity owned by the holding company – the cash had to be paid into GunnAllen Financial by the holding company. If the holding company didn't want to fund GunnAllen, it didn't have too. The cash could be used by the owners of the holding company however they chose.

While there was plenty of cash and, while the owners of the holding company were the same as the owners of GunnAllen, this wasn't a problem.

When there was no more cash, it would be a *huge* problem. When the new owners of GunnAllen's holding company decided to not invest any more money, it would be fatal.

To Sell or Not To Sell

GunnAllen had a New Product Committee ("NPC") that was responsible for reviewing and approving *all* new investments that were to be sold through the firm.

In order for a new investment to be considered, it had to be sponsored by a staff member and presented to the NPC. The NPC had a rotating list of members. However, I'm not sure that list was ever actually published or disseminated or communicated in any way. In fact, I'm not sure if the NPC members even knew who they were or when they were supposed to meet.

In any event, Rick called me one day. He wanted me to meet with and consider sponsoring a company called Vacation Ventures. This firm claimed to own a portfolio of exclusive estate homes in very desirable locations. The business model was to solicit investors to invest in a membership interest in Vacation Ventures ("VV"). This membership interest would grant an investor access to these exclusive properties – along with a gourmet chef, butler, and maid service – at a date and time of their choosing (subject to availability, blackout dates, etc.). In addition to the lump sum initial investment, there would be annual dues (that could go up). Travel to and from the VV property wasn't included.

Rick told me he knew one of VV's founders and he thought it sounded like a great prospecting tool, to market to affluent investors. I respectfully responded that it sounded like a timeshare. I was told to be open minded and Rick requested that that I meet with the principals. This type of request was not unusual.

Accordingly, I called the firm, asked for some information, and offered to have a meeting at their convenience. The very next day, I received a really cool-looking brushed aluminum briefcase, embossed with Vacation Ventures in huge letters. It was a great marketing gimmick:

Inside the metal-looking briefcase was a brochure loaded with slick photographs of super-good looking people, enjoying themselves at exquisite properties. There was a CD, a fountain pen, and – best of all – an elegant keychain, symbolizing the keys to success, or to financial freedom, or access to the exclusive VV club or...

Anyway, this full metal briefcase impressed me so much I still have it, as a token of things that can look *really* good – but go horribly wrong.

I called my staff together and we reviewed the offering and the structure of the investment. The product principal (quasi-analyst) reported that the investment structure was all wrong, the rate of return couldn't even be calculated, and there was no real ownership interest in anything. The analyst simply didn't like it. I kept my thoughts to myself. At the time.

The following week, Rick called. I was already in Tampa and out to dinner. He apologized for interrupting my meal and asked if I could go to Clearwater, FL, to have dinner at a Vacation Ventures estate property on the beach. He informed me that the firm's top-producing broker, Frank Bluestein, was there with his wife, Mona. He politely but firmly requested I go.

As I happened to be at dinner with the quasi-analyst that reviewed the deal, and since the analyst lived in the same town in which the property was located, I volunteered to eat another dinner, as long as my analyst could also attend. A deal was made, I paid for dinner number one, and my analyst and I were off to dinner number two, with Frank, his wife Mona, the Vacation Ventures chef, wine expert, and host.

The house was magnificent. The food was fantastic. The wine was superb. Frank was his exceptionally funny self. I was completely hammered. That was clearly the plan. As the evening drew to a close, I vaguely remember shaking everyone's hand and thanking them all for a wonderful evening. I recall walking out and hearing Frank yell, "Hey, Mona, let's do it on the spiral staircase."

The next day, I dutifully reported my Vacation Venture experience to the CEO. He was an excellent judge of the situation. Without having to ask, he could discern, through my hangover, that I was not impressed with Vacation Ventures as a potential investment. After a little polite conversation and a few laughs, I thought I was done with VV.

Not so fast.

Approximately one month later, on a Thursday morning, I received a call from the Executive Vice President who ran the firm's investment banking division. Since we were going to have our weekly senior business meeting later that afternoon, he wanted to give me a "heads up" courtesy call. Unbeknownst to me, his investment banking team had reviewed Vacation Ventures. They had bankers and analysts who reviewed deals all the time. The investment banking team thought it was a great investment. He knew

I was looking at it and he said he hoped I wouldn't mind if he took the ball and ran with it. I thanked him for the call and wished him the very best. I was done with Vacation Ventures.

Later that afternoon, in the executive boardroom, we all piled up our plates with the regularly served free lunch and sat down to discuss the critical issues that were not on any agenda. Eventually, the head of investment banking spoke up. In his typically upbeat and enthusiastic manner, he proudly explained that his team had an exciting new firm to represent, called Vacation Ventures. His division had already generated $50,000 in revenue for the firm by accepting a retainer to help Vacation Ventures sell its investments through our brokers.

The CEO let this positive announcement sink in and looked around for any reaction. There was none. So, in a classic power move, the CEO called on me and said: "David, I know you were looking at Vacation Ventures. What do you think?" The message was clear: he wanted this product sold and investment banking was going to sell it. I got the message. I simply didn't *get* the investment. I didn't care for Vacation Ventures and I certainly didn't care for this charade.

Since I hadn't answered, the CEO again asked me what I thought. "Well," I said, "since I thought we were in the investment business and not in the timeshare business, I'm glad someone else chose to take this ball and run with it."

It only took a moment for my words to sink in before the CEO started yelling, "Since when did you get the right to tell me what to sell? This is *my* firm. Just because you don't like something doesn't mean we're not gonna' sell it! Do you understand? Is that clear?"

Since I thought the question was rhetorical, I chose not to respond. Feeling the need to make his point more clear, the CEO added, "This is *my* fucking firm. If I decide we're gonna' sell mops, then we're gonna' sell fucking mops! Is that clear?"

I knew we would never sell mops. That was simply ridiculous. No one gets paid a $50,000 retainer just to sell mops. Since I'd turned down the $50,000, the executive decision was made to find someone else at the firm to take it. I looked at the CEO, felt all the eyes on me, and decided it was time to leave. I was paid a lot, but not enough for this shit. I cleared my plate, left the room, returned to my office to get my things and hopped on the next flight home to south Florida.

This was the first time I walked away from the firm. I should have stayed away. However, later that night, the CEO called and convinced me to stay with a very sincere private apology and his reassurance that he valued and needed my opinion, intellect, and integrity at the firm. I could've used a mop at that moment.

I later learned the firm never sold any investments and Vacation Ventures sued to get back the $50,000 retainer.

2007: GunnAllen's National Conference

2007 was GunnAllen's finest year. The market was soaring. Assets were peaking. Revenues hit a record high. We'd cut a few bad brokers and we'd landed a whale. The sale of the building also left the founders holding a pile of cash.

Against this backdrop, GunnAllen held its annual national conference at the J.W. Marriott, in Orlando. Consistent with the effort to upgrade the firm's image, the CEO decided Orlando was more family-friendly and more upscale than Tampa. There were just too many strip clubs, too much debauchery, and too many crazy memories from prior conferences in Tampa.

By now, GunnAllen's management was violently dividend. There was the old guard, comprised of executives who were previously waiters and/or bartenders – and the new guard, comprised of myself and other professionals with years of experience. There wasn't much love between us. The head of business development was the champion of the old guard. He'd recruited most of the brokers and administered their deals. He was cozy and tight with a lot of the "bad" brokers. He and I were clear and vocal in our mutual dislike and distrust.

GunnAllen was a house divided.

So, like two opposing teams taking the field, we all gathered in Orlando. The conference was attended by many quality vendors who paid tens of thousands of dollars to exhibit and speak to our brokers. A record number of brokers also attended this event. GunnAllen truly had peaked. Despite the tension among management, we all pulled together. The mood was great.

On the last day, I was given a small chance to get involved in the conference. Instead of the usual workshops that brokers were bribed to attend, I decided to conduct two sessions with brokers as panelists and myself as the moderator. I set up four chairs onstage, in the main auditorium, and called for a general assembly of all brokers.

One session focused on top producers. The other session focused on top practices. For each session, I asked three top brokers to sit on stage. The event was unscripted, although I'd advised the brokers of the types of questions I would ask.

My goal was to share with all the brokers what they *really* wanted to know. I wanted top-producing brokers – as peers – to share how they'd become top producers. I wanted them to share how they built their businesses. I wanted all the other brokers to hear and learn how they could be better. These two events turned out to be standing-room-only.

Naturally, I had Jay Gunn, the firm's President, as a panelist. He was a top producing stock broker. He'd built a large client base with substantial assets under management. He said the right things with sincere emotion and passion.

I also asked Frank Bluestein to participate in both sessions. By all accounts, Frank was a top producing broker and he'd built one of the most successful financial services practices at the firm. If only I knew then what we would all know soon enough...

During the day, Frank had been wearing shorts, sandals, and a hideous Florida-style print shirt. Thankfully, he dressed up for the "Top Practice Panel." I asked Frank, "Apart from being a sharp-dressed man by day, how do you get your clients?"

"Well," Frank said with a smile, "when you're short and fat and ugly like me, you have to be smart. You see, I don't have the movie star good looks or picture-perfect hair like your President. So, I need to really impress clients with my knowledge of product and strategy. I'm able to quickly tell an investor exactly how I can help them."

Frank Bluestein is on the Left. I'm on the right.

It was classic Frank. Funny, charming, endearing. Every alpha male in the room hated the guy before he spoke. He won all these awards. He made more money than them. Yet, in one sentence, the "short, fat, and ugly" guy won them over. His charm and self-deprecating humor were his calling card.

After he insulted himself, he charmed you and disarmed you; then, he explained how great and smart he was. It was funny, impressive, and seductive. *That's* how Frank got new clients.

Frank had a room full of aggressive skilled salesman in the palm of his hand. It was easy to see how he could impress any investor. It was one of Frank's finest moments.

Soon, it would be his worst.

2007 started as GunnAllen's best year. It would end as one of GunnAllen's worst.

The Beginning of GunnAllen's End

I was home in south Florida on a Tuesday night when Frank Bluestein called me on my cell phone. "David. It's Frank. We need to talk. It's serious," he said. Frank's normally overly-enthusiastic tone of voice and his quick wit were completely gone. I was listening to the voice of a dead man talking.

"Listen," Frank said. "I got involved in something that I think has gone bad. You have to believe me when I tell you that I believed in this product. I still do. It literally saved people's lives. In a down-and-out economy where workers lose their jobs every day, this product replaced people's entire income. But, something went wrong and the product didn't pay any dividends this past month or two..."

I interrupted him. "Frank – *what* product? What is the name of this investment?"

There was a long silence that told me almost everything. "It's not a GunnAllen product, if that's what you're asking," said Frank. "It's something I got involved in years ago."

"So basically, what you're telling me is that you sold a product away from the firm and now it's gone bad?" I asked. This was *very* serious. It's against the rules to sell *any* product that's not expressly approved in writing by your broker-dealer. What Frank was telling me was that he had "sold away." He was confessing to a major violation of securities rules and regulations. "How many clients...how much money is involved?" I think I yelled into the phone.

"It's not like that!" Frank yelled back. Then he calmed himself and added, "You don't understand. This is a real investment. I've been involved in this for years. This paid more than anything else. My clients have made a fortune with this. I don't know what went wrong or why, but I need some time to figure it out. I wanted to let you know, because I think one or two clients might call the firm. I wanted to give you the head's-up."

I wanted a few minutes to collect my thoughts, but my mouth was already moving: "Listen, Frank," I said. "I'm glad you called. I appreciate the 'head's-up.' But, here's what happens next. As soon as we hang up, I'm calling the CEO. I'm sorry Frank – but I have to. You know it. Next, you get on a plane. You get to Tampa as soon as humanly possible. What you need to do is to be humble and be honest and tell everything. Everything, Frank. There's no room to fuck around here. Do you understand? We're in this together. If you get sued, we get sued. If there's a legitimate way to defend ourselves and work this out together, we'll figure it out. If you screwed us, then you're done. You're gone and you know it."

"Can I ask a favor?" asked Frank. "Will you call me and let me know how your call with the CEO goes?"

"Of course," I said, softly.

We hung up and I hit my speed-dial, to call the CEO.

I relayed my call with Frank to the CEO. He was quiet. He asked me when Frank would be in Tampa. I told him either tomorrow or by Thursday. I suggested we suspend Frank immediately, until we got more information and completed an internal review. I could tell he wasn't too enthusiastic. While I knew this was bad, I think the CEO was already considering that this could possibly kill his firm.

I wasn't surprised when he said, "I want you here in Tampa when he gets here. We need to figure out how to deal with this."

I replied, "My input is that we suspend Frank immediately, notify the regulators that we have a problem, and work with the regulators to investigate this together. If we're completely transparent, we can get their help and show we knew nothing about whatever Frank did. I know I might be jumping the gun, but this is potentially a life-or-death situation.

In my opinion, Frank sold away. No matter what, he's a dead man walking. Unless we work this out with the regulators, they might kill us, too. So that's how I recommend we handle the situation."

We talked a while longer. After the conversation, I decided I wouldn't attend any meetings in Tampa. I had made my position clear. It appeared to me that another course of action was going to be pursued.

Afterwards, I called Frank back. "Frank, get to Tampa by Thursday. I suggest you get a good lawyer." It was one of my last calls with Frank Bluestein.

Unbeknownst to me, around the same time, one of Frank's clients had already called into GunnAllen. The call was routed to Daniel Ortega, the firm's assistant director of supervision. This client explained that he hadn't received a dividend check and he wanted to know if everything was ok with his account. Dan asked the client for their account number. The client had an account. Dan looked into the client's account. He asked the client for the name of the investment that didn't pay any dividend. There was no such investment in the account.

The alarm bells went off.

When the client told Dan about these "special" investments that Frank offered in lavish seminars at the Detroit Palace, Dan immediately knew there was a problem. Dan didn't know anything about these "special" investments. Dan didn't know about any seminars at the Palace. If Frank had done what he was required to do, Dan would have known something. What Dan *did* know was that something really bad was going on.

Dan took all of the client's information and wrote up a memo. He documented the client's claims of investing in something that wasn't showing up in any account. Dan documented the client's claims of attending seminars that were not known about or approved in writing, as required by the firm. Dan concluded the memo by recommending the immediate suspension of Frank and his staff. He recommended an immediate branch audit, to thoroughly review the client's allegations.

Dan followed up on his memo every day. He was told "management" was reviewing it and would make a determination. After several weeks, Dan was finally sent to audit Frank's office in Michigan.

Frank's son, daughter, and wife all worked in the office. The presence of family members within the same branch is often a warning sign. Family members keep secrets. Family members protect one another.

From that point forward, the Frank Bluestein "issue" was elevated to the highest levels of management. While I don't know exactly who comprised this "highest" level of management, I do know it didn't include either myself or Daniel Ortega.

In fact, we were – for all practical purposes – excluded.

SCAM ALERT – ADVISORS: Ponzi "Private Placements"

The shit hit the fan with Frank Bluestein's involvement in a Ponzi scheme. Although it started in 2007, it wasn't until the end of 2009 that the SEC went public with their allegations. By then, the fan was completely buried by the amount of shit that hit it.

U.S. SECURITIES AND EXCHANGE COMMISSION

Litigation Release No. 21223 / September 28, 2009

SEC v. Frank Bluestein, Civil Action No. 2:09-CV-13809 (E.D. Mich.) (Friedman, J.)

The Securities and Exchange Commission today charged Detroit-area stock broker Frank Bluestein with fraud, alleging that he lured elderly investors into refinancing the mortgages on their homes in order to fund their investments in a $250 million Ponzi scheme.

http://www.sec.gov/litigation/litreleases/2009/lr21223.htm

Rogue brokers like **Frank Bluestein** (*photo,*) a GunnAllen broker in Michigan, lacked oversight at the same time he was, according to the Securities and Exchange Commission, soliciting 800

investors who placed $74 million in an **alleged Ponzi scheme** that went bust in the summer of 2007.

Case 2:09-cv-13809-BAF-MKM Document 1 Filed 09/28/2009 Page 1 of 18

Frank Bluestein ("Bluestein") was the single largest salesperson in a $250 million Ponzi scheme perpetrated by an individual named Edward May ("May") and May's company, E-M Management Company LLC ("E-M").

From 2002 to 2007, Bluestein, while employed as a registered representative of a broker-dealer and an associated person of a registered investment adviser, raised approximately $74 million from over 800 investors in connection with the sale of about 110 supposedly separate E-M private offerings.

Bluestein misrepresented to investors that the investments in E-M securities were low risk investments. He made these statements even though he had no basis for doing so. In addition, Bluestein misrepresented to investors that he conducted adequate due diligence with respect to the investments when, in fact, he did little to investigate the legitimacy of the E-M offerings. Bluestein failed to investigate even when confronted with serious red flags regarding the existence of some of the transactions underlying the E-M offerings.

Bluestein's misconduct was particularly egregious when he solicited investors using unscrupulous tactics such as: (1) specifically targeting potential investors who were retired and/or elderly; (2) luring these retired or elderly investors through so-called "investment seminars"; and (3) encouraging many of these investors to refinance their mortgages for their homes in order to fund their investments.

Bluestein misled investors about the compensation he received from the E-M offerings by not disclosing that he received at least $2.4 million in commissions from May and E-M.

Bluestein also received an additional $1.4 million in disclosed compensation from investors in the form of fees for his company Fast Frank, Inc. ("F.F. Inc.").

---

http://www.sec.gov/litigation/complaints/2009/comp21223.pdf

While regulatory gears move slowly, legal gears barely seem to move at all. While certain Industry publications caught wind of the story and publicized it early on, it took years before there was any public action by the regulators. Frank had been terminated from GunnAllen and the Ponzi scheme was being unraveled. No more investors would be victims of this specific situation.

But, there was no public warning about this problem to investors. The Industry's investigative process is quiet and confidential. Until there is a press release announcing the bold brave actions by the regulators, investors are left to go about their business without any warnings. During this time, other investors were surely defrauded by other brokers in other scams.

As for Frank, he was smart enough and knowledgeable enough to know better than to destroy his career with a scam. He was successful without having to rip off investors. As a money manager, his performance – at least during the short time I observed it – was excellent. He knew products inside and out.

For lack of a better explanation, I believe Frank had a character defect. I'm not trying to be polite or to pull any punches. Frank was either blinded by greed or by his own bullshit. Perhaps the short, fat, ugly guy (as he referred to himself) was a short, fat, ugly boy who tried to overachieve and overcompensate as he grew up.

As for GunnAllen, the firm didn't know Frank was engaged in fraudulent misconduct. In hindsight, there were red flags. However, GunnAllen audited Frank twice. While he was affiliated with GunnAllen, FINRA audited his branch multiple times; the SEC audited his branch; the state of Michigan audited his branch *multiple* times. Prior to joining GunnAllen, he'd also been audited by his former broker-dealer, along with the SEC and FINRA. His scam went undetected by all.

Ultimately, Frank's story reveals that a highly motivated scammer can trick the system. Unfortunately, the investors who got scammed didn't know how to protect themselves from investment fraud.

When you're done reading this book, you *will* know exactly how to protect yourself.

In 2013, on a trip to the movies with my daughters, I saw Frank Bluestein standing in line for tickets. So – while investors lost millions, Frank was off to the movies.

If that doesn't reinforce the need to protect yourself, I don't know how else to help you.

<u>**Safety tip 5:**</u> **Protection & Loss Prevention Is Critical Since the Odds of Recovery are Very Low.**

There is no protection against fraud and there is no insurance reimbursement in cases of fraud.

If a firm can prove the broker committed fraud, independent of the firm's reasonably-designed supervisory policies and procedures (as determined by the Industry), there is no firm liability.

The Industry and firm supervisory systems are not designed to detect fraud. By its very deceptive nature, fraud can be nearly impossible to detect. There are clear red flags and certain warning signs that will be discussed later.

Notwithstanding the above, statistics show less than half of all customer complaints result in some monetary recovery for harmed investors. Even worse is a statistic that shows those harmed investors who *do* recover funds typically get less than half of what they sought.

For all of Frank Bluestein's victims, there would be virtually no recovery, since there was no insurance protection and both Frank and GunnAllen declared bankruptcy. The money lost was simply...gone.

2008: The Storm Worsens

GunnAllen entered 2008 still reeling from Frank Bluestein's involvement in a Ponzi scheme. The firm lost Frank's significant legitimate revenue and gained massive liabilities as a result of his misconduct. The liabilities were twofold: current expenses from legal fees and arbitrations, and future expenses from settlements or arbitration awards.

Costs were mounting daily.

Each customer complaint resulted in an arbitration filing which cost several thousand dollars, just to process. With over 250 complaints, the administration costs quickly exceeded $1,000,000. Legal fees were over $200,000 per month and growing. In addition, the cost of responding to various regulatory inquiries was mounting. In addition to FINRA and the SEC, the state of Michigan and several other states all piled on.

A Ponzi scheme is a *big* deal.

To top it off, the stock market started the year down by 10%. The housing bubble was about to burst. As the values of homes started to fall, the mortgage loans secured by those homes became more risky. If a house was worth less than what was owed on it, there was little incentive to make mortgage payments. Ripples were spreading throughout markets around the world.

Every month was worse than the last. Revenues were declining, losses were mounting, and liabilities were escalating. GunnAllen was losing money and burning through most of the profits from the sale of the building.

The firm's initiative to form a bank had stalled. The firm's prior negative history with broker-dealer regulators was known to banking regulators. When GunnAllen submitted a letter to bank regulators indicating the firm was going to apply to become a bank, bank regulators apparently responded by advising GunnAllen to not bother applying. That initiative cost the firm over $1 million and never went anywhere.

Revenues were declining, costs from liabilities were mounting. In addition, the firm now had a huge monthly rental payment for its gorgeous new headquarters.

Something *had* to change for GunnAllen to survive.

The CEO's Last Stand: The Not-So-Elite retreat

Opinions regarding GunnAllen's founder and CEO, Rick Frueh, vary wildly. Some think him the embodiment of all things evil. Others call him a slick car salesman. I think of him as a smart guy and a good leader who tried his best.

Maybe I'm too kind.

The CEO could motivate. He could build a team. He sought out talent to run areas of the firm that were beyond his expertise. He was an entrepreneur and he was willing to take risks. Unfortunately, I think, at times, his risk compass gave bad readings. Especially when it was time *not* to do something. I admire his willingness to take a stand. I regret his willingness to try to figure out how to do some things that should simply not have been done.

He had to grow GunnAllen to survive. So, he recruited and grew. Unfortunately, he grew too fast. That's normally not a crime in business. In fact, rapid growth is ordinarily hailed and praised. Had he been a branch manager at a large firm with infrastructure and supervisory systems, his rapid growth would have made him a rock star. However, at his own firm, without adequate infrastructure, staff, or systems, it was his downfall.

He knew damn well bad brokers were hired. He created a process to hire them without being directly involved. He trusted the firm to watch them. When management asked for expensive systems to adequately supervise the brokers, he provided funds. However, too much time had passed. Too much growth had occurred. There wasn't enough time or money to play catch-up. Unfortunately, the money, systems, and staff should have come first.

Many of the firm's missteps were clearly caused by growing pains. Proper policies and procedures would have prevented tremendous pain. Yet, while bad hiring practices and a lack of adequate supervisory systems can be blamed for GunnAllen's downfall, I believe it was a series of very unfortunate events that actually destroyed the firm.

The seeds may have been sown in the firm's "bad" hiring practices, but the "bad" transactional brokers didn't kill GunnAllen. They might have, over time. But, in my opinion, it was the "low-risk" planners that were primarily to blame.

Transactional brokers tend to work in an office with a manager and supervisor. With transactional business, i.e. brokerage accounts, a firm can closely monitor activity and take corrective action. That presumes the firm has systems to detect problems and management that is willing to resolve them.

Many financial planners and investment advisors tend to work in remote offices and visit clients in unsupervised settings. Planners tend to sell one or two products in large dollar amounts. There's less activity, different products, and different paperwork than transactional business and/or brokerage accounts. Advisory accounts, mutual funds, variable annuities, life insurance, and direct products are all considered to be less risky than traditional brokerage business. Yet, these types of products and this type of business generally require additional supervisory systems and personnel. Otherwise, this business can flow through a firm with less scrutiny than stock trading.

Like a silent heart attack, it's what you don't know that can kill you. In my opinion, it was the unauthorized, unsupervised activity of a couple of "trusted" local financial advisors that ultimately killed the firm. *Not* the slick transaction-oriented New York City stockbrokers.

A really bad market contributed, too.

Nonetheless, each year, GunnAllen hosted an "elite" retreat. This event was primarily for the top transactional brokers and branch managers. I'd never been to one of the early elite retreats, but rumor has it they were fun. As in, off-the-chain wild. A real celebration of success.

This year was different. FINRA was all over GunnAllen for the prior misconduct of its transactional brokers. This weighed heavily on the CEO. There was little room for any repeat offenses. Word was out about Bluestein. Brokers were concerned that Bluestein's involvement in a Ponzi scheme could kill the firm.

I sat in the back and watched the CEO deliver his opening speech. It went something like this:

"I want to thank you all for coming. I know your time means money and I appreciate you giving up your time to be here. I know you are concerned about the future of the firm. So – let's jump right into it and discuss our future. The few of you gathered here in this room generate over 50% of the firm's revenue. You are the elite because of your production. Production we value greatly. Yet, the same brokers and branches represented by the people in this room also account for over 80% of our customer complaints. Our litigation risk comes from the people in this room. Our errors and omissions insurance premiums keep going up because of the people in this room. Each and every day, I hear complaints about rising costs. Each and every day, I hear complaints about hiring. Well, it stops now. Recruit a good broker without a history of customer complaints and he's hired on the spot. We'll even help finance your growth and expansion. We are one of the largest and best firms for transactional brokers. We remain committed to serving your business. What we can't do going forward is pay for your mistakes. So, we're going to spend this time together figuring out what we can do to reduce risk, reduce costs, and make more money."

Brokers are aggressive types. Alpha-males. They hunt in packs. Every pack has a leader. At times like this, when a group gets together, a "pack" leader quickly emerges. It only took a moment before a pack leader jumped up and yelled: "How dare you speak to us like this? We make you money and you want to criticize us? You gather us here to give us shit in your fancy building with all your fancy cars? Fuck you!"

The rest of the pack attacked. The CEO bobbed and weaved. He managed to not get torn to pieces. He survived what would be *his* last Elite Retreat.

The broker that led the pack didn't survive. He was asked to leave the firm immediately. He was told to take all his brokers and find a new firm.

Changes were coming. Some of those changes would include the departure of some more of the not-so-Elite brokers.

To Hire Often but Fire Rarely

Hiring brokers or, rather, hiring "bad" brokers, was one of GunnAllen's core problems. Since I regularly opened my big mouth about the firm's hiring practices, it was only a matter of time before I was offered the opportunity to put my money where my mouth was. I was asked to join GunnAllen's hiring committee.

I lasted about a month.

GunnAllen's hiring committee was responsible for reviewing potential recruits who wanted to join the firm. By the time I joined the firm, the hiring process generally relied upon recruiters. Prior to my employment, the firm's National Sales Manager had been a pied piper, of sorts. He single-handedly recruited hundreds of brokers in a wild hiring spree over just a few years. Offering brokers almost anything they wanted, including up-front bonuses, very high payouts, and "special" deals, the pied piper led wave upon wave of brokers to join the firm.

The President's college roommate, who was also his brother-in-law, was the executive in charge of recruiting – or Business Development, as he called it. Prior to working in the brokerage Industry, I believe he was a bartender. I don't know if he was his brother-in-law's bartender. I never bothered to ask. I will refer to the executive of Business Development as "BD."

BD was fond of proclaiming, "It takes a craftsman to build something special. Anyone can wield a sledgehammer. It takes no skill to demolish. But, to build, it takes creativity, ingenuity, hard work, and skill."

I didn't see much skill in his recruiting, but there was an abundance of creativity. He was able to offer up-front money with very high commission payouts and still show how his "deals" made money for the firm. I think, by his creative math, there were more than 100 cents in each dollar.

Very creative, indeed.

Almost every day, there were calls or home office visits with potential recruits. The firm would roll out the red carpet for home office visits. Recruits would be flown in and put up at a nice hotel. After a tour of the firm and meetings with staff, there would be dinner at one of Tampa's many fine steakhouses. Cocktails and wine would flow. Brokers definitely know how to have a good time. Tampa, often referred to as the strip club capital of the US, certainly knows how to show visitors a good time. Brokers with a fistful of golden bucks (strip club funny money) were always treated well.

Aside from rolling out the red carpet and impressing potential recruits with professionalism and dedication, certain information had to be collected. This included:

1. A business mix and production profile
2. A background check – including criminal history and credit report
3. An Industry report, including any and all customer complaints and disciplinary history

The business mix/production profile would enable the firm to project the profit margin on the recruit's business. This was the amount the firm could expect to make if the broker joined the firm. It had nothing to do with whether the recruit was a good or bad broker. It was purely economics.

Background checks tell whether the broker previously committed any crimes. Hiring criminals is frowned upon – even by the Industry.

Credit reports indicate the financial health of the recruit. A broke broker is not a good sign. If a broker can't manage his own finances, it's reasonable to question that broker's ability to manage client money. It also presents an increased risk of financial misconduct, as a broker with bad credit and loads of debt might place generating a quick buck ahead of an investor's best interests.

An Industry report shows the broker's employment and disciplinary history. A broker who has worked at many firms (three or more) in just a few years (five or less) would trigger certain concerns regarding stability and conduct. A broker sometimes "jumps" firms, to get an up-front signing bonus, or to try to leave behind a problem. A broker with a history of customer complaints or regulatory violations would obviously raise serious concerns regarding conduct and performance.

When you're presented with a broke broker with bad credit who worked at multiple firms in a just a few years with several prior historical customer complaints, some pending customer complaints, and a regulatory sanction, a rational decision would be to **not** hire that broker. As I found out, GunnAllen's hiring process was definitely *not* rational.

Due to GunnAllen's less-than-stellar reputation, recruiting was difficult. The firm was most often presented with recruits who had a story as to why they "left" their prior firm, or why they liked GunnAllen better than some other highly-regarded firm. Basically, GunnAllen was ideal for transactional brokers with some "issues" who couldn't get hired by firms with better reputations. Or by firms with hiring standards more stringent than simply determining if a broker could fog a mirror.

As small firms collapsed, or when really bad firms actually got shut down by Industry regulators, GunnAllen's recruiters would swarm in to pick up the scraps. The scraps were generally not ideal. Nonetheless, other firms' misfortunes filled GunnAllen's recruiting pipeline – and created many of GunnAllen's future problems.

To remedy GunnAllen's "quality control" problem, management determined it would be wise to change the members of the hiring committee.

I was surprised when I was asked to join the Hiring Committee because I was generally considered to be a prima donna by my peers. The thought of me voting for anyone with any negative marks was laughable. I thought I was finally going to help the firm solve one of its core problems. If we hired better quality brokers, we would gradually transform the firm's DNA and ultimately become a better quality firm. I actually believed that.

Naturally, the firm stacked the deck against me. I was placed on the hiring committee with one executive who would likely vote against "bad" brokers and two other executives who, in my opinion, would consider hiring axe murders and rapists – *if* they generated enough gross production.

A deadlock was virtually guaranteed. Management by committee to perfection. The hiring committee chairman would only vote in the event of a tie.

Prior to my first hiring committee meeting, I was provided with a packet on each of the recruits to be considered. The recruiter would walk us through each recruit's packet and explain any "issues." After six or seven presentations, I learned how common it was for brokers (particularly in their early years) to have a misdemeanor for DUI, possession, disorderly conduct, etc. Brokers tend to live life aggressively.

GunnAllen's prospective recruits seemed particularly aggressive.

My idealistic notions of reviewing Harvard-educated brokers with the highest quality employment pedigree and pristine records were shattered. Quickly. Violently. I became more and more despondent with each meeting of the hiring committee. Recruit after recruit, presentation after presentation, story after story, explanation after explanation; it was just too much. Fortunately, there was the incredibly comedic performance of one of my favorite senior recruiters.

To this day, I never met anyone who could present as well or with as much humor.

It was common for him to explain, "First of all, this isn't nearly as bad as it looks. The first arrest was over a decade ago. You know, college stuff – nothing serious. The more recent arrest was apparently a misunderstanding with the police that is in the process of being cleared up. We wouldn't want to judge this candidate guilty when the whole issue might get dropped. As for the reason he recently resigned from his old firm, I can explain that, since I investigated it thoroughly. It turns out his sales assistant was simply trying to help an elderly client complete some paperwork. There was no intent to alter documents or falsify information. It was a total misunderstanding with a supervisor who's never actually worked with clients. You know how strict that other firm can be. And the entire incident had nothing to do with our recruit. It was the sales assistant who made a mistake and we're not hiring her! Anyway, this broker's bad luck can be our good fortune if we hire him and monitor his activity carefully. He does great numbers. I say we hire him, get him to transfer in his client accounts, and watch him closely. If it doesn't work out, we can always let him go. We can always re-assign any accounts that come over to one of our good brokers."

The logic was solid. The presentation was compelling. Yet, there was always a whiff of something that never smelled right. After a while, I started to suspect the recruiters would deliberately present a really bad recruit at the beginning of each hiring committee meeting. After presenting a marked up broker with a ton of customer complaints and multiple felony arrests, the next few recruits wouldn't look so bad by comparison.

After around three weeks of rejecting every prospective recruit, the head of business development – BD – decided to attend. He was frustrated. He explained that he was getting feedback from his recruiters that the new members of the hiring committee were making it too difficult to hire good brokers. He explained that, as one of the firm's founders and senior-most executives, he felt obligated to advise us that we were demoralizing the recruiters and hurting the firm. While we might think we were doing the "right thing," hiring new brokers was the only way to grow. Broker revenues paid our salaries. Adding brokers would grow the firm, increase our business, and enable us all to make more money. He explained that we were jeopardizing the firm and the livelihood of the firm's employees.

He sat back after his speech. He was clearly pleased with his delivery and he brimmed with confidence in his powers of persuasion.

Well, as I said, BD and I never did see eye-to-eye. However, I didn't expect what was coming next. BD said he was personally going to present the next recruit, to make sure we were all clear about doing our job right for the firm.

As I recall it, this recruit worked at more than five firms in three years, had six customer complaints and two more were still pending. He had a prior disciplinary action from the regulators and he'd been terminated for cause (fired for something bad) by his last firm.

BD started by explaining that he personally knew this recruit and, "...while this guy might look bad on paper, he's a solid broker and great individual." Someone should have told that to this broker's ex-wife, who had a court order to collect back child support.

I decided it was time to send another message to the head of Business Development. I was going to stop this madness, once and for all. There was no better moment to make my point, so I interrupted BD's presentation and said, "Listen. I heard what you had to say about the hiring committee and I really appreciate where you're coming from. It's critical we don't demoralize the recruiters. After the meeting, we should all go out for a few drinks to better connect. As for this candidate, I hate to interrupt your presentation, but I'm going to have to tell you there is simply no way I could ever vote to hire him. I can't speak for any of my colleagues, but I would be absolutely shocked if *anyone* in this room would vote to hire this broker."

Done. Speech delivered. Case closed – or so I thought – until I was rudely interrupted by the hiring committee Chairman. "David. We all appreciate your passion and position on this matter. However, it's not appropriate for you to interrupt the presentation or to broadcast your vote. Every recruit deserves to be heard. No one – not even you – should try to alter anyone's opinion or create any negative bias. In the future, I hope I won't have to remind you of this or ask you to refrain from speaking out."

I had just been spanked. In front of my colleagues. For trying to be a leader, I got shot down. To top it off, I saw BD smile, and some of my other colleagues look away. I knew then the fix was in. I just hadn't received the memo. This recruit was going to be hired, no "ifs, ands, or buts" about it.

With that realization, I decided my services were no longer needed on the hiring committee.

My response was simple. "Listen. I hear what you said. However and, with all due respect (which actually meant 'go fuck yourself'), my vote is 'no.' It's a 'no' now and it'll be a 'no' later. And anyone who votes 'yes' for this character is a coward. That's just my opinion. We don't get many moments in our business where the right answer is perfectly clear. This is one of those moments. This hiring process is supposed to have integrity. If we were to actually vote 'yes' and hire this character, we would be making a mockery of our process and ourselves. I won't be a part of it. My vote is 'no.' I will now remain silent. However, if you vote to hire this bad broker, I will immediately resign from the hiring committee."

"David!" yelled the hiring committee Chairman. "That's more than enough. I will not have my integrity questioned and you will wait your turn to vote. We have policies and procedures and you will respect them."

Approximately one minute later, the voting was complete: three "yes" votes to hire against my one "no" vote. Then, in a brilliant move to make matters worse, the Chairman said: "As you all know, I only vote in the event of a tie. In this instance, since a majority voted to hire the broker, I don't have to vote. However, off the record, if I had to vote, I would have voted against hiring this recruit."

Hearing those words, and being the calm, cool, reasonable, passive-aggressive, spoiled prima donna that I am, I lost it. I turned to the Chairman and yelled, "You should be ashamed. As the Chairman, you should vote on each and every recruit. You should lead and *own* the decisions made by this committee, because we all have to live with the brokers this firm hires! This is a joke. This committee is a joke and your leadership is a joke. I'm done."

With that, I started grabbing my files and stood up to leave.

"Where do you think you're going?" asked the Chairman.

"I told you I was done," I said. "At least one of us will keep his word."

"David," he said. "Stop. We have other candidates to review."

I turned to him and said: "Then it looks like you <u>will</u> have to vote, now."

As I started to leave, BD said: "That's right. Go ahead. Take your ball and go home."

He was loving this moment. I never liked him. Especially not at that moment. So, I stopped, and said, "Just because you married the President's sister and think you're one of the founders of this firm, doesn't give you any special rights, in my book. You're a moron. Hiring bad brokers is killing this firm. You're just too stupid or too greedy to see it. So I'll go. And why don't you go fuck yourself!"

With that new highlight firmly added to my list of professional (or not) accomplishments, I walked out, went to my office, grabbed my computer and my suitcase and drove straight to the airport. I caught the next flight home to south Florida. As I drove out of the parking garage, my cell phone rang. It was the CEO. He heard what happened. He couldn't believe it. He was very disappointed and thought he had no choice but to terminate me for insubordination. In that calm moment of clarity, all I could say was: "Do what you have to do. I was wrong for how I conducted myself – but my intentions were right."

That was the second time I walked away from GunnAllen. Again, I should have stayed away.

Two days later, the CEO called. He'd thought about my situation and said, "I've decided to accept your resignation...from the hiring committee. I value your insight and advice and I'd like you to stay with the firm. However, I expect you to apologize to the chairman of the hiring committee and to BD."

I considered it briefly. I'd lost it during the meeting and, no matter what, on a professional level, I owed my "colleagues" – even BD – an apology. On a personal level, I could think whatever I wanted to think, but I would act like a professional. Even though, deep down, I knew I *should* walk away, I rationalized my decision by thinking I could still try to change some things at the firm to make it better.

When I returned to Tampa, I got a hero's welcome. The story of my cursing out BD had already become legendary. I was looked at differently and looked up to by many employees.

I actually thought I won that battle.

GunnAllen Fined $750,000 by FINRA

The long slow-motion regulatory investigation that started in 2004 finally hit home. It took over four years. Finally, FINRA took aim and fired. The shot hit; but it wasn't a fatal blow.

For virtually all of the firm's violations up through 2006, the regulators agreed to accept a fine. GunnAllen was offered a settlement that included a $750,000 payment to FINRA. GunnAllen's founders were spared from any serious disciplinary action. The firm would survive. The founders, executives, and managers would survive. There would be a written slap on the wrist and a large fine.

Without any special conditions, GunnAllen was free to go about its business. Sign the settlement agreement, neither admit nor deny wrongdoing, and pay the fine.

That's the Industry's way of protecting investors.

FINRA's press release is below. The total disciplinary action can be found online here (http://www.finra.org/Newsroom/NewsReleases/2008/P038461). However, the most interesting aspect of the disciplinary action will be discussed at the end of this chapter.

NEWS RELEASE

For Release: Thursday, May 8, 2008

GunnAllen Financial Pays $750,000 to Settle Charges Involving Former Head Trader's Trade Allocation Scheme, AML, and Supervisory Deficiencies, Additional Charges

Washington, DC— FINRA announced today that it has fined GunnAllen Financial, Inc., of Tampa, FL $750,000 for its role in a trade allocation scheme conducted by the firm's former head trader, as well as for various Anti-Money Laundering (AML), reporting, record-keeping and supervisory deficiencies. Kelley McMahon, the former head trader's supervisor, was suspended for six months from association with any FINRA-registered firm in any principal capacity and fined $25,000, jointly and severally with the firm.

FINRA barred Alexis J. Rivera, the former head trader, in connection with the trade allocation scheme, in December 2006. FINRA found that in 2002 and 2003, the firm, acting through Rivera, engaged in a "cherry picking" scheme in which Rivera allocated profitable stock trades to his wife's personal account instead of to the accounts of firm customers. Rivera garnered improper profits of more than $270,000 through this misconduct, which violated the anti-fraud provisions of the federal securities laws and FINRA rules. Rivera was barred in December 2006.

"Broker-dealers have an obligation to supervise their registered representatives with a view to preventing them from engaging in conduct that violates fundamental rules, such as the anti-fraud provisions of the federal securities laws," said Susan Merrill, FINRA Executive Vice President and Chief of Enforcement. "The supervisory deficiencies here permitted the firm's trader to perpetrate a scheme that allowed him to benefit at the expense of the firm's customers, and contributed to serious violations in other areas of the firm's business. One such area was the investment banking department, where the firm's failures resulted in an absence of procedures to prevent the misuse of material, non-public information."

In connection with the firm's investment banking business, FINRA found that prior to March 2005, GunnAllen never put any stock of a company on a restricted or watch list even though the firm was conducting investment banking business with these companies. During the same period, GunnAllen failed to inform its own compliance department of the investment banking activities in which the firm was involved.

FINRA also sanctioned GunnAllen for failing to report to FINRA that its parent firm had entered into a consulting contract with an individual who had been previously barred by FINRA. In addition, the firm was sanctioned for failing to preserve e-mails and instant messages, for failing to implement an adequate AML compliance program and for supervisory and complaint reporting deficiencies. Supervisory deficiencies included a failure to ensure that markups and commissions charged on equity transactions were reasonable. In reviewing markups on equity transactions, the firm did little more than ensure that commission charges did not exceed 5 percent. GunnAllen and McMahon settled these matters without admitting or denying the allegations, but consented to the entry of FINRA's findings.

Investors can obtain more information about, and the disciplinary record of, any FINRA-registered broker or brokerage firm by using FINRA's BrokerCheck. FINRA makes BrokerCheck available at no charge. In 2007, members of the public used this service to conduct 6.7 million reviews of broker or firm records. Investors can access BrokerCheck at www.finra.org/brokercheck or by calling (800) 289-9999.

FINRA, the Financial Industry Regulatory Authority, is the largest non-governmental regulator for all securities firms doing business in the United States. Created in 2007 through the consolidation of NASD and NYSE Member Regulation, FINRA is dedicated to investor protection and market integrity through effective and efficient regulation and complementary compliance and technology-based services. FINRA touches virtually every aspect of the securities business – from registering and educating industry participants to examining securities firms; writing rules; enforcing those rules and the federal securities laws; informing and educating the investing public; providing trade reporting and other industry utilities; and administering the largest dispute resolution forum for investors and registered firms.

The irony of this settlement is that FINRA had every opportunity to shut GunnAllen down. The scope of misconduct was vast. The evidence was clear. There were multiple violations. The violations were all serious. Moreover, since the settlement negotiations started, back in 2004, there were multiple new problems. Yet, the settlement negotiations had more to do with agreeing upon the amount of the fine and the language that would be used in the settlement agreement.

Once again, GunnAllen was punished and FINRA would get paid. However, one of the interesting aspects of the settlement was that the fine was payable over many years, in installments. Despite all the significant violations, FINRA accepted an IOU and allowed GunnAllen to continue to operate. The regulators would allow GunnAllen to pay for its past misconduct with future revenue.

While it may seem unfair to look back now, with the benefit of knowing what was to happen next, I think hundreds of investors who lost millions of dollars after this settlement would beg to differ. Over the next few years, despite changing management, adding staff, acquiring some of the leading supervisory systems available, GunnAllen would miserably fail its clients, investors, and creditors.

So, too, would the regulators.

FINRA had the chance to close GunnAllen. Instead, FINRA staff showed its commitment to enforcement by getting tough and fining GunnAllen – in installments. FINRA generated more money for its own coffers. Not one cent of GunnAllen's fine was ever paid to harmed investors. FINRA kept all the money. Mitch Atkins, the senior executive of FINRA's Boca Raton, FL office, would be promoted for a job well done.

Previously harmed investors got screwed. Over the next few years, even more investors would get screwed.

But, so would FINRA. Since GunnAllen's fine was payable in installments, once the firm declared bankruptcy in 2010, even FINRA didn't collect. The majority of FINRA's fine never got paid. The regulators' decision to allow the firm to stay in business was a colossal blunder. It certainly did nothing to protect investors.

FINRA let GunnAllen pay a fine for harming old investors by earning money and harming new investors.

That sounds like a Ponzi protection scheme.

In any event, the regulators cleared GunnAllen to go about its business.

The large fine was the price of admission. The stage was all set for GunnAllen's next act.

The performance was tragic.

SCAM ALERT – Certified Financial Predators

Just two months after announcing its settlement with FINRA, another GunnAllen broker was arrested and charged with stealing money from elderly investors via a Ponzi scheme.

Jeff Southard was a mild-mannered seemingly conscientious certified financial planner based in New Jersey. He would frequently call GunnAllen, to request guidance and obtain approval for his business activities. That behavior, alone, should have been a warning. In hindsight, I believe all those calls were indicative of a guilty conscience.

In reality, Jeff was a criminal.

With some brokers, there are warning signs. With Jeff, there was a failure to warn. As it turns out, Jeff had been investigated at his prior firm before joining GunnAllen. In 2003, Southard was working for American Express Financial Advisers (now Ameriprise Financial, Inc.), when he was accused of selling unregistered securities and combining client funds with his own money.

I don't believe this information was disclosed to GunnAllen. Had the system worked, had one firm documented and warned another, investors could have been protected. However, at the time Southard's prior firm started investigating him for stealing from senior citizens, Southard accused American Express Financial Advisors of falsely accusing him of misdeeds. When American Express started to investigate Southard for misconduct, Southard had the balls to sue them. Southard alleged American Express acted unprofessionally and violated his personal confidentiality. The inmate sued the asylum.

Southard manipulated the system and caused his prior employer to remain silent about his alleged misconduct. Consequently, Southard's scam was covered up, instead of being exposed and disclosed to investors and prospective employers.

Southard's scam was remarkably simple. Some of his clients wanted income. At the same time, Southard also wanted more income. So, he made up a fake bond with a fake tax-free yield. Southard would raise money by selling the fake bonds. He would use some of the money he raised to pay "interest" to the investors and he would keep the rest.

When Southard needed to make interest payments, he would raise new money by offering more bonds to new investors. The high tax-free yield on the new fake bonds attracted new money from new investors to make payments to old investors.

A classic Ponzi scheme.

A Ponzi scheme can continue as long as prior investors continue to get paid. This includes interest and principal, when demanded. However, when there is no real investment, and when the money is used to pay for private schools, meals, or other unauthorized uses, there's no "principal" left to return to investors.

Eventually, the money runs out and the scheme gets exposed.

Southard took advantage of his client's trust. Cloaked with a professional designation that conveyed integrity, Southard took advantage of clients' legitimate desire for yield and created an illegitimate product. He sold investors fake bonds. He printed fake statements for the fake bonds. Since the fake bonds were tax-free, there was no IRS reporting. The scam was simple, but effective.

Had clients been informed and educated, Southard's misconduct would easily have been detected. Any legitimate investment should be able to be deposited in a bank or brokerage account. When a legitimate firm takes custody of an investment, that firm – also known as the custodian – will issue a statement with a position and a value, on a regular basis. A fake bond can't be deposited in a legitimate account at a real bank or brokerage firm. A real bank or brokerage firm won't produce a fake statement showing a fake position.

Southard's clients also had to pay for the fake bonds with real money – by check or by wire. Unless payment is made to a legitimate company, the transaction is suspect. Southard's clients could have and should have asked for the bonds to be held in their bank or brokerage account, and they should have asked for one institution to pay for the bonds by sending funds to another institution. Any of these basic simple steps could have protected Southard's clients.

The irony is that it wasn't GunnAllen, or a defrauded client, or FINRA, or a state regulator that finally exposed Southard's misconduct. It was the IRS.

During a routine audit of Southard's tax returns, the IRS found money coming in and going out of Southard's bank accounts that he couldn't explain. His "supplemental" income had to come from somewhere. The deposits and withdrawals were in plain sight. The noose was tightening. While the Industry's entire supervisory system failed to detect and protect investors, a random routine IRS audit actually uncovered Southard's scheme.

The IRS audit ultimately exposed Southard's theft of client money. Faced with the guilt, shame, and embarrassment of his crime, Southard attempted suicide. Twice. He didn't succeed. Either time.

Ponzi scheme nets Salem County investment broker Jeffrey J. Southard 15 years

FRIDAY, 04 DECEMBER 2009 17:01 -- A Salem County investment broker was sentenced to state prison Friday for defrauding South Jersey investors out of $1.8 million through a Ponzi scheme...

http://www.newjerseynewsroom.com/state/ponzi-scheme-nets-salem-county-investment-broker-jeffrey-j-southard-15-years

Southard sold fake bonds and stole client money. According to the article:

Instead of purchasing "Ohio Bonds," Southard laundered and converted the funds through a series of financial transactions, using the funds to pay for personal expenses, including $236,678 in private school tuitions for his five children; $270,142 toward his mortgage; $58,334 in car payments; $87,002 in ATM withdrawals; and $36,175 in debit card purchases.

While at American Express/Ameriprise, there were several complaints against Southard that were denied. These minor violations were indicative of things to come. When there were more complaints against Southard, a pattern started to emerge. American Express started an investigation. Southard voluntarily decided to leave.

This is another one of those moments when the Industry failed. American Express had an obligation to document, report, and disclose Southard's misconduct as a warning, to both investors and to other potential employers.

In fairness to American Express, GunnAllen might still have ignored the warnings. GunnAllen was aggressively hiring and Southard's **_reported_** disciplinary actions didn't look that bad.

Yet, had American Express fully documented and reported their findings, and had GunnAllen better scrutinized Southard's disciplinary history, a bigger problem could have been avoided. After Southard was arrested and investigated, New Jersey regulators stated that American Express Financial Advisors failed to properly disclose to clients the problems that could have arisen from working with Southard.

The regulators' order also accused Southard of misleading his clients. Many of them switched to GunnAllen when he left American Express Financial Advisors, after he told them he was leaving to pursue better opportunities. The New Jersey regulators say that, while working at GunnAllen, Southard continued to engage in broker misconduct by selling fake bonds as tax-free investments.

Sometimes, simple is better. For example, if GunnAllen could have called American Express and candidly discussed Southard's employment history, better information might have been communicated. If American Express or GunnAllen had called some of Southard's clients and asked some questions, better information might have been obtained. Southard had already stolen money from clients by offering fake bonds. Some phone calls might have identified his prior crimes, prevented his future misconduct, and protected investors from losing money.

In fairness, any broker who's been around for any significant period of time may have something on his or her record. Between major market corrections and life events (like divorce), things happen. In *any* business, there can be errors and mistakes. Between people, there can always be miscommunication or misunderstanding.

However, while one or maybe two issues might be explainable, any pattern must be reviewed carefully. Researching a broker's background and looking up the broker's firm are the first steps any investor must take before entrusting someone with their money.

Just because a broker is licensed doesn't mean he or she is any good. An investor cannot simply assume the Industry has done its job and refused or revoked the license of a bad broker.

An investor also should not assume that a licensed "investment professional" is either knowledgeable about investments or even professional. Investors need to ask questions and get referrals.

Part 2 contains a section on how to select a financial professional.

Safety tip 6: There are _No_ "Special" Investments

For victims of both Southard and Bluestein, there was a common factor. Investors were told about a "special" investment program that their trusted broker had some exclusive access too. THE IS A WARNING FLAG! Any time a broker or advisor refers to _any_ type of "special" investment program or their unique, private, and confidential relationship with some great investment – RUN LIKE HELL!

Bluestein had the balls to tell clients to keep his "special" investment program quiet, since it was limited and, if they talked, the program would fill up and the investor wouldn't get the chance to invest. Many good hardworking people fell for it.

The trusted relationship, the broker's apparent success, their network of contacts, any special credentials, religious, or military affiliations that lend credibility – all need to be double-checked.

Simply ask your broker/advisor if you can take the **_written_** information about any proposed investment to **_your_** accountant or attorney for a second opinion. Any legitimate broker or advisor will not and should not have a problem with having an accountant or attorney review a legitimate product – as long as you promise to invest through that broker, if everything checks out. You're not committing to invest; you're only committing to have your people help you review the proposed investment.

Just make sure the attorney or accountant you go to isn't affiliated in any way with the investment or the broker/advisor.

Back to Southard – he was ordered to repay harmed clients: not by FINRA, but by a Judge. Unfortunately, Southard had no money. That's why he stole in the first place. Now that he's in jail, at least he can't steal more money from new clients to repay old clients. That would be another Ponzi scheme.

It's kind of like FINRA letting GunnAllen pay a fine for harming old investors by earning money and harming new investors.

Again, that sounds a lot like a Ponzi Protection scheme.

The Tide Turns

2008 was the year the tide turned. GunnAllen was losing money. Fast.

Not only had the firm burned through most of the cash from the sale of the building, expenses were running wild. There were mounting costs from regulatory inquiries, customer complaints, legal fees, settlement payments for broker misconduct, technology expenses, etc. In addition, the firm now had a massive monthly rent payment for its exquisite corporate headquarters.

GunnAllen's incredibly rapid growth came at a very steep price, indeed. As the firm's financial condition began to deteriorate, the founders began looking for more capital.

Fortunately for GunnAllen, capital was nearby. GunnAllen would be saved – but only for a short time.

The financial and human cost would prove to be too great.

The Calvary Arrives

 It didn't take long and GunnAllen didn't have to go far to find more money. John Sykes was a successful and wealthy man. He'd built up a call center business from scratch. He took it public and made hundreds of millions. John Sykes was named to the Forbes 400 list of the wealthiest people in America after his call center business, Sykes Enterprises, went public in 1996.

John had a firm named after him, his name was in big bright lights on one of Tampa's tallest buildings, and he had his own private jet.

Sykes has been recognized by numerous organizations for his business accomplishments and community involvement. Some of these awards include the 1996 Florida Entrepreneur of the Year, and the 1997 Innovator of the Year award.

Sykes made his permanent mark on the city of Tampa when, in 1997, he made a ten million dollar donation to the University of Tampa. He topped this gift, in 2000, by donating an additional 28 million dollars, thought to be the largest gift ever given to a Florida University as of that time.[1] In honor of his generous contributions and in recognition of his achievements, the University of Tampa renamed its College of Business to the **John H. Sykes College of Business**. He also holds two honorary doctorates from the University of Tampa – one in Business Administration and another in Humane Letters. – From Wikepedia.

While you may not have heard of John Sykes or Sykes Enterprises, chances are you've heard of Raymond James. Most know Raymond James as a large financial services firm. Others know of Raymond James for the Football stadium that bears its name. Either way, Raymond James got it right. Timing, business model, recruiting, growth strategy – you name it. Raymond James was built and managed properly. It was a firm to be envied. And envied it was.

Sykes may have had his name in big bright lights at the top of one of Tampa's tallest buildings, but Raymond James had a *stadium* that was on national TV almost *every week*.

While John's former business, Sykes Enterprises, was a public company with a market cap of over $600 million, Raymond James was a public company with a market cap of more than $5 billion. There was money in the call center business, but there was a *lot* more money in the financial services business.

Despite all his wealth and success, John Sykes showed no signs of slowing down. He had recently become Chairman of a local bank. He was forming an insurance company. He had also dipped more than just his toe into financial services.

When the opportunity arose to take control of GunnAllen and turn it around, John jumped at the chance.

InvestmentNews
The Leading News Source for Financial Advisers

John Sykes to take reins of GunnAllen
By Bruce Kelly
September 5, 2008

GunnAllen Financial has a new owner.

John H. Sykes, founder and chairman emeritus of Sykes Enterprises Inc., based in Tampa, Fla., will assume the role of chairman of the board of Gunn Allen Holdings Inc., based in Tampa, Fla., the parent of GunnAllen Financial, also based in Tampa, Fla.

Mr. Sykes leads the investment group that now has the single largest position in the parent company of the independent broker-dealer which earlier this decade was one of the fastest growing firms in the industry.

The size of the investment, which needs to be approved by regulators, has not been disclosed, the company said in a statement issued yesterday.

He will assume his new position within 60 days.

Mr. Sykes will name four of seven members of the reorganized company's board. Gunn Allen founder Rick Frueh will stay on as a board member and president of the holding company and chief executive of the broker-dealer, GunnAllen Financial.

Mr. Frueh said that Mr. Sykes was the only outside investor he recently had spoken to about investing in the firm.

"John and I started having conversations probably five or six months ago," he said.

Mr. Frueh said he was looking for a "strategic investor" that could "help pull the organization along."

Mr. Sykes has "a long track record of making successful business selections," he said.

"I think he likes the prospects of the financial services industry."

The new investment "allows us to continue to accelerate growth" in the company's platform and pursuit of "high quality" financial advisers to GunnAllen's platform, Mr. Frueh said.

GunnAllen currently has 750 affiliated registered reps in its network. Last year, it was the 22nd largest independent-contractor broker-dealer in terms of gross revenue, and reported $151 million in revenue, according to rankings tabulated by *InvestmentNews*.

I met with John and members of his due diligence team, prior to his investment in GunnAllen. I believe GunnAllen's CEO tried to limit my interaction with John's due diligence team, for fear of my big mouth. The CEO was afraid I would say there were too many bad brokers and a lack of adequate supervisory systems. Both problems were easily fixed, so I didn't know why being honest about fixable problems would be a bad thing – other than for the obvious reason that it was embarrassing for current management to admit to mistakes, flaws, and mismanagement.

Basically, knowing what I knew, I couldn't understand why anyone would invest directly in GunnAllen. I still believed in the firm's potential. I desperately *wanted* GunnAllen to survive. However, years of mismanagement had created so much liability; I couldn't understand why *any* investor would risk capital and assume GunnAllen's liabilities.

In my opinion, management changes *had* to be made and a different structure was necessary in order for GunnAllen to survive. Essentially, I thought GunnAllen should sell its assets and infrastructure to a new, clean broker-dealer. The name had to be changed. The sins of the past had to be buried. The inglorious history had to be left behind.

Ultimately, I shared these thoughts with members of John's team. During conversations with John's due diligence team, it became clear they valued information and candor. They wanted the truth. Good, bad, or ugly, John and his team wanted information and facts. They knew they bought into a mismanaged firm. Even though I was a part of that management, I opened my big mouth.

If we were all going to be fired, at least I would go out swinging.

2009: Bad to Worse

The market correction that started in early 2008 turned into an all-out crash in the fall. For the year, the major US stock market indices were down by more than 30%. The stocks generally favored by GunnAllen brokers were down by 40% or more. Much of this decline occurred within the last four months of the year.

Right when John Sykes invested.

Year	Beginning Price	Ending Price	Gain or Loss	Percent Gain or Loss
DJIA 2008	13,264.82	8,776.39	-4,488.43	-33.84%
S&P 500 2008	1,468.36	903.25	-565.11	-38.49%
NASDAQ 2008	2,652.28	1,577.03	-1,075.25	-40.54%

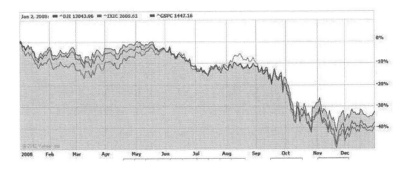

John finalized his investment around the end of September, 2008. In October, the market essentially collapsed. In an unprecedented move, the US Treasury and the Federal Reserve stepped in to bail out major banks and some other financial service firms. Some broker-dealers were permitted to reclassify themselves as banks, in order to receive bailout funds from the Federal government. Not GunnAllen.

With the market's collapse, GunnAllen's revenues fell off a cliff.

Of the initial $10,000,000 invested by John Sykes, about $7,000,000 went up in smoke in his first month of ownership. It was the worst month in the firm's history. Within a few more months, GunnAllen had to change clearing firms. This cost approximately $3,000,000 in additional "unforeseen" expenses. On top of that, operating losses continued a monthly basis. Almost immediately, John had to reach into his pocket to invest more money, to keep the firm afloat.

Welcome to GunnAllen.

John was dismayed, but undeterred. He had a vision. Most of all, John demonstrated either unshakable faith or incredible arrogance in his ability to succeed.

John had a plan.

John gave every GunnAllen employee a copy of the book, *From Good to Great*. He sent more copies, with handwritten notes, to each branch owner, and to GunnAllen's top brokers.

With all GunnAllen's problems, with the market crashing, the message was welcomed and well-received. John called for all employees to meet in the corporate auditorium. Then he stood, side by side with Rick Frueh, GunnAllen's founder and CEO. He commanded the room. He was a great speaker. John told us all that we had built something good and it was now time to be great. He acknowledged that mistakes had been made.

Then John summed it all up by saying, "I can't change the past. I can't change yesterday. I can't change 30 seconds ago. What we can all do is work together to change today. Together, we *can* be great. You have built something good. *Really* good. If we all work *really* hard, we can be *great*. Who among us wants to go from good to great? Who is with me?"

Everyone wanted to be great.

From Good to Great

My first trip on the road from good to great was actually on a private jet. Shortly after John invested in GunnAllen, I got a call from his personal assistant. "John would like you to be at the airport in the morning. Wheels up at 6:00 am sharp. Do you know where his hangar is?" With directions, I found my way to John's private jet, which was in his private hanger. A select few executives were going to New York, to visit the top branches with John. While going with John didn't guarantee anything, not going virtually guaranteed the end of your career at GunnAllen.

It was time for the brokers to meet the new owner of the firm. Rumors were running wild. Fears were high. Brokers were worried changes might affect their management relationships and – even worse – their economic relationship with the firm.

We landed in New York, got picked up by a fleet of limos, and were whisked to a nearby hotel on Long Island. John conducted meetings during the day and hosted a short cocktail reception in the afternoon.

Throughout the day, John and his lead executive, Gordon Loetz – known as Gordie – met with various brokers and branch owners. Gordie had conducted much of John's advance due diligence on GunnAllen. I'd had many prior conversations with Gordie before, during, and after John Sykes' investment in GunnAllen. I found Gordie to have very strong opinions – but he was a great listener, too. Most important, Gordie showed the ability to actually *hear* what was said.

Gordie and John would talk to someone and, periodically, come over and pull me aside to ask, "What's his deal?" John and Gordie repeated this process with me and a few others.

By the afternoon, it was time to interrupt the informal "meet and greet" with a formal presentation of the new owners by the old owners. John and Rick stood side-by-side and addressed the crowd. Rick praised John's wisdom for investing in GunnAllen and congratulated him for all his prior successful investments. John commended Rick for building a successful firm and explained how honored and privileged he was to have the opportunity to help a good firm become great.

Then the brokers started asking questions: "Are you gonna' change our deals? We heard you were going to make cuts? Who is going to run the firm? Will you reduce our payouts? Are you going to raise our costs? We have contracts, you know? You can't just come in here and change things!"

Many of those questions had already been asked privately. But, the broker pack mentality took over and the wolves tried to attack. Like a consummate professional, John defeated every attack by answering questions with grace and charm. He told everyone that he *would* make changes, but only changes that would make the firm healthier and stronger. He *would* change deals, but only if the changes made sense and were agreeable. He explained that he invested in GunnAllen because he saw value. He valued each and every one of them and their business. He was looking forward to getting to know them and to hearing from them what he could do to make GunnAllen great.

John won the day. He was rich and successful and his team was now clearly in charge. By the end of the evening, John and his team had successfully opened private dialogues and started building relationships with most of the major brokers and branch owners.

Rick, the founder and CEO, looked awfully lonely and alone.

Risky Business; Business Risks

By the end of 2008, GunnAllen had lost almost all of John's original investment and the firm faced another major challenge – and a potentially catastrophic business risk. GunnAllen had to convert its clearing business from Pershing to another firm.

As an independent broker-dealer, all of GunnAllen's brokerage accounts were opened with a clearing firm. The clearing firm actually had custody of the clients' assets. GunnAllen and its brokers could simply trade the investments in an investor's brokerage accounts. All customer securities and cash were held by Pershing, which was (and is) an independent custodian. When a GunnAllen broker executed transactions, the purchases and sales of securities was handled by the independent clearing firm that held the client's assets.

Since 2005, GunnAllen had used Pershing as its clearing firm. In the independent broker-dealer business, the two finest clearing firms are generally considered to be Pershing and National Financial Services – a Fidelity Investments Company.

> **Safety tip:** investors should always know the name and financial condition of the firm that acts as custodian. A broker or advisor should be able to trade securities and manage assets within an account; but – for safety and protection – the client's funds should always be held by a known and reputable custodian, i.e. NFS, Schwab, Fidelity, Pershing, Merrill Lynch, Morgan Stanley, or a Bank or Trust company.

After GunnAllen's $750,000 settlement with FINRA, after Frank Bluestein's Ponzi scheme was exposed, and after numerous other issues, GunnAllen and Pershing decided to part ways.

GunnAllen's CEO always maintained that it was GunnAllen's decision to change clearing firms. However, it's my belief that Pershing came to GunnAllen and gave GunnAllen a choice: either change the firm's hiring practices and cut bad brokers – or leave.

The choice was simple, but not easy. GunnAllen needed to cut bad brokers and hire good ones. By hiring good brokers, the firm could replace the revenue it would lose by firing bad brokers. Even if the firm couldn't hire good brokers, the firm could have fired bad brokers and cut expenses, to maintain profitability. There were many options.

A year later, I believe the choice Pershing gave GunnAllen became an ultimatum. While the firm hired fewer brokers, it still hired "bad" brokers. While the firm cut existing "bad" brokers, it didn't cut enough. Cutting brokers reduced sales. GunnAllen desperately needed to *increase* sales.

Pershing had given GunnAllen a choice: be good or be gone. Pershing gave GunnAllen time to do not only what Pershing wanted – but what was clearly necessary for the survival of the firm. GunnAllen didn't get it done. The choice was gone. The opportunity to be good was gone.

Consequently, GunnAllen now had to convert all 70,000+ brokerage accounts to a new, lesser-quality clearing firm. All systems would have to be converted to a new back office. Supervisory systems, commission systems, trading systems – all had to be set up, programmed, installed, and tested.

Significant time and resources were spent preparing for a conversion. Significant costs were incurred to change to a lower-quality platform.

Had those same resources been focused on cleaning up the firm's brokers and operations, GunnAllen might have had a chance. Had all the time and money been spent on deploying new systems or on operating current systems better, GunnAllen might have survived.

Instead, another straw was placed on GunnAllen's back. With past regulatory problems, Bluestein's Ponzi scheme, a crashing market, declining revenues, and the pending business interruption to come from changing clearing firms, it was only a matter of time until GunnAllen's back broke.

As the months passed and the conversion deadline approached, it was clear to me and a few others that GunnAllen's conversion would be nearly impossible. First of all, the new clearing firm's broker workstation – the system used by every broker to enter customer trades – couldn't process approximately 70% of GunnAllen's business. If brokers can't trade, the firm can't serve customers or generate revenues. Not only was the trading system not fully functional, the few GunnAllen brokers who were testing it *all* hated it. It was a potential disaster.

Moreover, GunnAllen had no time to test all the other systems that had to be converted. GunnAllen would have to convert first and find out if multiple systems worked later. From trading systems, to supervisory systems, to operational systems that processed business, to accounting systems that reconciled financial transactions, there were multiple systems that simply would not be fully functional by the conversion deadline.

No business should ever convert *any* system – let alone multiple core systems – without sufficient testing. This includes running both systems simultaneously. By running systems in parallel, problems can be identified, diagnosed and fixed – *prior* to any conversion.

I'd been very vocal about the impending problems. Finally, Rick acknowledged and addressed one: the trading system problems. He selected an alternative broker trading system, from an Industry-leading systems provider. It was a solution I'd been recommending for months. Unfortunately, the decision was made too late.

You might ask why it was so hard and took too long to make the decision to procure a new trading system, when the need was so obvious. By now, you should know the obvious answer: money!

The new clearing firm's trading system was free. While the system was provided to GunnAllen for free, GunnAllen turned around and charged each broker to use the system. The economics of charging more than 700 brokers about $100 per month was significant. GunnAllen was looking at making a pure profit of more than $800,000 per year by using the clearing firm's "free" trading system. The fact that this system didn't work for GunnAllen's business didn't seem to matter.

I believe that, in "selling" GunnAllen to John Sykes, certain financial projections represented that the firm would realize cost savings and gain other financial benefits by converting the business to the new clearing firm. Among those other financial benefits was a projection for an $800,000+ annual gain. This gain could only be realized if GunnAllen used the free trading system.

In my opinion, the system was a material item in convincing John to invest in GunnAllen. Consequently, the motivation to try to use or fix the free system was extremely high. When the realization finally sank in that a new trading system was required, the decision was costly.

First, the new system came with a large up-front installation fee and a high monthly cost per broker. Installing a properly working trading system would now cost the firm hundreds of thousands of dollars in additional fees. It would also virtually wipe out the previously-projected $800,000+ annual profit GunnAllen expected to make by using the new clearing firm's free system.

In addition, since the decision to select the new trading system was made so late, there was no way it could be installed and programmed by the conversion deadline. GunnAllen had to beg Pershing for more time, to delay the conversion deadline. This extra time came at an incredibly steep price.

Under the original terms of GunnAllen's mutually agreed-upon departure, several "exit" fees were going to be waived by Pershing. Once GunnAllen asked for more time, Pershing agreed to give GunnAllen a little more time, as long as GunnAllen agreed to now pay for the previously waived fees. By some estimates, these fees amounted to more than $2 million. This was on top of the installation costs for the new trading system. It was also in addition to the loss of the previously anticipated $800,000+ annual profit from the abandoned "free" trading system.

These details — and the negotiations surrounding them — played out over several months, prior to and leading into the clearing firm conversion. There were many spirited conversations and outright arguments in management meetings. John had various people in the room — but, I don't know if they fully understood at the time the economic impact of these decisions. When the financial results came in, there was no longer any question about the economic costs of procuring the trading system and requesting more time to convert.

When GunnAllen finally *did* convert, most accounts transferred successfully. All in all, it wasn't a total disaster. There were, however, *many* problems. Brokers were pissed. Clients needed to sign many new forms and there was a *lot* of confusion.

Entire branches and many brokers started to leave. Hiring was at a standstill. Costs were rising, revenues were still falling. Instead of going from good to great, things went from bad to worse.

The conversion process began before John invested. It was completed after his money was at risk.

Gordie Leads the Charge

Once John's initial investment was wiped out, and after he had to put even more money at risk, he decided to take over management control of GunnAllen Financial. Since John and his investors controlled GunnAllen's parent holding company, John and the holding company's board of directors effectively controlled the GunnAllen management team.

GunnAllen's original management started with Rick Frueh and Jay Gunn. Despite all the executive management additions and departures, Rick Frueh ran GunnAllen. Jay Gunn was the President but, to me, he seemed like a non-factor in management decisions.

Either way, GunnAllen's original founders had a vision: to build a firm for brokers run by brokers. They understood transactional business and created a firm and a platform to support brokers and clients who wanted to actively trade stocks. Unfortunately, that business is inherently risky and volatile.

Transactional business also was under increasing regulatory scrutiny — even at firms that were run well. There was increased competition from discount brokerage firms that enabled clients to avoid commission-based brokers, like those at GunnAllen. Moreover, the Industry placed a higher value on the distribution of such products as mutual funds, variable annuities, and life insurance, to name a few.

The business had changed. While GunnAllen's founders sought to change with the business, the new owner(s) determined it was time to change management. It was time for someone else to lead the charge.

InvestmentNews
The Leading News Source for Financial Advisers

Ultrawealthy use business acumen to buy into indie B-Ds
Lack of direct experience didn't stop Sykes' big wager on
GunnAllen
By Bruce Kelly | **January 25, 2009 – 12:01 am EST**

Who would be better at running an independent broker-dealer than an independent rep?

That's the thinking of investor John Sykes, who put his personal financial adviser, Gordon Loetz, in charge of his latest investment, GunnAllen Holdings Inc.

Mr. Sykes, who is chairman of the company, and Mr. Loetz, its chief executive, have big plans for Tampa, Fla.-based GunnAllen Financial, the company's broker-dealer subsidiary, which has 750 affiliated representatives and produced about $120 million in gross revenue last year.

"If it was just an independent-broker-dealer business, we probably wouldn't have done it," said Mr. Sykes, who at 72 is a newcomer to the business. "I said to Gordie, 'If I got a bank involved, take a look at it, and then in the back of your mind, think of Raymond James [& Associates Inc. of St. Petersburg, Fla.].'"

Mr. Sykes is far from the only notably wealthy investor with no experience at an independent firm who recently placed a big wager on independent broker-dealers.

He said that he was buying the controlling stake in GunnAllen in September, just as the market began its historic collapse.

Mr. Sykes plans to align the firm with a variety of other financial services offerings, such as NorthStar Bank in Tampa, where he is also chairman and the largest shareholder, and potentially a trust company.

With that in mind, he sees no reason why GunnAllen's advisers won't generate $500 million in annual revenue by 2014.

"I've given Gordie my vision. It's up to him to execute it," Mr. Sykes said with a laugh.

He made his fortune in the call center business through equity in Sykes Enterprises Inc., also of Tampa, which he no longer controls.

Outside of the call center business, Mr. Sykes has already put large sums of money to work in a variety of ways.

In 1997, he branched out into racehorse breeding, buying the 1,000-acre Clover Leaf Farms II Inc. in Reddick, Fla., reportedly for $5 million.

Mr. Sykes has been generous to educational institutions too.

He and his wife have donated $38 million to the University of Tampa and more than $10 million to Queens College of Charlotte in North Carolina.

According to local business reports, Mr. Sykes is known around Tampa for his inability to stay retired, and he clearly intends to shake things up at GunnAllen.

Also, a name change is in the works, and a new brand will be announced soon.

Mr. Sykes knows how to create wealth. In 1996, when he was still running the call center company, he made the Forbes 400 list, with an estimated net worth of $520 million.

Some in the independent-brokerage business scoff at the notion that even the wealthiest interlopers can make a successful run at a highly competitive business known for thin margins, long hours and compliance that many believe focuses on the picayune.

But others say the bet is too good to pass up.

"I know it's a terrible time in the market, but that doesn't change the demand for advice," said Dennis Gallant, president of Gallant Distribution Consulting of Sherborn, Mass.

"That's attractive to an outsider," he said. "Outsiders often have a fresh perspective."

And those supplying that fresh perspective are also supplying the coin.

Like Mr. Sykes, Dr. Phillip Frost, a member of the Forbes 400 who made his fortune in pharmaceuticals, has been making a mark in the independent-brokerage industry.

Dr. Frost is the largest shareholder of Ladenburg Thalmann Financial Services Inc. of Miami, and during the past 18 months, that firm has acquired two independent broker-dealers, first Investacorp of Miami Lakes, Fla., and then Triad Advisors Inc. of Norcross, Ga.

According to Forbes, Dr. Frost, 71, was worth $2.2 billion last year.

Other recent wealthy investors come from other areas of the financial advice business. Philip Purcell, 65, and David Pottruck, 60, were chief executives of Morgan Stanley of New York and The Charles Schwab Corp. of San Francisco, respectively.

The two are among a group of investors who launched a new independent broker-dealer and registered investment advisory firm in the fall, HighTower Advisors LLC of Chicago.

Both had tens of millions of dollars' worth of shares of company stock, along with millions in severance, before leaving their firms.

Aligning a variety of businesses, including offering tax returns to clients on a discount, is a key part of Mr. Sykes' plan for GunnAllen, he said.

"The more that we're able to grow [NorthStar] bank, the more we're able to capture the monetary value of GunnAllen to the bank" through products such as cash sweep accounts, he said.

Tim Smith, InvestmentNews *data editor, contributed to this story.*

E-mail Bruce Kelly at bkelly@investmentnews.com

If John Sykes was the cavalry, Gordie was now the general leading the charge. From the top of the firm on down, changes were coming. As the firm fought to survive, so, too, did members of the firm's management team.

My Good to Great Meeting

About one month after the clearing firm conversion, Gordie called and asked me to meet him and John at a hotel in Fort Lauderdale. I was asked to keep the meeting confidential.

I was not at all prepared for the conversation I was about to have with John and Gordie. First, I sat with John. He told me Gordie had described me as being honest and candid. John said that, according to Gordie, I'd been right in my assessment of the firm's situation and I'd been courageous and vocal enough to share the truth. John told me they wanted a guy like me on their team. Someone who knew the business and wasn't afraid of the truth.

In short, they wanted to offer me a deal. If I served them well and proved myself, I could be next in line to run the firm. Gordie smiled and said, "In five years, I want to be able to turn over the reins. You're in the frontrunner position. The job is yours, if you earn it."

I had bonded with Gordie, but this was a total shock. I looked at John. He gazed at me with his wise old eyes. I stared back. This was a very uneasy moment. John and I stared at each other, trying to size each other up. I was flattered, but I thought this was too much too soon. The best case was that I would have some time and get the chance to prove myself. The worst case was that I would be used and ultimately discarded. The decision was easy. I still believed I could make a difference and help GunnAllen survive.

John and I stood up and shook hands. Then we got in my car. John and Gordie had a meeting with FINRA in Boca. On the short drive from Ft. Lauderdale to Boca, my phone wouldn't stop ringing. With the conversion, there were a *lot* of problems. Brokers were constantly calling me for help. My phone kept ringing off the hook. I apologized. John told me I should answer my phone. He asked me to put the calls on speaker. He wanted to hear what brokers had to say. Speaker or no speaker, the screaming could be heard outside of the car.

A branch owner from New York was calling to complain. He couldn't trade mutual funds. How could we convert to a system that wouldn't let him trade mutual funds for his clients? He was screaming.

I let him vent and said, "Listen, I hear you and I agree. The current system isn't yet configured to handle mutual fund trades. It will be soon. We put out an announcement and we set up an alternate system. I'm sorry we didn't communicate this alternate system to you better. All you have to do is call your trades into our desk. It's that simple. I'll have the desk call you to take care of your orders. Going forward, just collect all your orders and make one call at the close of business and we'll process all your mutual fund trades. Ok? And – one more thing. We'll waive your ticket charges for the entire month, to try to make this up to you. Hang in there. We'll get it right."

I hung up. John and Gordie looked at each other. "Is it true that mutual fund trades can't be entered through the new system?" John asked.

"Yes," I replied. "That programming hasn't been completed. We had to get equity trades programmed and working first, since they dwarf the number of mutual fund trades. Mutual fund trading is expected to be online within 2 months."

There was a moment of silence as they digested this information. Then Gordie spoke up, "You gave them a month of free tickets. How much will that cost the firm?"

I ran some numbers in my head. "If they normally do 200 trades in a month and our cost is $10 per trade, our cost would be $2,000. Since I gave them free mutual fund trading for the entire month, they'll probably do 300 trades, which would normally cost $3,000. However, our new clearing firm is giving us a few months of free trading, so it'll actually cost us nothing."

I could see John smile. Gordie actually laughed out loud. Then he said, "With your permission, I'm going to borrow a page from your playbook. We're gonna' offer all the branches free trading for a month or two."

Then Gordie turned to John and said, "See, John. I *told* you he was smart."

With that, John was temporarily convinced of my abilities. He said, "Gordie, after our meeting with FINRA, I want you to drop me at the airport. I'll fly back solo. I want you and David to drive up to Tampa together. I think there's a lot you two can figure out by spending four hours in a car together."

John was right. Gordie and I had a great time driving to Tampa. I had more broker calls and Gordie saw first-hand what was really going on. We went for dinner. We had drinks. We laughed like hell. After dinner, Gordie looked at me and said, "I don't think John or I had any idea how much of a burden you tried to take on. I know it's been rough. I'm gonna' ask you to trust me and John. Have faith. Dig deep. We will fix this firm. I have a plan. You'll play a big part in that plan. Together, we can do this."

I was blown away. I still believed GunnAllen could be great. For the first time in years, I felt hope. I believed Gordie and John would bring the money and the will-power to right all the wrongs.

It was late. Gordie gave me a big hug and smiled his goofy grin before he lit one of his cheap cigars and got in his car.

"Drive safe," he shouted. "I need you. We have a lot of work ahead of us, partner."

Indeed we did.

Only – we never got the chance.

No Time for Goodbyes

A short time after meeting with John and Gordie in Ft. Lauderdale, Rick Frueh, GunnAllen's founder and CEO, quietly disappeared. To this day, I still don't know exactly how or why – or when it happened – but Rick was gone.

For many, it seemed necessary. Rick was the firm's CEO. The blame for all of GunnAllen's misfortune fell on him. So did the axe. I understood the logic of removing Rick. I see why John's management team wanted him gone. Rick had made mistakes. Yet, in my opinion, getting rid of Rick was a mistake.

Rick had strong relationships with the brokers. I thought those relationships would be critical in keeping good brokers and re-negotiating bad deals with other brokers. Rick wanted to save his former firm. He still had a sizeable ownership interest in GunnAllen and an even greater personal and professional interest in seeing the firm succeed.

Many core issues, such as bad hiring, spotty supervision, and a failure to fire, could have been solved. GunnAllen could stop all hiring for a while. The firm had installed excellent supervisory systems and was even improving upon them. Bad brokers could have been fired immediately. Rick could have been removed from all of this. He could have remained helpful to the firm.

There were rumors of issues with the "deal" between Rick and John. There were disagreements over certain information that may or may not have been communicated accurately or represented fairly. These rumors – and any substance to them – were outside of my direct knowledge. I was not involved in Rick and John's deal-making.

What I *do* know is that the firm was badly broken when John arrived. He conducted extensive due diligence for a fairly long time. During that time, GunnAllen's condition deteriorated ever more rapidly. As the firm's condition changed, so did the deal terms. John drove a harder bargain and Rick had no choice but to agree.

No one knew the financial markets would collapse the same month John invested. The entire world changed. The financial crisis wasn't Rick's fault. It wasn't John's fault. GunnAllen wouldn't have survived it – with or without Rick. It certainly wouldn't have survived without a capital infusion by John.

I was never in the room with Rick and John, but I think Rick would have taken direction from John's management team. Perhaps Rick disagreed or argued too much with Gordie. A lot of distrust and animosity had been building. Ultimately, as the financial crisis worsened, and as GunnAllen's condition continued to deteriorate, things got so bad change *had* to occur.

Like everyone else, I found out Rick was gone – and there was no time for goodbyes.

It was also communicated to me that it would be unwise to have any further contact with Rick. I understood the warning. Regardless, I called Rick – and we spoke. He never said anything negative or disparaging. He asked me to keep my eye on the ball and do my best to make things work. He also asked me to look after certain people as best I could. I offered to meet up for a drink. He declined – I think to save me from the risk of getting caught.

It was awkward and sad.

Surviving the Cuts

Rick's departure was just the beginning. A wave of layoffs was coming. I would get to ride the wave.

I was summoned to meet privately with Gordie. It was late in the day, on a Wednesday. Gordie asked me to come into his office and told me to close the door. In my experience with Gordie, he was either tough and serious or loud and joking.

That day, he was *very* serious.

He looked up and said, "You've been very outspoken about the need to make changes at this firm. Tomorrow, you will get your chance. We *have* to reorganize the firm. I'm meeting privately today with five executives that will help shape this firm's future. Tomorrow, I want you and this team to go in your office. I will provide each of you with a list of all current employees. Your job tomorrow is to define the ideal structure for this firm and to select the best of our employees to work within the new structure. The current number of employees is 140. This *must* be reduced to no more than 70. The current total payroll is $6.5 million. This *must* be reduced to $3.5 million. There is no flexibility or room to negotiate these numbers. This _has_ to be done. Of course, I have my own thoughts as to how to achieve these figures. But, I want you to have input in this process. This is a critical task. Do you have any questions?"

I don't think I even blinked. I had no questions – none that I would verbalize. The request was clear. Gordie knew I understood. He watched me closely, to see my reaction. None was necessary. It was an awful request and an awful job. We could have exchanged words, to show how much we cared. We could have said such cliché things as, "...to save many, we have to let go of a few..." Instead, I simply nodded and got up to leave. As I opened the door, Gordie said, "Be in your office by eight sharp. You might want to hang paper to block the windows, so no one can see what you're up to."

He wasn't kidding.

He stood up and put his hand on my shoulders. It was close to a hug. I knew Gordie's heart was in the right place. He wanted to reassure me. This was not an act of cruelty. He took no pleasure in this. Cutting staff was, unfortunately, a necessary response to our firm's financial condition.

The next morning, I was in my office by 8:00 a.m. – sharp. Not one minute sooner. Within minutes, four other executives found their way to my office. One commented that he'd stopped by earlier, but I wasn't there. No shit. There was no surprise as to who was there. There were a few notable absences. Someone brought coffee and donuts.

No one felt like eating.

Gordie walked in with the firm's chief financial officer. They handed each of us a list of employees, by department, with each person's salary next to their name. Gordie spoke up, "Gentleman, you all know your task. We need to build the ideal broker-dealer. We need to reduce the head-count and total payroll expense. We want our ratio of employees-to-brokers to be 1:9. This is a tough job, but we need it done today. As a group, we'll review and finalize your recommendations this afternoon. I expect to make these layoffs tomorrow. There are a few names on the list that are exempt from cuts. They are highlighted in bold. You are *not* to discuss those individuals – regardless of your feelings. They are exempt from cuts. They are safe. *For now.* You all are safe, too. Does anyone have any questions?"

Not wanting to miss the opportunity, I asked, "Is the CFO next to you safe?" Gordie looked at me and then he looked at the CFO. I knew damn well he was safe. I just had to ask. I think the CFO blinked. He might have been amused – or pissed. All I got was a blink. Gordie looked back at me. He shook his head and smiled.

With no further questions, Gordie and the CFO left us to our task.

Despite the expected amount of lobbying to protect colleagues and friends, the job went quickly. Divisions were reviewed, staffing levels discussed, individuals selected and others cut. It was distasteful work and we all wanted it done quickly. With a few exceptions, we were done by 1:00 p.m.

At 2:00 p.m., we all gathered in the executive boardroom. As always, lunch was served. As we ate a free lunch, dozens of employees lost their jobs. We argued back and forth about the need to reduce the head count, versus the need to shrink the total payroll.

I insisted we could keep more employees and maintain service levels if we cut pay across the board and/or eliminated some higher-paying jobs. The CFO explained that, while I was correct, there were Industry-standard ratios that we needed to meet. GunnAllen simply had too many employees, compared to other broker-dealers.

He was correct. GunnAllen also lacked automated systems, as compared to other broker-dealers. If you lacked adequate automated systems, you needed manpower. When you had to process a high volume of transactions without automated systems, you needed extra staff.

While the firm had invested considerably in acquiring automated systems, installation of these systems took time. Unfortunately, we'd run out of time. The ongoing projects to install expensive automated systems would have to be put on hold. There would be less staff to process business and the remaining staff would have to work harder.

It was necessary, yet hopeless. We needed to install systems to reduce staff. We lacked the budget to install the required systems. Now we were cutting the required staff. Gordie and the CFO had supreme faith that we would somehow figure it out.

One or two of my closest colleagues and I knew it couldn't be done. The firm had grown too fast. We had achieved a volume of business that required a certain amount of systems and staff to operate properly. The systems came too late. This was a downward spiral. Current revenues simply couldn't sustain our current payroll expenses. With less staff, we wouldn't even be able to support or sustain the reduced sales levels. The business had to scale down, in order to survive. To me, it was like trying to catch a falling knife. According to the CFO, we would be smaller and more profitable, thanks to our good work.

I'd held my tongue long enough. I'd worked diligently on this "rightsizing" initiative in good faith long enough. Finally, I leaned forward and said, "If we're cutting staff, we need to cut brokers, too. If we're going to 'right size' this firm, let's cut out the high-risk, high-maintenance brokers who cause us regulatory problems. We have certain brokers and several branches that generate too many customer complaints. We need to cut the bad brokers and branches. We can't continue to handle customer complaints, or incur legal fees, or tie up employees with responses to regulatory inquiries. If we're cutting staff, we need to cut the broker count, too. Let's get this firm down to a manageable level of more profitable production."

Everyone agreed. My closest colleagues nodded violently in agreement. Finally, we would really address the core problem and fix this firm. Keep good brokers and fire bad ones.

Finally.

I looked at Gordie. Gordie looked at the CFO. The CFO looked back at me and said, "That sounds fine. But, if you cut brokers – even bad ones – you have to cut more staff. We need to stick to a ratio of 1 employee per 9 brokers."

I heard what he said. I just couldn't believe it. In the best fake calm voice I could manage, I replied, "You do realize that just being in the securities Industry, regardless of broker count or sales volume, requires a certain level of infrastructure and staff? There are certain systems and certain staff levels that are required, to support even the smallest firm in this business. We don't have all the systems. Either invest in proper systems or keep a certain level staff. In our case, we need to keep staff until the systems are fully installed and working properly."

The solution was simple. A little more time and money would enable us to install the systems and reduce staff to "reasonable" levels. "I understand," the CFO said. Then he looked around the room and said, "I think we're done here. The cuts will start tonight."

We were out of time and money. We were screwed. We just didn't know how badly.

Starting on Friday, the cuts would begin. Administrative and operational staff first. Executives by the close of business.

That was the plan. Now – I'm sure the original owners of the building, Tropical Sportswear, had a plan before they went bankrupt.

They made clothes. They built an auditorium inside the building to host fashion shows. The auditorium had a stage and multi-colored lights in the ceiling. They never got to use the auditorium. GunnAllen actually did get to *use* the auditorium. Unfortunately, we used it to fire employees – in waves. Employees were summoned down in groups into the auditorium to lose their jobs.

Normally, since I commuted to Tampa from south Florida, I would leave on Thursday afternoon, so I could return home to my family. Instead, I extended my trip and stayed. On Friday morning, I first met with each staff member who was being let go. I tried to explain that it was nothing personal. The company's revenues had declined. Expenses were greater than revenues. We had to cut staff, in order to survive. I told everyone how much the firm appreciated their service and I personally thanked each and every employee. Most took it better than I did. Some just wanted to get the hell out.

All had to go to the auditorium and hear a speech from the director of human resources. There were nominal severance packages. Counseling was offered. Arrangements had been made with several local placement agencies to help employees find new jobs.

Once my direct reports were let go, I met with the remaining employees and tried to offer some reassurance. I told them I understood if any of them felt the need to go on interviews and find a new job at a more stable firm. I would help and support them any way I could. I just asked that we all buckle down and do our best as long as we could. I told them I believed there was a chance we could survive – but I told them clearly I could make no promises. What had been beyond my control before was way out of my hands now. I knew it. They knew it. There were tears and hugs. Then I left. I turned off my office lights, locked the door, and walked through the halls of a mammoth building that was nearly empty. I drove to the airport. Got home and went to bed.

The next morning was Saturday. My daughters asked me to take them to a water park. We needed to have some fun, so we headed out to Rapids Water Park, in Palm Beach. We were having a great time going on all the different slides. My daughters were experts. I was a rookie. They knew the best slides. It was a good day. Around lunch time, we went to get my wallet from a storage locker. My phone was vibrating. I ignored it. It kept vibrating. It started ringing. It kept ringing *and* vibrating.

Finally, I looked at my phone. There were dozens of missed calls, multiple voicemails, tons of emails, and texts. I listened to the first message, which said, "Did you hear about Gordie? Call me ASAP."

There were six more messages that asked the same question. I called the President of the firm. It took a while, but he answered. "What's going on?" I asked.

I remember a very long pause. I heard him take a deep breath. "We're trying to keep this quiet" he said. "I'm not sure how news got out. But – yesterday, Gordie died. Apparently, he went fishing in Puerto Rico on Friday. The boat capsized and he drowned. We don't have any more details. We'll meet on Monday, to discuss our next steps. Please keep the news of Gordie's death to yourself until further notice."

Friday, when the cuts were being made, Gordie was killed in a boating accident.

"Dad? Daddy?" I heard my daughters calling me. "What's wrong? Why are you crying?" they asked. I looked at them and realized the personal and professional toll GunnAllen had taken was just too much. I hugged them both. My two young girls. Gordie would never hug his children again. Or his wife. The whole damn thing was sickening. I told them everything was going to be fine. I explained that daddy just got some bad news about a friend. There would be no more fun at the water park that day.

I haven't returned to the water park since. But, at least I was able to go home and be with my family.

GunnAllen Financial CEO Gordon Loetz drowns

By Mark Albright, Times Staff Writer

In Print: Friday, April 3, 2009

TAMPA—Gordon Loetz dived under thrashing waves off Puerto Rico to save his wife. She survived. He did not.

It was a final act of generosity that his friends said was just what they would have expected of him.

The 59-year-old chief executive officer of GunnAllen Financial drowned Friday after a fishing charter boat capsized.

Gordie's Last Ride

On Monday, I flew to Tampa. By now, everyone knew Gordie had died. No one knew what would happen next. The executives gathered in Tampa. Many of the "old guard" who were gathered around the table were supposed to have been cut on Friday. Apparently, Gordie told the CFO to start with the administrative staff and he would personally let the executives go upon his return from his fishing trip. That would have been this very day.

The CFO spoke up. He was emotionless and monotone. "As you all know, Gordie was killed over the weekend. John loved Gordie like a son. He was my closest friend. He was our leader. The board of directors called an emergency meeting over the weekend. I have been named acting CEO. Our mission has not changed. We all have work to do. We'll put out a statement to employees and brokers. We'll have a meeting today, at the close of business, for all staff, in the auditorium. Gordie's funeral details will be provided later."

The CFO told me, "David. Please communicate to staff that we'll hold a meeting today, at 4:15 sharp. Please deal with any media or press inquiries. No comment for now. We'll have a statement later."

Around that time, John Sykes had flown his private jet to Puerto Rico. I believe he brought a doctor, to help tend to Gordie's wife's injuries. He was flying them all back as soon as he could get Gordie's body released by the authorities.

That week passed in a blur. Details of Gordie's death emerged. He died a hero. In his final act, he saved his wife.

I've come to believe that nothing could have saved GunnAllen. I've been angry that Gordie decided to go fishing. I've questioned his judgment for going out to sea with his wife, son, and son's girlfriend in unsuitable weather. But that was Gordie. He lived life fully. He was gone too soon.

I was invited to the funeral. I received a call that John had room on his private jet and I was welcome to travel with him to Baltimore, where Gordie would be buried.

The same four other executives who were in my office the day we made the cut list were all at the airport. Jay Gunn was there, too. In five years, I barely spoke to Jay. We simply nodded. We wouldn't start talking today. There were some family friends, John's attorney, and – of course – John and his wife. Little was said as we flew to Baltimore. Limos picked us up and drove us straight to the church.

It was standing room only. I've never seen so many people attend a funeral. I had no idea how many lives Gordie must have touched. Several close friends and family members spoke. Gordie's son spoke. I stood near the CFO. He was stoic. John spoke. He was profoundly religious and his faith sustained him and many others during this time. He was always a great speaker. Today was no exception.

As John spoke, I heard some noises behind me. I turned and saw one of my colleagues crying and shaking. He'd lost it. He looked up and handed me a tissue. I was crying, too.

The procession to the cemetery was unlike anything I'd ever seen. A police escort led the way. The highway to the cemetery had been closed for Gordie's last ride. He was treated like a head of state.

Gordie was laid to rest. After a few more speeches, we got back in the limos and went to leave. John put his arm on me and escorted me to his car. I was still crying.

Gordon H. Loetz Obituary

LOETZ, Gordon H., 59, of Baltimore, Md. and Tampa, died while vacationing with his wife and oldest son in Puerto Rico in a boating accident, Friday, March 28, 2009. He was a business man, a Baltimore area resident and executive with business affiliations in Baltimore, Md. and Tampa. "Gordy, as most called him, was a very gregarious and fun loving family man" said, Ned Spilker, a best friend, "always there to lend a helping hand to his family and friends. He will be deeply missed by all who knew him." Mr. Loetz was born November 11, 1949, in Baltimore, Md. and grew up in Glen Burnie, Md. He was the son of Frank and Eileen Loetz. He was a 1967 graduate of Glen Burnie High School. It was there he met the love of his life, his high school sweetheart who later became his wife, Ms. Deborah Ann Carter. He earned a bachelor' s degree from The University of Baltimore in 1972. In the mid 1970s, Mr. Loetz founded Comprehensive Financial Services (CFS), a financial investment and advisory firm headquartered in Severna Park, Md. In addition to CFS, Mr. Loetz served on the board of directors at Sykes Enterprises, Inc., headquartered in Tampa, from November 1993 through 2001. Over the course of this period he held several positions including vice chairman, executive vice president and chief operating officer. More recently, Mr. Loetz became president of Gunn-Allen Financial, Inc., headquartered in Tampa. Further, as an Arnold, Md. resident over the past two decades, Mr. Loetz has served as chairman of the board of Chesapeake Academy in Arnold, Md. and on the Board of Summit School in Edgewater, Md. "While he was a brilliant business executive and financial advisor, Gordy was like a son to me" said John H. Sykes, a prominent Tampa, businessman and founder of Sykes Enterprises Incorporated. "He will be deeply missed by those whose lives he touched." According to his family and numerous friends, his real joy in life, besides his family, was boating and fishing. On any given weekend he could be found on the Severn River or Chesapeake Bay enjoying the fresh air, trying to land the "big one" and entertaining those that were with him. Visitations will take place 2-4 p.m. and 6-8 p.m. Friday April 3, 2009, at Barranco Funeral Home on Richie Highway in Severna Park. A memorial service will be conducted at 10 a.m. April 4, 2009, at Severna Park Methodist Church on Benfield Road, followed by burial at Meadow Ridge Cemetery. Gordy is survived by his wife of 32 years, Debbie; four sons, Carter, Chase, Chris and Colby; and his parents, Mr. and Mrs. Frank Loetz. The family requests donations in lieu of flowers, send contributions to the "Summit School, Gordon H. Loetz Fund." Send donations to 664 East Central Ave. Edgewater, MD 21037, www.thesummitschool.org.

Published in TBO.com on April 2, 2009

Halfway through the flight back to Tampa, John stood up and clapped his hands, then said, "Let's not forget this day. We shall never forget Gordie. Let us not forget our mission. Gordie was going to turn GunnAllen around. We will be successful. This will be his legacy. I am counting on you all to make GunnAllen a success. Let us celebrate the man we lost and rejoice in his memory."

John opened up draw after draw of a well-stocked liquor cabinet. He and his wife poured each and every one of us multiple drinks during the remainder of the flight to Tampa.

Once we deplaned, a few of us went out for dinner and more drinks. We asked for an extra seat, ordered Gordie's favorite drink, and placed it before his empty seat at the table.

Gordie had one last ride – in spirit.

Changing of the Guard

After Gordie's death, there was a brief quiet period. The CFO had been promoted to acting Chairman and the former Director of Supervision was promoted to acting CEO.

Picking up where Gordie left off, we were asked to make more cuts. We were also told some of the previously discussed cuts would be finalized. It was a very awkward meeting, considering several soon-to-be cut executives were sitting in the room.

They knew it. We knew it.

Within a few days, GunnAllen's "old guard" was essentially gone. The "new guard" was promoted. There was a new Chief Compliance Officer and new acting Director of Supervision, a new Chief Operations Officer. And me.

The vocal minority who had wanted to change the firm had survived.

Yet, it soon became apparent we were caretakers. There was no master plan; just administration and maintenance. We were role-players; not executives. It was quiet.

While John's small management team conducted meeting after meeting in private, my colleagues and I all waited for the next shoe to drop.

When it did, it fell hard.

Up in Smoke

As the stock market crashed, as the housing bubble burst, and as the US and global financial systems experienced a meltdown, interest rates also fell to record lows. There was no safe place to invest.

Fixed income investors were hit particularly hard. As interest rates declined, monthly interest payments to investors fell, too. Fixed income investors saw their incomes decline precipitously. Stocks were not an option. Banks were failing in record numbers. Interest rates kept plunging. It was a very scary time.

Against this backdrop, in this perfect financial storm, investors began to consider "alternative" investments. When traditional investments like stocks and bonds don't meet investor needs, the Industry will always create new and innovative products. Scammers and scoundrels will also rush to fill this void.

Offering low-risk high-yield investments during a time when risk was high and yield was low was a recipe for disaster. Forget the old adage that, "If it sounds too good to be true, it probably is." Thousands of investors poured hundreds of millions of dollars into alternative investments that turned out to be scams. Investors could buy "healthcare receivables" that would "yield" 12% or "oil and gas investments" that would "yield" 18%.

Many of these investments were total scams.

Among these scams was a high yielding "investment" in an oil and gas program call Provident Royalties, LLC. As a broker-dealer in Florida serving thousands of fixed income retirees who were looking to replace lost interest income, GunnAllen offered the high yield Provident program to its clients.

In 2009, Provident Shale Royalty Investments was determined to be a fraudulent Ponzi scheme and a criminal enterprise. This was after the company stopped paying dividends and after multiple complaints by multiple clients.

These oil and gas investments caused investors' funds to go up in smoke.

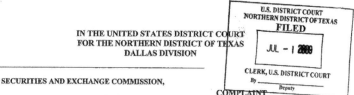

PROVIDENT EXPLODES:
SEC charges Provident Royalties in $485 million fraud

http://www.sec.gov/litigation/complaints/2009/comp21118.pdf

IN THE UNITED STATES DISTRICT COURT
FOR THE NORTHERN DISTRICT OF TEXAS
DALLAS DIVISION

U.S. DISTRICT COURT
NORTHERN DISTRICT OF TEXAS
FILED

JUL - 1 2009

CLERK, U.S. DISTRICT COURT
By _____
          Deputy

SECURITIES AND EXCHANGE COMMISSION,

PLAINTIFF,

COMPLAINT

v.

PROVIDENT ROYALTIES, LLC, a Delaware Limited
Liability Company, PROVIDENT ASSET MANAGEMENT,
LLC, a Delaware Limited Liability Company, PROVIDENT
ENERGY 1, LP, a Texas Limited Partnership, PROVIDENT
RESOURCES 1, LP, a Texas Limited Partnership,
PROVIDENT ENERGY 2, LP, a Texas Limited Partnership,
PROVIDENT ENERGY 3, LP, a Texas Limited Partnership,
SHALE ROYALTIES II, INC., a Delaware Corp., SHALE
ROYALTIES 3, LLC, a Texas Limited Liability Company,
SHALE ROYALTIES 4, INC., a Delaware Corp., SHALE
ROYALTIES 5, INC., a Delaware Corp., SHALE
ROYALTIES 6, INC., a Delaware Corp., SHALE
ROYALTIES 7, INC., a Delaware Corp., SHALE
ROYALTIES 8, INC., a Delaware Corp., SHALE
ROYALTIES 9, INC., a Delaware Corp., SHALE
ROYALTIES 10, INC., a Delaware Corp., SHALE
ROYALTIES 12, INC., a Delaware Corp., SHALE
ROYALTIES 14, INC., a Delaware Corp., SHALE
ROYALTIES 15, INC., a Delaware Corp., SHALE
ROYALTIES 16, INC., a Delaware Corp., SHALE
ROYALTIES 17, INC., a Delaware Corp., SHALE
ROYALTIES 18, INC., a Delaware Corp., SHALE
ROYALTIES 19, INC., a Delaware Corp., SHALE
ROYALTIES 20, INC., a Delaware Corp., PAUL R.
MELBYE, BRENDAN W. COUGHLIN, and HENRY D.
HARRISON,

DEFENDANTS,

and

SHALE ROYALTIES 21, INC., a Delaware Corp., SHALE
ROYALTIES 22, INC., a Delaware Corp., PROVIDENT
OPERATING COMPANY, LLC, a Texas Limited Liability
Company, SOMERSET LEASE HOLDINGS, INC., a Texas
Corp., and SOMERSET DEVELOPMENT, INC., a Texas
Corp.

Civil No.:

3-09CV1238-L

BACKGROUND

1. From approximately September 2006 until January 2009, Provident Royalties, LLC ("Provident") solicited investments and sold preferred stock through a series of fraudulent private placement offerings. Provident raised approximately $485 million from at least 7,700 investors nationwide. Provident promised high returns and misrepresented how investor funds would be used. Although a portion of the proceeds of the offerings were used for the acquisition and development of oil and gas exploration and development activities, investor funds were also commingled and investor funds raised in later offerings were used to pay "dividends" and "returns of capital" to earlier Provident investors.

2. Provident and its principals made material misrepresentations to investors in order to induce individuals to purchase preferred stock or limited partnership interests in the Provident private placement offerings. Investors were told that 86 percent of their funds would be placed in oil and gas investments. That representation was false. Investors were not told that their funds would be commingled with funds derived from the other private placement offerings and that the proceeds from later private placement offerings would be used to pay promised returns to earlier investors.

In short, Provident raised more money from new investors to repay old money from prior investors. It was a classic Ponzi scheme.

The SEC Audit Begins

In the aftermath of Bluestein, Southard, and Provident, it was clear there was still a major problem. There was something wrong with GunnAllen. Too many problems were occurring at one firm. One or two big problems every now and then are simply scandals. The Industry deals with those all the time. But, when there's a pattern of multiple severe problems at the same firm, something *must* be wrong.

So, the SEC showed up with a microscope. *This* exam was going to be different. The newly-empowered executives would show the SEC how much progress was made and how GunnAllen was operating better.

That was the plan.

Except – this plan was doomed from the start. In hindsight, the SEC came to conduct an autopsy while the patient was still alive. We were cut open and split down the middle. We poured out our insides and handed over file after file. We led the horse to water. The new Chief Compliance Officer and the new Director of Supervision showed how many things they actually caught and prevented. They showed all the new policies and procedures they had implemented. They presented their plans to install and deploy additional systems. They presented binder after binder of evidence that demonstrated a real commitment to investor protection.

The SEC staff didn't have to do much work or ask too many questions. The patient on the slab volunteered *everything*. GunnAllen spilled out its guts. If a patient could perform his or her own autopsy, GunnAllen did it.

It wasn't pretty.

Records were presented of accounts opened and trades executed for dead people. The files were received and reviewed by SEC staff with a blank stare. We literally had to *show* the SEC's staff that the person died six months prior to the account opening date. We showed the regulators that we caught the broker's assistant notarizing the signature of a dead person. By the way, the notary attested to the dead person being present when the account opening form was signed.

Boxes of files were presented that documented the detection of sales practice violations. Account documents that were falsified. Low income clients had suddenly become millionaires and were now supposedly eligible to invest in highly risky private placements with big commissions. There were memos that recommended firing certain brokers. Nothing was held back. The new guard came clean.

What was most amazing to me was not that we volunteered the information, but how the SEC staff processed it. Even when we provided files with specific examples of misconduct, the SEC staff often didn't seem to know what they were looking at. Often times, we literally had to connect the dots, to "help" the SEC staff understand what had transpired.

To me, this raised a serious question. If we were actually *showing* the SEC clear examples of misconduct and they didn't seem to understand, how could these regulators *ever* detect or prevent fraud on their own? No wonder so many scams went undetected. No wonder investors are so poorly protected.

Even when we provided clear examples of misconduct with total honesty, we got blank stares.

However, as we would soon find out, rigorous honesty would come with a steep price.

Cowboy Ethics

As 2009 was winding down, John Sykes and his team were apparently winding up the finishing touches on his new game plan. The market had rebounded. A rumored settlement was within reach with approximately half of the Bluestein claimants. Provident had exploded – but, somehow, I thought that was different. Since Provident lied to GunnAllen and 50+ other broker-dealers, I assumed Provident was less likely to be a problem than Bluestein.

That assumption might have been right; but I was wrong, either way.

John called me to his office. The acting Chairman and acting CEO were there, too. I was informed that John wanted to reassure the brokers about his commitment to the firm. He'd decided to host a weekend retreat at the Saddlebrook Resort, which was about 30 minutes northwest of Tampa. It was to be an all-expense-paid trip, for brokers only. No families. No girlfriends. No boondoggle. I was to prepare a private invite list for John's review. I had to justify who was invited and why I thought they should be invited.

Once again, John already had his own list. He just wanted to compare notes.

To help me with my task, John presented me with a book, titled *Cowboy Ethics*. It was written by a renowned hedge fund manager. It spoke to the unwritten "code" that existed in the old west. When there were open plains without fences, when cattle roamed onto another rancher's property, there was an unwritten code of moral and ethical behavior that governed.

According to John, the Industry was so screwed up that he wanted to revisit a simpler time. John believed that good "men" still existed. He believed there was a moral compass within us all that would separate good brokers from bad. He wanted to invite only those brokers who could relate to such a code. John wanted to build a firm around ethics. John's vision for his securities firm differed dramatically from the Wild West. His firm would require and rely on an honor system, based on *Cowboy Ethics,* in addition to Industry rules, regulations, and supervisory systems.

Previously, John explained that the firm of the future might be much smaller. GunnAllen's parent holding company had already acquired a second broker-dealer that was operating independently from GunnAllen. We all suspected John would move over GunnAllen's now excellent infrastructure with a select few brokers, branches, staff, and executives. John would right-size the firm and upgrade GunnAllen's broker DNA with *Cowboy Ethics.*

It was an ambitious – but deeply flawed – plan. It sounded good, in theory. It *looked* good on paper. Yet, in my opinion, it was doomed from the start. First, the other broker-dealer John acquired actually had worse DNA than GunnAllen. John was warned of this, but he ignored the warnings. Second, unlike the corporate world, in which John and his team of lawyers could flex their muscles and maneuver people around, FINRA had to approve and bless every move a broker-dealer made. I didn't believe FINRA would simply let John shut down GunnAllen and walk away from the firm's liabilities with any significant portion of GunnAllen's assets, brokers, or revenues.

FINRA was embarrassed by GunnAllen's public failings and misconduct. There would be a price to pay. In my opinion, FINRA would deliver a bill to John for GunnAllen's sins, wherever he went.

I liked John. I did not like it when John displayed what was either arrogance or blind faith. John had great moments of humility wherein he displayed *Cowboy Ethics.* In other moments, he made decisions with which I didn't agree or that I simply didn't understand. Yet, he was on a

Forbes rich list and I wasn't. I know he didn't get there by being nice and kind all the time.

I also knew John wasn't going to keep me around. Unlike the relationship I'd quickly forged with Gordie, John and I didn't connect the same way. John required complete obedience. I was not sufficiently obedient. I disagreed with some of John's decisions. John did not agree with some of my decisions.

I believed John had already selected my replacement – the founder and CEO of the other broker-dealer. It was only a matter of time. John left me in place to be a caretaker at GunnAllen while John's new guy planned to absorb GunnAllen's infrastructure and brokers.

I read *Cowboy Ethics*. I felt like I was doing my job, like the cowboys of old. Knowing my days were numbered, I still showed up and worked hard. With Gordie, there was communication. Gordie listened. Even when there were differences of opinion and disagreements, there was always mutual respect. With Gordie, I had someone to talk to, something to believe in and fight for.

It was not the same with John. I desperately wanted to fight and win. I just knew I wasn't going to be allowed to be in the fight. It was obvious what needed to be done. John saw some of it, but he was determined to do it his way. His way would not include me.

Nonetheless, I created a list of top brokers and branches. I presented the list to John, to the acting chairman and to the acting CEO. There was some discussion about who was on the list and who was not. To my surprise, John had me add several brokers and branches that didn't meet any of his selection criteria. The list was finalized, the invitations went out – with autographed copies of *Cowboy Ethics* – and the event was scheduled for late September.

A few days before the event, I received my official invitation. I'd begun to doubt whether I would even be invited. I was summoned to the acting

Chairman's office. He unceremoniously handed me a manila envelope. "Inside is your invitation and the itinerary for the event," he said. "I wanted to let you know we will be unveiling a new organization chart for the firm. For many reasons, this had to be kept strictly confidential. We expect you to keep it confidential. It would be improper for any of this to leak, prior to the event. Do you understand?" he asked.

"Of course," I replied.

"Well...open it," he directed me. There was not much inside. I already had a copy of the book. The invitation looked nice. The agenda was cryptic. I guess my expression signaled my lackluster reaction. Finally, the acting Chairman said, "As far as the org. chart goes, I will be named as the CEO, the former Director of Supervision will be named as the new President, and we'll be introducing you as the Executive Vice President and Director of Capital Strategies. We believe your deep product knowledge and exceptional broker relationships make you ideally suited to run the division that will be responsible for financial products and investment banking."

It sounded good. I thanked him and left his office.

I knew we were shutting down Investment Banking. I felt like I was being invited to my own funeral. The weekend at Saddlebrook would likely be my last hurrah. It would also be the end of GunnAllen, as we knew it.

At Saddlebrook, John presented his new vision for his new firm. The new firm just wasn't going to be GunnAllen. I subsequently learned that, about the same time that John was telling GunnAllen brokers he had no plans to abandon GunnAllen; he was already in the process of setting up his new corporation while preparing the legal maneuvers to close down GunnAllen.

As John was looking to the future, one of GunnAllen's ghosts was about to haunt him. And me.

SCAM ALERT – CFP: Certified Financial Predator

Neal Smalbach turned out to be one of the worst serial financial predators I've ever encountered. Smalbach committed a massive pattern of misconduct before, during, and after his time at GunnAllen. He left a wake of victims. The damage he caused still impacts people today.

Unfortunately, Smalbach's story reveals just how badly the Industry fails to protect investors. Since there are many other "Smalbachs" out there, there's no better case to show clients exactly how to protect themselves.

I recall first meeting Neal Smalbach on a cruise. GunnAllen had decided to run a sales contest. The winners would go on an all-expense-paid trip, from Fort Lauderdale, FL, to the Florida Keys, to Mexico, and back. In my opinion, the sales contest was rigged to make sure certain top producers, including Smalbach, would win.

The former head of client services ran the sales contest. It was his turf and I wasn't allowed to get involved – even though I was more familiar with the many rules and regulations that governed sales contests. My knowledge and help was neither asked for nor wanted.

The sales contest had to be designed according to Industry rules and regulations. This prohibited running a sales contest that provided an award for sales of a *specific* product. It becomes a disclosure issue, if brokers are offered any form of supplemental compensation for selling one product over another. Accordingly, the firm simply awarded points for sales of different *types* of products. Brokers with the most points would win.

Obviously, a broker wouldn't improperly generate commissions *just* for a sales contest. Certainly, a broker wouldn't just start selling a certain type of product, *just* to win some points. Even if those points were in addition to the normal commission but now also counted toward a sales contest in which they could win an all-expense-paid cruise.

Once again, the Industry created stupid rules that do nothing to protect investors. Allowing *any* kind of sales contest with commission-driven brokers is like throwing gasoline on a raging inferno.

Anyway, Smalbach had been a top-producing broker and – to no one's surprise – he won a spot on the trip. He even decided to bring along his wife and kids. It seemed nice to me, at the time. Little did I know, his wife worked in his office and "allegedly" helped him falsify account applications, to trick GunnAllen into approving inappropriate client transactions. More on that later.

Halfway through the trip, Jay Gunn conducted an awards ceremony. The ceremony was after lunch, but before dinner. Anyone who's been on a cruise knows this time is generally reserved for drinking outrageous quantities of alcohol – or for napping after having consumed outrageous quantities of alcohol. I sat in a conference room and watched as brokers appeared to do both during the awards ceremony.

Some passed out, while others kept going back to the bar for more.

The President proudly read each winner's name, handed out a trophy, and smiled for a picture. If you've ever visited your broker's office and saw a lot of trophies and top-producer awards, don't be fooled. Those awards were paid for at your expense. You sent that broker on a cruise or a ski trip or to a Caribbean island.

Toward the end of the award ceremony, the President called Smalbach's name, to collect his award. "Neal Smalbach," called the President. We all looked around. "Neal?...Neal? Has anyone seen Neal?" asked the President.

At that very moment, the doors burst open and Smalbach strolled in, having just returned from a private fishing trip. Neal smiled to the crowd, walked straight up to collect his award, took a photo and, just as quickly as he'd entered, he walked right out of the room. Perfect timing. A grand entrance and a comedic exit. Classic traits of a top broker. And clear warning signs, too!

For several years, Neal Smalbach was one of the firm's top producers in central Florida. His business model was simple. He advertised in local papers and conducted frequent dinner seminars at local steak and seafood restaurants. Smalbach primarily marketed to elderly unsophisticated investors who wanted income – without risk. No matter what investment an investor already owned, Smalbach could recommend a product that was safer and which also paid more yield.

Smalbach could smarm and charm, tell and sell. He was a smooth talker and skilled financial predator. He operated the perfect business model during the perfect storm caused by low interest rates: free dinner seminars for unsophisticated income-oriented investors. I will let FINRA's words tell the story:

> Smalbach concentrated his customer prospecting on the senior citizens who populated the west coast of Florida and solicited them to invest with him by offering free dinners at investment seminars. Smalbach held investment seminars on an almost daily basis and advertised the sales seminars to the investing public. For new investors, the sales seminars were held at popular local restaurants like steak houses and seafood restaurants located near the homes of the prospective clients. At the seminars, Smalbach generally spoke about his many years in the securities business and the success he had investing money on behalf of clients. Smalbach regularly emphasized that he was a certified financial planner and had the credentials, expertise and experience to invest their money in the right financial products.

FREE SEMINARS ARE <u>NEVER</u> FREE – THAT MEAL COULD BE *VERY* EXPENSIVE.

DON'T BE IMPRESSED BY SEEMINGLY IMPRESSIVE CREDENTIALS.

LOOK UP YOUR BROKER'S BACKGROUND.

LOOK UP THEIR FIRM'S HISTORY.

For clients with FDIC insured certificates of deposit, Smalbach offered variable annuities. For clients with variable annuities, Smalbach offered "better" variable annuities that paid a higher rate of "interest." Except, every investor should know that variable annuities, as the name implies, pay variable rates of return – not fixed interest rates, like a CD. That didn't stop Smalbach; he told investors what they wanted to hear and sold variable annuities just like they were CDs. Instead of an interest rate, he told clients the variable annuities had a crediting rate that was just like "interest" on a CD. Except, with a CD, you get paid interest and don't access your principal until maturity. With a variable annuity, every payment includes the return of some of your principal – plus any investment gains or losses. So, instead of living on interest, variable annuity investors were living on and using up their principal. In the case of Smalbach's clients, they simply didn't know that was the case.

So, basically, Smalbach would tell clients his variable annuities were like CDs, paid more than CDs, and had a money-back guarantee that was better than CDs. What he didn't tell clients was that, unlike a CD, you could lose your principal; that, unlike a CD, you didn't get interest payments; and, also unlike a CD, you had to die to get your principal back – at which time, it generally would do you no good. Unlike a CD, a variable annuity doesn't come with a maturity date; you have to expire – without making any withdrawals – in order to get a guaranteed return of principal.

Some annuities *do* provide excellent forms of protection, such as a lifetime income. But others, if you live too long, may require annuitization, which would eliminate *any* return of principal at death. Variable annuities can be excellent products, but they have many features and benefits that can be very complicated to understand. Many financial professionals don't truly understand the details behind many of the available variable annuities. Either way, neither details nor facts mattered to Smalbach.

With each free meal, Smalbach always offered a better, safer product – with a higher yield.

Once the customer decided to invest with him, Smalbach primarily placed his customers in annuities and direct participation products. Smalbach would regularly tell his new customers that the equity, annuity, mutual fund, bond or certificate of deposit that was currently in their portfolio was not appropriate for them and the annuity or direct participation product that he was offering was a better investment with better features.

> **NEVER TAKE GENERAL ADVICE.**
>
> **REQUEST A PROPOSAL IN WRITING – VIA MAIL OR EMAIL.**
>
> *ALWAYS* **GET A SECOND OPINION.**

For clients who wanted even more yield than what a CD or fixed annuity would provide, Smalbach sold private placement (illiquid) investments in the highly speculative oil and gas program sponsored by Provident.

Provident was a private placement. These types of investments were *only* to be sold to accredited investors who had at least $200,000 in annual income or more than $1 million in liquid assets. The risk of loss and the risk of illiquidity were so great that these investments could *only* be offered, by rule, regulation, and law, to wealthy and sophisticated investors who could withstand a total loss.

The federal securities laws define the term accredited investor in Rule 501 of Regulation D relevant to the issues in this Complaint as: (1) a natural person who has individual net worth, or joint net worth with the person's spouse, that exceeds $1 million at the time of the purchase; (2) a natural person with income exceeding $200,000 in each of the two most recent years or joint income with a spouse exceeding $300,000 for those years and a reasonable expectation of the same income level in the current year; or (3) a trust with assets in excess of $5 million, not formed to acquire the securities offered, whose purchases a sophisticated person makes.

Provident promised investors a yield of approximately 18% a year. Who knew that holes in the ground could pay so much money? Who knew that a business with no operating cash flow could pay a return of 18%? Still, Smalbach sold a highly risky illiquid investment as a *safe* product with a high yield:

> Smalbach virtually guaranteed his customers that they would receive the yearly 18% dividend and the return of their principal after three years. Smalbach buttressed his claim that Provident Shale was a safe investment by stating to customers that Provident Shale had never had a dry well; investing in Provident Shale was like investing in a certificate of deposit; the customer could not lose; the company had been in business for years; and it was a liquid investment which was easily sold, none of which was true.

In every great lie, there's a grain of truth. At the time, rising gas prices, the explosion of "fracking," the credible location of these holes in the ground – all made it seem *possible*.

Until it wasn't.

> Smalbach also rebutted customer fears about the risks discussed in the Provident Shale subscription agreement by analogizing the investment's disclosures to the warnings given on a Tylenol bottle which warn of possible death for taking the drug but Smalbach would retort that "you never hear of anyone dying from taking Tylenol". Smalbach fraudulently induced customers to invest in Provident Shale by falsely minimizing the risks of the investment that were disclosed in writing by Provident Shale.

My apologies to Tylenol.

READ. READ. READ.

ASK QUESTIONS.

> **DOUBLE-CHECK THE ANSWERS.**
>
> **IF IT SOUNDS TOO GOOD TO BE TRUE, IT PROBABLY IS.**
>
> **IF A DOCUMENT SAYS THERE ARE RISKS, THEN THERE ARE RISKS.**

Initially, there were two problems with Provident:

1) It was a highly risky illiquid private placement, and
2) It could only be offered to sophisticated accredited investors.

However, Smalbach had a solution to *both* of these problems: he lied.

Smalbach lied to clients and said Provident was safe. Smalbach lied to GunnAllen and said the investors were accredited. He tricked clients into investing and he tricked GunnAllen into approving unsuitable transactions.

> **UNDERSTAND WHAT YOU INVEST IN.**
>
> **DON'T INVEST IN SOMETHING YOU DON'T <u>FULLY</u> UNDERSTAND.**
>
> **THERE IS NO HIGHER RETURN WITHOUT HIGHER RISK.**
>
> **IF SOMETHING PAYS SO MUCH MORE THAN ANYTHING ELSE – RUN.**

In short, Smalbach misrepresented the product to clients. He downplayed the risks of loss and illiquidity and oversold the yield. That was bad enough but, in order to get the firm to approve these transactions, Smalbach would have the client sign blank documents and then fill in false information regarding the client's income, assets, net worth, risk tolerance, and other required details.

Once a customer agreed to invest in Provident Shale, Smalbach asked the customer to sign a **blank** GunnAllen Client Information form and Provident Shale subscription form in his presence and then he took it with him. He typically justified his request by telling customers that he was late for another appointment.

Smalbach would make up or alter client information, to make clients eligible for these products and to make the products seem suitable for these clients. With an 8% commission on the line and with his wife and mother-in-law working as office staff – it was a family affair.

> **ASK HOW YOUR BROKER GETS PAID.**
>
> **START SMALL WITH ANYTHING NEW.**

Smalbach also completely, totally, knowingly, willingly, recklessly, and deliberately lied, omitted, and misrepresented investors to his employer.

Later, an administrative assistant assisted Smalbach in completing the blank Client Information forms and Provident Shale subscription form that had been signed and/or initialed by the customer. Smalbach would leave the signed in blank forms at the office and instructed the administrative assistant to complete the forms by referring to handwritten notes with customer financial information that were provided by Smalbach. The administrative assistant wrote the information provided by Smalbach on the Client Information and Provident Shale subscription forms that had been signed in blank by the customer.

> **NEVER, <u>EVER</u> SIGN BLANK FORMS.**
>
> **NEVER, <u>EVER</u> SIGN FORMS WITH INCORRECT INFORMATION.**

In fact, if an investor didn't have the appropriate net worth, or risk tolerance, or a suitable time horizon, or sufficient liquidity, Smalbach and his staff would simply make up numbers, to "help" the client appear to be a suitable candidate for the investment.

After the administrative assistant completed the forms, Smalbach reviewed them and sometimes made changes to the documents. Once the documents were reviewed and approved by Smalbach, the administrative assistant submitted the completed forms to GunnAllen. Smalbach instructed the administrative assistant that if Finn compliance or a securities regulator came to the office, that the administrative assistant was to hide and withhold the folders that held the signed in blank Client Information forms and Provident Shale subscription agreements from their examination.

This kind of "help" is called fraud. Smalbach knew the firm wouldn't approve these transactions, so he made up figures and/or altered documents, to trick the firm into granting approval.

If an investor actually reviewed the completed forms and noticed inaccurate information, Smalbach had an answer for that, too.

Smalbach told customers who reviewed the Provident Shale subscription forms and confronted him over inaccurate information in the application that they "should not worry about it"; "it is just paperwork"; and "you have to put this information in the paperwork in order invest in Provident Shale".

CALL YOUR BROKER'S EMPLOYER WITH ANY QUESTIONS.

CALL THE PRODUCT VENDOR, TO DOUBLE-CHECK INFORMATION.

GET A SECOND OPINION.

DON'T BE AFRAID TO ASK QUESTIONS.

Smalbach's helpfulness knew no limits. In his ongoing commitment to help his clients, Smalbach called Charles Schwab, where an investor had an account. On a recorded line, Smalbach was caught *impersonating* the client, in an attempt to gain access to the client's money. Schwab's compliance called GunnAllen's compliance and presented the tape-recorded evidence.

Faced with recorded evidence, direct action from another firm's compliance department, and the prospect of potential regulatory action, GunnAllen finally moved to fire Smalbach. Yet – even *that* didn't go down right. In a not-at-all funny replication of a scene right out of a movie, Smalbach ran and grabbed a piece of paper, wrote a letter of resignation and screamed: "You can't fire me; I resign."

Smalbach should have been fired years earlier. Time and time again, his conduct was suspect and his procedures were unacceptable. However, his substantial revenues blinded management to the enormous future risks.

There were many warning signs concerning Smalbach's misconduct with clients. When he was hired by the firm, in early 2005, he already had numerous customer complaints on his license. The staff charged with supervising him placed him on "special supervision," which meant that, due to prior bad acts, *all* new business from him would be more highly scrutinized. However, over the next few years, as "irregularities" were identified in paperwork and product sales, warnings about Smalbach's misconduct fell on deaf ears.

Smalbach made a *lot* of money for the firm, so every courtesy was extended to him, and *not* to the investors he placed at risk. There were multiple memos written by supervisory staff to management, attempting to address Smalbach's misconduct. There were multiple memos by supervisory staff recommending Smalbach's termination.

However, while supervisory staff could *see* the problems, they couldn't *fire* Smalbach. Only management could take this action. In a classic case of short-term greed versus long-term gain, the firm placed a higher value on current cash flow than it did on protecting investors and the firm's reputation.

GunnAllen failed to fire Smalbach and the Industry failed to stop Smalbach promptly. Most of Smalbach's clients lost all the money they invested in Provident. Had Smalbach been fired, who knows how many clients might have been spared becoming victims of Smalbach and the Provident fraud?

Starting in 2006 – and for more than 3 years – Smalbach placed over $4.3 million from at least 94 other clients into the Provident Ponzi scheme. The victims included dozens of unsophisticated elderly retirees in Florida who, in return for a free dinner from Smalbach, lost most or all of their investment. The dinner was not nearly free. In fact, for many victims, it was the most costly meal of their lives.

Even after being fired by GunnAllen, the Industry allowed this broker to destroy investors for several more years. Ultimately, it wasn't FINRA or the SEC that finally stopped Smalbach. It was the state of Florida and the criminal court system. Smalbach's fraudulent serial predator spree wasn't stopped until 2013 – by which time dozens of additional investors were victimized for millions in additional losses.

JEFF ATWATER, CHIEF FINANCIAL OFFICER
FLORIDA DEPARTMENT OF FINANCIAL SERVICES

Home   News   Contact Us   About the Agency   Español   Search

Press Release

4/10/2013

CFO Jeff Atwater and Attorney General Pam Bondi Announce Conviction of Senior Scammer for $2 Million Investment Fraud

TALLAHASSEE—Florida Chief Financial Officer Jeff Atwater and Attorney General Pam Bondi announced today the conviction of former insurance agent Neal Seth Smalbach, 50, of Palm Harbor, for grand theft in misrepresenting details of financial products to more than 30 senior clients who suffered losses of more than $2 million in unsuitable financial investments.

"This is a great victory in the fight to protect seniors from financial crimes," said CFO Atwater. "I applaud the fraud investigators, prosecutors, and all those involved in bringing this criminal to justice. This case sends a clear message that if you prey on seniors or anyone who is vulnerable in Florida, you will be put behind bars."

"We put this criminal behind bars by working together, and we were able to obtain restitution for consumers who were affected by these shady deals," stated Attorney General Pam Bondi. "Smalbach profited from knowingly misguiding elderly investors into making risky investments they did not qualify for, and these dishonest business practices will not be tolerated."

An investigation by the Department of Financial Services' Division of Insurance Fraud revealed that Smalbach misrepresented factual details of investment products to multiple senior citizens for personal gain. As a result of Smalbach's misrepresentations, an estimated $4.6 million was invested by seniors in products that were unsuitable for them.

http://www.myfloridacfo.com/sitePages/newsroom/pressRelease.aspx?ID=4157

The Last Straw

Despite churning, front-running, multiple supervisory failures, Bluestein and Southard's Ponzi schemes, FINRA's massive fine, Smalbach's extensive pattern of misconduct, opening and trading in accounts of dead people, a brutal SEC exam, and numerous other miscellaneous violations of securities rules and regulations, GunnAllen still had a chance of survival.

If that doesn't show how fucked up the financial service Industry is, I don't know what else to say.

Except – when Provident blew up and GunnAllen now faced *additional* customer complaints, *another* mountain of unknown liabilities, and the certainty of increased legal costs – it *was* the last straw.

Even then, it still wasn't the regulators who closed GunnAllen.

John Sykes had already lost his entire initial investment in GunnAllen. Almost all new capital went to legal fees and potential settlements with harmed investors. John's money wasn't going toward building a new or better firm. John was paying for the sins of GunnAllen's past.

As an investor, as an entrepreneur, you require a return on your money. With Provident, the potential losses John faced just increased. The potential liability was unknown – but significant. The outcome was uncertain. The only known fact was that there would be more arbitrations and legal fees.

The hole John faced just got deeper. John had to decide if he was throwing good money after bad. John and his team had to decide if GunnAllen was worth saving. John had to decide if Provident was the last straw. Would he dig in deeper to save GunnAllen, or would Provident prove to be the straw that broke GunnAllen's back?

"It's Over."

My day started with a phone call: "It's over. John called a board meeting last night. He resigned. His whole team resigned. It's over."

Confirmation followed. Then more phone calls – wave after wave of phone calls. Employees called, pleading for their jobs; brokers called to ask what they should do next. I wondered the same thing.

The Leading News Source for Financial Advisers

John Sykes quits GunnAllen board, CFO walks
Questions surround the beleaguered firm after owner and chairman resigns, chief financial officer quits
By Bruce Kelly | **December 3, 2009 – 12:49 pm EST**

GunnAllen Financial Inc. appears to be in serious disarray and faces questions about its future after its owner and chairman quit the company's board of directors.

It was not clear when John Sykes, who bought the beleaguered firm last year, resigned. Industry sources said a number of other directors at the firm quit as well.

Mr. Sykes did not return phone calls to comment Thursday morning.

Scott Bendert, CFO of GunnAllen Holdings and acting chairman of the broker-dealer, also resigned, sources said.

Fred Kraus, the broker-dealer's president and acting CEO, sent an e-mail to the firm's brokers on Thursday afternoon and said that, despite the turnover of senior management, it will be "business as usual" for the brokers, according to a rep who read the e-mail to

InvestmentNews. The firm would also call on its founders, Rick Frueh and Jay Gunn, for advice and support going forward, the e-mail said.

The firm's advisers were scheduled to have a conference call with management late Thursday.

Mr. Sykes is the founder and chairman emeritus of call center operator Sykes Enterprises Inc. of Tampa, Fla. He led the investment group that acquired a controlling position in the parent company of the independent broker-dealer, which earlier this decade was one of the fastest-growing firms in the industry.

Mr. Sykes was chairman of Gunn Allen Holdings Inc. of Tampa, the parent of GunnAllen Financial. When he bought GunnAllen last September, the amount he paid for the firm was not disclosed. Mr. Sykes named four of seven members of the reorganized company's board.

GunnAllen continues to grapple with lawsuits and litigation stemming from a rogue broker, Frank Bluestein who sold investments in what turned out to be a $250 million Ponzi scheme, according to a Securities and Exchange Commission complaint.

The firm was also one of the independent broker-dealers that sold securities of Provident Asset Management, a series of oil and gas deals that the SEC this summer charged with fraud. Investors have begun to sue firms and advisers over the Provident investments.

According to the most recent InvestmentNews survey, GunnAllen Financial had 726 affiliated reps, with 285 of those producing more than $100,000 in fees and commissions.

In March, Mr. Sykes used a tragic occasion to confirm his desire to keep the company on course.

GunnAllen Holdings and GunnAllen Financial's CEO, Gordon Loetz, died in a boating accident. Mr. Loetz was a close personal friend of Mr. Sykes, as well as his personal financial adviser.

After Mr. Loetz's death, Mr. Sykes said in a statement: "The firm will continue and we are committed to seeing Gordie's vision for the firm fulfilled."

That appears to no longer be the case.

John and his team were done dealing with excessive costs, pre-existing debt, mounting customer complaints, and ever-increasing liabilities. GunnAllen's multiple legacy problems and the market's severe downturn were too much for Sykes to bear.

The emotional impact of parting with GunnAllen after Gordie's death is something I can't imagine. However, Gordie wasn't GunnAllen and, in my opinion, it was better to let GunnAllen and Gordie each rest in peace. Separate them once and for all. Gordie's legacy could be fulfilled another way. It was time to take GunnAllen off life support.

Unfortunately, the end would be anything but peaceful.

Can You Lend A Hand?

After John resigned, the firm's current President reached back to GunnAllen's founder and former CEO, Rick Frueh, for help. Rick immediately jumped back into the swing of things, to try and help find new investors or a buyer for GunnAllen.

For many, it was strange. So much blame had been piled on Rick, it was as if the prodigal son returned and no one knew whether to be glad or mad. For the remaining desperate employees, there was only one choice: hope for the best.

Rick worked feverishly with all his resources and contacts. He sought out and found several interested parties. I was flying back and forth and participating in new rounds of due diligence meetings. With all the liabilities, it soon became clear that finding a new investor was a virtual impossibility. They would be buying into the massive claims and liabilities that John Sykes correctly decided to leave behind.

However, there were several prospective buyers for GunnAllen's "assets": client accounts, systems, staff, and etc. FINRA and the SEC would have to approve any transaction, and that would take time and money. GunnAllen was running out of both.

John Sykes was among those interested and willing to make an offer for GunnAllen's assets. I believe the general consensus was that FINRA might not have approved of a transaction where John got any sizable portion of GunnAllen's assets while escaping its liabilities. I know John presented several offers in writing. Apparently, these offers were ignored or rejected and John was never given the chance to try working a deal with GunnAllen and the regulators.

Instead, Rick worked on a deal that would sell the rights to service all of GunnAllen's customer accounts to another broker-dealer that was essentially a shell. This new broker-dealer would also acquire and transfer all GunnAllen's brokers, systems, and staff. It was an ambitious plan to essentially change the name on the door. Rick and Jay would try to re-emerge and rebuild as a new firm under a new name. It was a time-tested play from his old playbook: change the name on the door, but keep the same space and phone number.

Since we had recently converted GunnAllen's business from one clearing firm to another, we were ready for another fire drill to affect a wholesale transfer of operations. Unfortunately, we had a fraction of the staff that was needed. This was our last chance to save what was left of GunnAllen. The firm was dying. It was terminal. There was no possible cure. No miracle could save GunnAllen. The crushing debt, current liabilities, onslaught of new complaints and the enormous monthly rent for the glorious office had overwhelmed any hope of survival.

There was also no ability to use the legal system to file bankruptcy. If a broker-dealer files bankruptcy, it is immediately liquidated. GunnAllen couldn't buy time or renegotiate its rent, debt, or liabilities under the normal protection afforded other non-broker-dealer corporations under a bankruptcy proceeding.

There was one shot and one shot only for GunnAllen's survival. It was a long shot.

The SEC Audit Results

Unfortunately, the SEC shot first. It was up close and personal, too. On March 2, 2010, the SEC delivered the results of its last examination of GunnAllen. Basically, in a ten-page confidential report, the SEC determined that GunnAllen had no business being in *any* business, let alone the highly regulated securities business.

All the information we willingly volunteered to the SEC can and was used against us. The problems we detected and corrected were used to convict us. It's a good thing we spent the time explaining the problems to the SEC. At least, after we connected the dots, the SEC staff was able to understand enough to write us up as if *they* were the ones who detected the problems.

Now – here's the really sad part. In 2009, we showed the SEC about a bond trading scheme that took advantage of terminally ill investors. We stopped this on our own. We presented the evidence to the SEC. Yet, the SEC did **nothing** about it – for years!

The following announcement was recently released by the SEC September 20, 2013:

U.S. Securities and Exchange Commission

SEC NEWS DIGEST

Issue 2013-182
September 20, 2013

ENFORCEMENT PROCEEDINGS

Commission Files Injunctive Action against South Carolina Father and Son for Fraudulent Program Designed To Profit from Fate of Terminally Ill

The Securities and Exchange Commission ("Commission") today announced the filing of a complaint in federal district court against Benjamin Sydney Staples ("Benjamin Staples") and his son, Benjamin Oneal Staples ("Oneal Staples") (collectively, the "Defendants") of Lexington, South Carolina for operating a fraudulent investment program designed to profit illegally from the deaths of terminally ill individuals.

The complaint alleges that Defendants deceived bond issuers out of at least $6.5 million by lying about the ownership interest in bonds they purchased in joint brokerage accounts opened with people facing imminent death who were concerned about affording the high costs of a funeral. According to the Commission's complaint, Benjamin and Oneal Staples operated what they called the Estate Assistance Program from early 2008 to mid-2012. They recruited at least 44 individuals into the program and purchased approximately $26.5 million in bonds from at least 35 issuers.

The Complaint further alleges that Defendants required the terminally ill individuals to sign documents relinquishing any ownership interest in the assets in the joint account, including the bonds that Defendants later purchased. According to the complaint, Defendants purchased discounted corporate

Of the $6.5 million that was bilked out of bond issuers and stolen from terminally ill investors, how much occurred after 2009, when we provided evidence of the scam to the SEC? Most of it.

In any event, the SEC sent a copy of its GunnAllen exam findings to FINRA's office in Boca Raton.

It was a kill shot.

2010: THE CLOSING BELL: FINRA Shuts Down GunnAllen

Within two weeks after receiving the SEC's examination report, FINRA determined that GunnAllen lacked sufficient capital to continue operations. FINRA had staff on site at GunnAllen's headquarters for weeks prior to receiving the SEC's report. GunnAllen's books – including its capital reserves – had been reviewed daily. Suddenly, the game changed.

Prior to the SEC's report, negotiations for a deal were in the works. FINRA had been reviewing a proposed transaction. I can't say FINRA would have approved the deal. But, now all bets were off. GunnAllen had been walking the plank. With FINRA's sword in its back, and no more room in front, GunnAllen was doomed.

The Leading News Source for Financial Advisers

Finra shuts down GunnAllen
Embattled firm said to be in net capital violation after eleventh-hour effort failed to raise fresh funds
By Bruce Kelly | *March 22, 2010 – 9:17 am EST*

Time has apparently run out for the crippled broker-dealer GunnAllen Financial Inc. and its 400 reps and advisers, as regulators informed GunnAllen late last week that the firm did not have enough capital to open for business this morning.

According to several sources with knowledge of the matter, the **Financial Industry Regulatory Authority** Inc. told GunnAllen it would be in a net capital violation as of Monday morning—if the firm did not receive an infusion of cash over the weekend.

David Levine, executive vice president at GunnAllen, confirmed that the firm had a net capital violation. Executives told employees they were losing their jobs this morning at the company's Tampa, Fla., headquarters.

The largest problem facing GunnAllen is the raft of lawsuits lodged against the firm. Investors are seeking as much as $50 million in damages, with many of those claims stemming from the activities of Frank Bluestein. Mr. Bluestein was a rogue broker who allegedly steered clients into a Ponzi scheme that eventually went bust in 2007.

GunnAllen, which bulked up on brokers in the last decade—and was one of the fastest growing firms of the era, with a significant but obscure operation in New York—is also facing client lawsuits over the sale of Provident Royalties LLC private placements.

Last week, Finra expelled the broker-dealer instrumental in marketing those deals, Provident Asset Management, for its role in a $475 million Ponzi scheme, the regulator said.

Finra's action does not mean that GunnAllen's client accounts were in any danger, sources said. GunnAllen's clearing firm, Ridge Clearing & Outsourcing Solutions Inc., will take over the accounts.

Mr. Levine stressed that customer accounts were safe at Ridge.

Herb Perone, a Finra spokesman, said the industry's self-regulator had no comment about the GunnAllen matter.

GunnAllen has faced serpentine and sometimes bizarre twists and turns of late, including serious questions about whether it had enough capital on hand to do business.

GunnAllen teetered on the edge of insolvency in December, when John Sykes, chairman and largest shareholder of the firm's holding company, GunnAllen Holdings Inc., abruptly resigned from the company's board.

Finra regulators scurried to the firm to comb its books, pronouncing the broker-dealer fit to remain open for business. Mr. Sykes then acquired a separate B-D, **Pointe Capital Inc.**, from GunnAllen Holdings, saying he intended to focus on the wealth management business.

On Sunday afternoon, Mr. Sykes said that he could not respond to questions about GunnAllen.

Reps and advisers commenced leaving the firm as the broker-dealer searched for a new partner. At the end of January, Progressive Asset Management Inc. said it intended to acquire the firm.

It now appears that the bid failed to stave off the end for the once high-flying GunnAllen.

The Post-Mortem: Who – or What – Killed GunnAllen Financial?

Did FINRA really step in because GunnAllen lacked sufficient capital or was it because GunnAllen could not make the installment payments on its FINRA fine? After years of monitoring GunnAllen's misconduct, FINRA suddenly decided, one day, that GunnAllen didn't have enough capital?

FINRA pulled a chicken shit move. Time ran out for FINRA, too. The SEC's exam findings were also an indictment of FINRA, for its failures to properly supervise GunnAllen. FINRA simply didn't do its job. Like a naughty child who got caught in the act of wrongdoing, FINRA attempted to cover its ass. So, FINRA "quickly" stepped in to shut GunnAllen down. This was years after not doing enough.

FINRA's feeble attempt to cover up its own incompetence is just as much a part of this story as GunnAllen's misconduct.

The Leading News Source for Financial Advisers

Who – or what – killed GunnAllen Financial?
Failed B-D left behind unfulfilled promise, overwhelming litigation
By **Bruce Kelly**
Mar 28, 2010 @ 12:01 am (Updated 3:30 pm) EST

As the stock market was climbing to its historical peak in late summer 2007, GunnAllen Financial Inc. executives told people that the firm was working to put the worst elements from its brief, intense past of breakneck growth behind it.

David Levine, then the firm's national sales manager, was touting an aggressive recruiting package dubbed "100% for Life." He was also talking up the quality of financial advisers making inquiries about the firm.

It appeared that he had good reason to be so chipper. The independent broker-dealer peaked—along with the stock market—that year with $151 million in gross revenue.

At the same time, GunnAllen appeared to be getting a handle on its compliance problems.

Behind the scenes, company lawyers and executives were working with the **Financial Industry Regulatory Authority** Inc. to reach a wide-ranging settlement for the sins of the firm's incredible expansion, including supervisory issues and lax anti-money-laundering systems and record keeping.

Mr. Levine's upbeat, hopeful version of GunnAllen's future never came to pass.

LACK OF CAPITAL

Last Monday, Finra shut down the firm, stating that it lacked sufficient capital to conduct business.

The action left many wondering who—or what—killed GunnAllen.

No one answer emerged. GunnAllen brokers, top executives, industry recruiters and lawyers had a series of answers, focusing on ethically challenged brokers, investments that went bust and ill fortune.

In the end, GunnAllen appeared to be a firm that couldn't get out of its own way.

Was the killer one broker, Frank Bluestein? He, the **Securities and Exchange Commission** alleges, was responsible for soliciting about 800 investors who invested $74 million in an alleged Ponzi scheme that went bust in the summer of 2007, just as Mr. Levine was touting the firm's renaissance.

Last year, the SEC charged Mr. Bluestein with fraud, and he has more than 130 customer complaints on his employment record. The SEC's case against him is pending.

Perhaps, the real killer was the recent fallout that the firm suffered from selling $39.5 million in private placements in oil and gas offerings from Provident Asset Management, which Finra expelled from the securities business this month and the SEC charged with fraud last year.

Industry observers said that it could have been the culture of the firm. To that point, during its peak growth period, GunnAllen hired advisers with histories of compliance problems and had some who had multiple marks on their employment records.

In 2005, 4.5% of the firm's brokers were on heightened supervision by the compliance department because they had three or more knocks—or "yes" answers—on their U4s, the registration form for registered representatives.

By comparison, just 0.6% of reps registered in 2005 with NASD— Finra's predecessor organization—had three affirmative answers on their records. Former employees and industry observers will be left to decipher what caused the firm to fold.

What isn't open for debate, however, is that the firm's legacy is one of unfulfilled promise and insurmountable litigation.

GunnAllen executives and outside attorneys said that the firm could have between $35 million and $50 million in liabilities in client lawsuits stemming from brokers such as Mr. Bluestein and investments—namely Provident private placements—that have blown up. Legal costs crushed the firm, which was spending $500,000 a month on lawyers, executives said.

At its peak at the start of 2005, 970 reps and advisers were affiliated with the firm. About 400 were left to receive the news March 22 that the firm was shutting down.

In an effort to shake off its checkered past, the firm made significant strides by investing in compliance systems and hiring compliance personnel. GunnAllen executives, however, remained beholden, at times, to certain reps and branches with dubious ethics and business practices, said David Jarvis, the former general counsel.

"You cannot let the inmates run the asylum, and that's where the firm failed," said Mr. Jarvis, whose comments echoed those of other GunnAllen executives, brokers and industry recruiters. "It let the inmates run the asylum."

Donald "Jay" Gunn, the firm's co-founder, was aiming high, telling brokers that he envisioned the firm as what **Merrill Lynch & Co. Inc.** should be—a place where a broker can be left alone to do his or her business, said one GunnAllen rep, who asked not to be identified.

"I think a lot of brokers lied to his face about their background and intentions, and he believed them," said the broker, who was deciding last Tuesday about which broker-dealer he would join.

"Jay wants to believe people. During that time, stories [were being] written about guys' being blackballed by broker-dealers," the rep said.

Advisers with marks on their employment records turned to Mr. Gunn and co-founder Richard Allen Frueh, he said.

"Brokers probably said to Jay, 'It's not my fault,'" the rep said.

Mr. Frueh and Mr. Gunn, producing brokers who are moving their registration to **J.P. Turner & Co.** LLC, both made their careers in the securities business as successful, transaction-oriented brokers.

The firm mirrored that type of business. It opened in 1997 and bulked up on brokers from 2002 to 2005, adding a whopping 750 in that time frame. At its peak, the firm had close to 1,000 brokers.

Many were transaction-oriented reps and some, as noted earlier, had besmirched employment histories.

During the first quarter of 2004, about 7% of the firm's gross revenue came from fees, with 88% coming from transactions. By contrast, the average independent broker-dealer generated about 20% of its gross revenue from fees.

In an interview last week, Mr. Frueh dismissed notions that the firm looked the other way in hiring brokers with bad track records, or that the legacy of early hiring did the firm in. GunnAllen "grew fast but added all kinds of compliance and supervision, and spent millions on that," he said.

Instead, Mr. Frueh pointed to a variety of reasons for the firm's demise, including the historic market downturn and the change in the firm after it was sold in September 2008 to John Sykes.

At the time, the firm ceased recruiting, and brokers with $34 million in production eventually left.

"How do you make up that production?" Mr. Frueh asked.

What's more, Mr. Bluestein hornswoggled GunnAllen because he didn't tell the firm that he was selling private placements that have been called fraudulent by the SEC, Mr. Frueh said.

Mr. Frueh had remained with GunnAllen as a broker after Mr. Sykes bought the firm, and when the latter abruptly resigned as chairman in December, Mr. Frueh and Mr. Gunn informally reasserted their presence.

They are now trying to lure some brokers to follow them to J.P. Turner.

"Frank Bluestein was a 22-year veteran without a single mark on his license when we hired him," Mr. Frueh said. He "had a beautiful book of business, and he was an incredibly good money manager," running almost $1 billion in client money, he added.

"We didn't know anything about [the] Ed May [private placements], nor did two other broker-dealers" Mr. Bluestein worked with prior to GunnAllen, Mr. Frueh said.

In fact, someone at GunnAllen knew that Mr. Bluestein was selling the Ed May offerings, said David Foster, Mr. Bluestein's attorney.

Mr. Bluestein testified in an arbitration hearing last year that in 2005, just before he joined the firm, he told Dave McCoy, then a GunnAllen recruiting executive, that he was selling the deals.

Mr. Bluestein is unemployed, according to Mr. Foster.

"Did Frank kill GunnAllen?" Mr. Foster asked. "The seeds for GunnAllen's demise were planted when GunnAllen made an intentional decision to expand their company by hiring many registered reps with questionable records and then took the position of sales and profits regardless of costs."

A deal with a potential buyer, Progressive Asset Management, was announced at the end of January, but the negotiations were never finalized or approved by regulators.

"At the core of GunnAllen were extremely dedicated employees that tried their best—each and every day—to create a firm where brokers wanted to be," Mr. Levine said.

Meanwhile, the biggest-producing branch from GunnAllen is heading to independent broker-dealer, Aegis Capital Corp.

The New York branch is in the process of moving roughly 70 brokers to Aegis. Sources estimate the branch has as much as $500 million in assets.

0

GunnAllen's demise was unfortunate, but well-deserved. So many things could have been done better.

Bad brokers should never have been hired. Bad brokers could have been fired sooner. The implementation of adequate supervisory systems should have come first, before hundreds of questionable brokers were hired. While money was spent on top-quality systems, it was too little too late. Playing catch-up in a transactional business with moving markets is simply a recipe for disaster. If you want to take a risk and hire brokers with a bad history, you better be able to watch them closely. If you hire bad brokers knowing you really can't supervise them properly, you deserve to get shot.

There were many good brokers at GunnAllen. There was also an incredible group of loyal employees who always tried to be better. In my opinion, the firm's bad reputation created a chip on everyone's shoulder that made people care more and work harder. To this day, I've never worked for any firm that had a core group of employees that cared as much for their firm. But, it wasn't *their* firm. They couldn't stop the madness or make the necessary changes. Day-in and day-out, these hard-working employees watched overpriced executives make horrendous decisions.

I stayed at GunnAllen because I believed we could be better. I thought I could make a difference. I know, at times, I did. Still, there was simply too little time to overcome all the bad decisions.

One of the worst decisions of all was made by the Industry regulators – the very regulators who were tasked with protecting investors. While FINRA's Boca Office – the office responsible for supervising GunnAllen – grew in size and reputation, GunnAllen buried client after client. While officials in FINRA's Boca Office rose in stature and pay, GunnAllen's investor losses increased in size and severity.

The disconnect between FINRA's lack of action and GunnAllen's broker misconduct was staggering. Only after the losses became too high, after the publicity became too great, after the political pressure became too unbearable, did FINRA finally step up to deal with GunnAllen.

But – it was *how* FINRA finally chose to deal with GunnAllen that deserves closer examination. By now, you've seen examples of executive mismanagement. You've seen multiple examples of broker fraud. In any other business, that would have been enough.

Not in the Industry.

GunnAllen was not shut down for broker misconduct, or failures in supervision, or for securities fraud. GunnAllen was shuttered for failing to maintain sufficient net capital. In the end, GunnAllen was shut down by FINRA for a technical rule violation of what is essentially an accounting requirement.

The Industry requires broker-dealers to maintain a certain amount of capital (money) in reserve. The amount is tied to the size of the firm's business. It includes a requirement to hold additional reserves when there are customer claims against a firm. As claims against GunnAllen mounted, so, too, did the firm's capital requirement. Ultimately, FINRA determined the firm simply didn't have adequate capital to continue.

In a move that screams of an epic failure to supervise, FINRA caused GunnAllen to close, not for its extensive history of violations that FINRA should have watched more closely and tried harder to prevent. FINRA closed GunnAllen for an accounting problem. Does that mean GunnAllen could have raised more money and gone on its merry way? Would money have solved all of GunnAllen's problems?

No – and no.

FINRA failed to properly supervise GunnAllen. GunnAllen failed to properly run many aspects of its business. In an Industry that claims to protect investors, FINRA screwed up. FINRA gave GunnAllen enough rope to hang itself – which it did.

Yet, FINRA's job is to regulate broker-dealers. FINRA's job is to *protect* investors. FINRA shouldn't allow a bad firm to grow and thrive at investors' expense. FINRA shouldn't give a firm more rope. FINRA should use rope to create a noose and *hang* bad firms and bad brokers.

FINRA is supposed to protect investors and *not* broker-dealers.

Investors lost millions. GunnAllen is closed and bankrupt. Clients have virtually no hope of recovering their losses. FINRA continues on its merry way.

The Industry goes on.

Still, you can now do something to protect yourself. Unless you want to continue to entrust your money to a system and an Industry that looks after itself first, there is an alternative. There are tools you can use to control your finances and to help protect your investments.

Part 2 will further document how the Industry abuses investors at virtually every firm, in virtually every product.

As a result of my experience with GunnAllen, in addition to writing this book, I've decided to make available directly to investors many of the very tools the Industry claims to use, to supervise firms and brokers.

However, *now* these tools can be used directly for *your* benefit.

I've started a business called InvestorProtector® – www.investorprotector.com. You can enroll virtually *any* online account. It doesn't matter whether you direct your own investments or work with a broker or advisor. Your account can be at any firm. InvestorProtector® will safely and securely aggregate all of your account information. With

InvestorProtector®, you'll receive an interactive personal financial Website that will help you organize and better control your financial well-being. In addition, InvestorProtector® will provide continuous independent monitoring of the activity, fees, risk exposure, performance, gains, losses, and many other factors. You'll receive automated alerts when certain account changes require your immediate attention.

Best of all, there is a "no sales/solicitation" and privacy guarantee. You can enjoy independent monitoring with automated alerts without any interaction with brokers or sales people. Salaried customer service representatives will answer your questions with honesty, professionalism, and integrity.

InvestorProtector® is a first-of-it's-kind subscription-based service. You support us; we protect you.

If you wish to get advice or recommendations, we can refer you to an appropriate and highly qualified professional – but only at your request and only with your explicit authorization.

In the meantime, you can try InvestorProtector™ for free. Your broker/advisor will never even know. Our team of professionals has seen it all and will look out for you – *without* any hidden fees or commissions.

We can help. We can watch. Make the call.

InvestorProtector
Get Connected. Be Protected.

www.investorprotector.com

Epilogue

In June of 2013, Bloomberg ran the following story: "Finra Regulator Resigns after 1993 Bingo Fraud Is Leaked."

A top official for the Financial Industry Regulatory Authority resigned after the agency was informed he was indicted for felony theft and charitable bingo fraud in 1993, the year he joined the agency.

Mitchell C. Atkins, a senior vice president who managed Finra's work in 11 states, quit after spending 20 years with the brokerage industry self-regulator and its predecessor.

An investigation by the Louisiana State Police found a health-care corporation formed by Atkins' father reaped more than $58,000 in bingo proceeds in 1991 and 1992, and that "no money was received by any charitable organization," according to the disciplinary board's summary of the probe. The company had more than $1 million in debt at the time and hadn't done any business since 1988, the board's record states.

In November 1993 Atkins agreed to plead guilty to charitable bingo fraud, a misdemeanor, and prosecutors dropped the felony theft charge, according to minutes of court proceedings from Louisiana's East Baton Rouge Parish. The conviction was "set aside" after Atkins showed that he carried out the terms of his sentence, including 100 hours of community service and a $500 payment to the United Way, according to the minutes.

PART 2: Products, Problems, & Protection

The Massive Cost of Failed Investor Protection

$150 BILLION is a staggering number. The extent, enormity, size, scale – the massive amount of money lost per year – is simply staggering. By some estimates, as much as $50 billion is lost to fraud and another $50 billion is lost to excessive Industry fees and bad products. Annually. That's each and every year.

> **Fraud, fees, excessive, and unnecessary charges cause $100+ billion in investor losses annually.**

The incidence of financial fraud in the United States is on the rise. Americans submitted more than 1.5 million complaints about financial and other fraud in 2011 – a 62% increase in just three years – according to the Federal Trade Commission's (FTC) annual "Consumer Sentinel Network Data Book."

As the incidence of fraud increases, the dollar amount that victims of all types of fraud reported grew sharply – from $343 million, in 2002, to $1.5 billion in 2011 – per the FTC's report.

> **Fraud costs victims $2,267, on average, in 2011 – based on the FTC's numbers.[1]**

That's just the tip of the iceberg. Amazingly, the FTC data doesn't capture the scope of financial-product fraud. The agency tracks only complaints submitted by consumers – and not convictions or civil complaints filed by

---

[1] The Rise of Financial Fraud: Scams Never Change but Disguises Do, by Kimberly Blanton, Feb. 2012

state securities regulators and federal and state law enforcement officials.[2]

According to a 2013 survey conducted for the FINRA Investor Education Foundation:[3]

- 84% reported being solicited with at least one of the 11 types of potentially fraudulent offers.

- 16% invested money in response to at least one of the likely fraudulent offers.

- 11% of all respondents acknowledged making an investment in response to one of these offers that turned out to be worth much less than they had been led to believe (and/or that led to them losing all or most of their money in the investment).

- 4% admitted to being a victim of fraud when asked—an under-reporting rate of over 60%.

The amount of under-reporting makes it impossible to calculate the true amount lost to financial fraud.

If only 4% of victims reported losses, the actual number of victims might well be over 37,000,000!

If each victim lost the average of $2,267, the total amount lost could easily exceed $85,000,000,000!

In addition to financial and investment fraud, you also must consider excess commissions and fees. These are losses caused by the unnecessary imposition of fees – when cheaper, lower-cost alternatives exist.

---

[2] The Financial Fraud Research Center The Scope of the Problem An Overview of Fraud Prevalence Measurement 2012

[3] Financial Fraud and Fraud Susceptibility in the United States Research Report – Prepared for the FINRA Investor Education Foundation September 2013

According to an article by Rudy Adolf, of *Focus Financial*: "Wall Street wirehouses destroy close to $50 billion of portfolio value each year with 'unnecessary fees and depressed performance based on poor product choices, or both.'"[4]

> **Add another $50 billion in estimated product fees and overcharges, to $85 billion, and the figure is well over $100 billion in losses to fraud and fees each year.**

Now – add another $32 billion that consumers paid in overdraft fees to banks in 2012, according to a study by Moebs Services.

This should bring you a little closer to understanding the annual cost of failed investor protection.

Now that you understand the amount at risk each year, it's important to know how hard it is to recover funds once they're lost.

You need to understand the value of protection – in advance.

---

[4] http://www.investmentnews.com/article/20131022/BLOG15/131029971?utm_source=indaily-20131022&utm_medium=in-newsletter&utm_campaign=investmentnews&utm_term=text

The Low Odds of a Little Recovery

Today's forecast: a high probability of loss with a low chance of recovery...

The odds of getting back money lost to misconduct are less than 50%. Even for those who prevail, the average award is less than 50% of the amount lost to the misconduct.

Once a loss has been realized, FINRA's arbitration process governs an investor's ability to recover lost funds – along with any damages and legal fees. According to FINRA's published dispute resolution statistics (http://www.finra.org/ArbitrationAndMediation/FINRADisputeResolution /AdditionalResources/Statistics/), 2010 was the best year for investors who lost money, because the percentage of cases in which customers were awarded damages reached an all-time high of 47%!

That means less than ½ of all harmed investor were able to recover anything. But, it gets even worse. According to data compiled by Securities Arbitration Commentator Inc., a Maplewood, New Jersey-based legal publishing and research firm, in 2010, the median amount won by investors through FINRA arbitration was $129,800, or 42 percent of the median amount of $310,000, in compensatory damages sought by investors who won. So – fewer than half of harmed investors only recovered 42% of their claimed loss.

The situation may go from bad to worse. A recent Bloomberg article titled, "Investors May Lose as Congress Saves Money on Adviser Oversight." stated:

> "Congress may hand oversight of almost 12,000 investment advisers to Wall Street's self-funded regulator [FINRA] as a cost-saving measure. The price could be paid by investors.

"The **Financial Industry Regulatory Authority**, deputized by the government to oversee brokers, is lobbying to replace the U.S. Securities and Exchange Commission as a regulator of registered investment advisers who manage about $40 trillion. Congress is considering the move as a cheaper alternative to increasing resources for the SEC, since Finra's $877 million **budget** is paid by the brokers it regulates."

While I have no doubt that the Industry would love to have greater control over how it regulates and supervises itself, it would be a disaster for investors. As the above article also points out:

"Less than 1 percent of [FINRA] arbitration cases on average have resulted in disciplinary actions against brokers or brokerage firms."

Simply put, investor protection cannot be entrusted to an Industry that self-regulates. Your odds of recovery are already less than ½ of ½; it would be unconscionable to see investor protection go from bad to worse.

THE MORAL OF THIS STORY, IS THAT AN OUNCE OF PREVENTION IS WORTH MORE THAN A POUND OF CURE.

DETECTION AND PREVENTION CAN HELP AVOID INVESTMENT LOSSES!

Why Investors Lose: The Unfortunately Large Truth

At the highest possible level, the Industry protects itself over investors. While the "fix" is in place to help the Industry make a profit, recent events and recurring financial scandals prove that, while individual investors can lose, the Industry *must* profit. In short, the Industry is "too big to fail." Specifically, the banking bailout and government takeover of certain businesses, such as AIG, Fannie Mae, Freddie Mac, etc., reveals that the Industry *must* survive – even at the expense of investors.

The Industry has recruited some of the brightest minds and largest personalities to separate investors from their money. These "great" minds serve as management of the firms that create the Industry's products and services. The pricing, structure, and actuarial assumptions that go into each product are controlled by few and understood by fewer. They are the brains of the Industry's operation.

Brokers, advisors, planners, and insurance agents are the brawn of the Industry's operation. These larger-than-life personalities market, sell, and distribute the Industry's products and services. Some of these salespeople are among the most sociable, funny, and amicable people you'll ever meet. Some were even famous. While many may be trustworthy, others may not be particularly well-educated as to products, strategies, tax consequences, etc.

Others are simply thugs and/or thieves.

Collectively, the brains and brawn of the Industry are committed to manufacturing and distributing products, generating fees and commissions, and gathering assets – whether you make money or not. Even though it's entirely possible to help investors make money while also generating profits, the Industry has chosen to place its collective profit ahead of investor protection.

Today, most financial services firms have become too big to fail. If Industry firms bet right, they win: via trading profits, higher sales, and increased fees and commissions. If they bet wrong, you lose: via higher future fees or taxes, to support an Industry bailout. The "public trust" in a functional financial services system is too important.

While public trust in the financial services Industry is paramount, it should not come at the expense of investor protection. The Industry's goals have nothing to do with *your* goals. The Industry is thinking about *its* profits – *not* yours. It's not a zero-sum game, as some might argue. The profits of the Industry must exceed the collective profits of investors. In short, you're entrusting your money to an Industry that, in actuality, isn't thinking about your financial future.

Time and time again, financial scandals occur. Investor confidence gets shaken. Time passes and memories fade. But, the rigged system remains intact. The Industry gets strengthened. Yet, meaningful investor protection remains weak. The irony is that, if investors were better protected, there would be more trust in the financial system.

There are two primary reasons why investors keep losing money:

1. Inadequate Protection: flawed systems & conflicted regulators

As soon as there were "securities" to be sold, there were problems. During the Depression, this country's wealth was destroyed, along with faith in capitalism, in general – and stocks, in particular. It was during this period that the government created the current framework of rules, laws, and regulatory agencies that were all *intended* to protect investors.

Recently, the Industry's failures were exposed again, in a very public and dramatic fashion. The housing bubble and the exposure of rampant mortgage-backed securities fraud almost resulted in the collapse of the US banking and financial system.

When scandals occur on a repeated basis, when fraud occurs on a systemic basis, when investors get ripped off on a continuous basis, there can be only one conclusion: the Industry's foundation is flawed. It doesn't protect *investors*.

The same issues that caused the Great Depression caused this financial meltdown: bad loans, easy credit, excessive lending and fraudulent representations in the creation and issuance of new securities (mortgage-backed debt). History repeated under the very rules, regulations, and regulators that were created to prevent history from repeating. Unless there are changes, it's only a matter of time until the next financial meltdown.

Understanding the Industry's fundamentally flawed and conflicted system of oversight and supervision is the key to understanding why there is no meaningful investor protection. The *Financial "Fix"* has already presented two key problems that undermine the Industry's ability to properly protect investors:

1. A flawed self-regulatory system, and
2. Overwhelming financial conflicts of interest

These two problems are deeply entwined. Unfortunately, they also form the core structure of the Industry. This core has radiated problems since its inception.

The Industry's current system of oversight, regulation, and supervision either needs to be completely reworked or rebuilt. Unless there is fundamental change, the house of cards will continuously collapse. Each time, it will be rebuilt, so it can collapse again.

Except – this isn't a *game*.

The financial health of the economy, of the Industry, and of every investor is at stake.

2. Greed: rampant fraud & unrealistic expectations

It's never wise to blame the victim. But – seriously, people? There is *no* free lunch. There is no such thing as return without risk. There is nothing paying a lot more than a certificate of deposit that's guaranteed. *Nothing!*

A lack of investor education does cause certain problems. However, I believe most problems occur when need meets greed. Some people just can't earn enough at the bank or in traditional safe investments. Consequently, a search for higher returns begins. The legitimate need to earn more frequently drives investors to illegitimate investments and outright scams.

Victims are created when investors who need higher returns encounter "brokers" driven by greed. All the education in the world won't help if investors can't remember one simple saying: "If it sounds too good to be true, it is." In general, the higher the promised return, the greater the likelihood you will never see your money again. Ever.

It's *that* simple.

Yet, time and time again, unsophisticated investors fall prey to false promises. According to Financial Fraud and Fraud Susceptibility in the United States, a research report by FINRA's Investor Education Foundation, a majority of people have been targeted by financial fraudsters, while nearly half were unable to spot classic red flags of fraud:

- More than 80% of respondents had been solicited to participate in fraudulent financial schemes.
- More than 40% of people found an annual return of 110% to be appealing.
- More than 43% felt "fully guaranteed" investments were appealing.

> **WARNING:**
> - **Nothing safe pays 110%. *NOTHING*.**
> - **Very few investments are fully guaranteed.**

Most scams follow a predictable pattern:

- The scammer is often introduced by a friend or acquaintance
- There are political/religious/military connections (sorry, people!)
  o The scammers tend to be pinnacles of the church/temple/community that they rip off
- The investment is a "special," "unique," "private," "limited," "time-sensitive" opportunity
- The investment cannot be held in a bank or brokerage account (run like hell)
- The check isn't payable to a major financial institution (again – run like hell)
- The return is high
- The risk is low

Yet – investors fail to see the signs. Many don't *want* to.

There's no stopping an investor who simply doesn't *want* to listen. For the investor who doesn't listen and loses, there's almost *no* hope of recovering lost funds.

How Investors Lose

You can't maximize returns by losing money. To help protect your money, I've broken down the most common causes of loss, into two categories:

1. **General Investor Problems**: losses that are not product-related, such as:
    - Excessive fees and commissions
    - Taxes
    - Investor behavior
    - Fraud

General investor problems affect large groups of investors. This section includes fraud – which is the most obvious and sudden form of loss. Despite being the most obvious, I'll deal with fraud last. That's because there are three more-common and insidious items I believe cause greater amounts of investor losses each and every year.

Some causes of loss are surreptitious, slow, and recurring – such as excessive fees and commissions, taxes, and investor behavior (death by a thousand cuts). Others, meanwhile, are obvious, rapid, and catastrophic – such as fraud (poof...it's gone!). Whether obvious or surreptitious, these general investor problems cause billions of dollars of investor losses annually.

2. **Specific Product Problems:** losses caused by the illegitimate use of legitimate products:
    - Brokerage accounts
    - Advisory/managed accounts
    - Mutual funds

- Exchange traded funds
- Variable annuities
- Equity indexed annuities
- Alternative Investments

Products aren't inherently evil. Investors become victims when products are misrepresented, mispriced, or used in an abusive manner. It's the hidden fees, excessive pricing, misunderstood features, misrepresented benefits, omitted risks, and outright misuse of products that causes losses.

It's the unsuitable use of products that causes losses.

Today, there are products that are so complex, the regulators issue product warnings; product manufacturers have to provide intensive training, so their own salespeople understand the products they represent; brokers have to undergo specialized training, to make sure they understand the products they sell to investors. In reality, many brokers don't fully understand some of the products they sell. In these cases, there's virtually *no* shot in hell the investors understand what they're sold.

General Investor Problems

1. Excessive Fees and Commissions

Paying lower fees is like earning higher returns.

If you earn returns of 6% and your recurring brokerage, advisory, or product fees are around 2% – which is very common – you'll lose more than 30% of your returns to fees. These recurring annual fees reduce your return and can erode your principal over time. What does this mean?

		Amount Lost to Fees		
Fee:	2%	1 Year	5 Years	10 Years
Investment:	$10,000	$200	$1,000	$2,000

High fees mean lower returns; conversely, lower returns mean fees will be higher – as a percentage of return. Consequently, one of the most important actions you can take is to avoid losses caused by fees and commissions. Reducing commissions and fees will protect your principal and improve your returns– without any additional risk.

That doesn't mean you need to become an investment guru yourself. Even if you have the time and inclination, there are too many financial strategies and investment products to know it all. No investor can know it all. In fact, no financial professional can know it all, either. For most investors, there's an appropriate balance between doing it yourself and receiving professional advice. Especially over time, as circumstances and needs change, even the most die-hard do-it-yourself investor can benefit from seeking some advice or at least getting a second opinion. The same holds true for the well served investor who has the utmost faith in a trustworthy advisor. Different times, needs, or circumstances may call for different products, services, or strategies.

Good advice has value. Many financial advisors deserve to get paid, if they provide good advice and excellent customer service. In my experience, most investors would willingly pay for good advice and excellent customer service. The problem is transparency and reasonableness. If the cost of service was clear and the price was reasonable, I believe many problems would be solved.

Instead of consistently delivering value, the Industry takes investors for granted. Instead of clearly disclosing fees, the Industry buries investors in paperwork. When fees are disclosed via a 50+-page prospectus, investors might as well be looking for a needle in a haystack. In addition, the Industry adds miscellaneous nuisance fees that nickel-and-dime investors almost to the point of disgust.

The amount of money lost to excessive fees, commissions, and embedded product costs is staggering. Just across the major "wirehouse" firms, one estimate calculates the cost to investors at almost $50 billion – per year! Rudy Adolf wrote and published an article titled, *The $50B Wirehouse Heist*, in *InvestmentNews*, published on October 22, 2013,[5] in which he states:

> "The result is shocking. I have done the math. Wirehouses destroy close to $50 billion in portfolio value each year. That's some 100 basis points in lost value that could be in their clients' portfolios, and isn't. It is $50 billion these clients are paying away in the form of unnecessary fees (which they may not even know are there), or depressed performance based on poor product choices, combined with high expense levels. Or both.
>
> "First, there are high-commission structured products: Rarely is there a sound investment reason for them to be there … Wirehouses virtually always sell these on a commission basis despite the existence of much-cheaper solutions designed for fee-

---

[5] http://www.investmentnews.com/article/20131022/BLOG15/131029971&template=printart

based advisers. We've analyzed at least 100 wirehouse structured notes and found none to be in the clients' best interests.

"Second, there are hugely marked-up bonds. The bonds in one pretty straightforward $40 million bond portfolio constructed by a well-known wirehouse had been marked up by $600,000 – about 1.5% on average.

"Third, wirehouses often significantly overweight clients in A-shares, instead of other more efficient share classes. Wirehouses rarely provide clients with access to the cheapest share classes, dramatically increasing the cost of money management."

Most mutual fund investors generally don't know their actual annual costs. A recent article in *Forbes* itemized annual costs as follows:[6]

Cost Summary

The following summarizes the average quantifiable costs described. Advisor and soft dollar costs are excluded due to the large range in advisory fees and the difficulty of quantifying soft dollar costs. When working with a financial advisor, it is important to add the advisory fee to the mutual fund costs listed below for an accurate depiction of total potential costs.

Non-Taxable Account	**Taxable Account**
Expense Ratio .90%	Expense Ratio .90%
Transaction Costs 1.44%	Transaction Costs 1.44%
Cash Drag .83%	Cash Drag .83%
—	Tax Cost 1.00%
Total Costs **3.17%**	Total Costs **4.17%**

---

[6] "The Real Cost of Owning A Mutual Fund", written by Ty A. Bernicke, CFP, published by Forbes on 4/04/201

As illustrated, hidden costs have infiltrated the mutual fund industry and are being paid by many unsuspecting investors.

What does this mean to you? The tables below show how much these fees would cost you, on a $10,000 investment:

Total Costs: 3.17%			Total Costs: 4.17%		
Amount Lost to Fees			**Amount Lost to Fees**		
1 Year	5 Years	10 Years	1 Year	5 Years	10 Years
$317	$1,585	$3,170	$417	$2,085	$4,170

The above costs do not include any additional fees from external commissions, loads, advisory fees, etc. Excessive fees and commissions cause *huge* losses – especially when the investor is unaware of recurring annual costs.

PROTECTION SOLUTIONS:

InvestorProtector.com provides free tools that can help you easily evaluate whether you're paying reasonable fees for the investment owned and the performance returned:

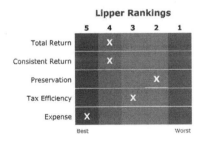 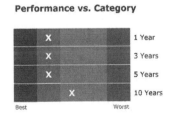

Source: InvestorProtector®, eMoney, Lipper.

Knowing your annual fees and expenses is just the beginning. Another solution is to actively seek lower-cost alternatives. Since many mutual funds charge up-front loads (commissions), many investors have chosen to avoid these types of funds by using no-load (no commission) funds. *All* mutual funds charge ongoing annual management fees – known as the expense ratio. Accordingly, many investors choose passively-managed index funds, which generally have lower annual expense ratios than actively-managed funds.

For mutual fund investors, one of the first actionable steps, to protect yourself and reduce the loss to fees and expenses, is to identify lower-cost alternatives. This is easy to do and there are services that can help – without charging you excessive fees to help you lower your fees!

According to Morningstar, Inc., the average of the most recent total operating expenses (or prospectus net expense ratio) among active U.S. mutual funds, excluding load-waive share classes and active U.S. Exchange Traded Funds (ETFs) are:

Category	Average Total Operating Expenses	
	Mutual Funds	**ETFs**
STOCK/EQUITY FUNDS		
US Large-Cap Stock	1.31%	0.47%
US Mid-Cap Stock	1.45%	0.56%
US Small-Cap Stock	1.53%	0.52%
International Stock	1.57%	0.56%
BOND FUNDS		
Taxable Bond	1.07%	0.30%
Municipal Bond	1.06%	0.23%

For equity funds, the annual cost savings can be 1.00% or more. For bond funds, the cost savings can be 0.75% or more. It all depends on the funds.

Remember: the expense ratio is just part of the fee. You must also be wary of transaction fees and tax costs. There's more information regarding the total cost of mutual fund ownership in the chapter that deals with mutual funds.

At InvestorProtector.com, you can find free tools that will help you protect yourself from fees.

FREE FEE SCORECARD: *Find out how much you actually pay in annual product fees by visiting:*

www.investorprotector.com

Fee Level Comparison Group
Moderate Allocation Front Load

Fee Level
Below Average

Expense Relative to Category   **ABCDE Fund**

● Fund   ● Category (Moderate Allocation)   ● Fee Level Comparison Group Median

History	2009	2010	2011	2012	2013
Expense Ratio	1.12	1.09	1.08	1.09	1.09
Morningstar Category Average	1.02	1.01	1.01	0.97	1.04
Fee Level Comparison Group Median	—	1.22	1.20	1.30	—

Maximum Sales Fees

Initial	4.75%
Deferred	—
Redemption	—

Total Cost Projections

	Per 10K
3 Years	805
5 Years	1,047
10 Years	1,739

Source: InvestorProtector®, Morningstar

OUR WEB-BASED SERVICE WILL REVIEW YOUR ACCOUNTS AND IDENTIFY THE ANNUAL AMOUNT OF FEES, COSTS, AND EXPENSES YOUR MUTUAL FUNDS ARE CHARGING.

HOW THE INDUSTRY MAKES MONEY & HOW YOU CAN SAVE MONEY

The Industry is all about the Benjamins. It's also all about the dollars, quarters, dimes, nickels, pennies, and even fractions of pennies – and the "points," or percentages, which Investors can be charged, up to: 15% for a direct participation program (i.e. REITs, oil and gas programs, etc.); 10% for private placements and limited partnerships; 10% for equity indexed annuities; 8.5% for a variable annuity; 5.75% for a mutual fund; 5% for a stock trade (per trade); 3% for managed accounts (per account, per year), etc.

Broker Commission/Fee per $10,000 Investment

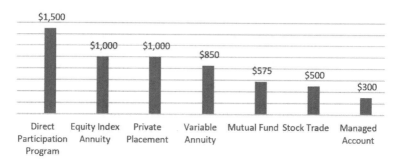

Brokerage Commission = Investor Cost

The above fees directly *reduce* the amount of your investment. Your $10,000 could actually start out only being worth $8,500. You must first earn back the fee, *before* you make a profit. Would you rather start out with your $10,000 investment being worth $8,500 or $10,000?

Investors should want to protect investments from commissions and fees. Brokers are drawn to sell products that pay commissions and fees. The higher the compensation, the greater the incentive to sell certain products. Investors want returns. Brokers want commissions. Therein lays the conflict.

In short, products are sold. Rarely does an investor wake up and jump out of bed exclaiming: "Today, I'm going to call my broker to see if I can generate a huge commission by investing in a variable annuity!" The reality is that some products are sold simply because they pay higher commissions than other products. In some cases, brokers will sell a product that's totally inappropriate for the investor, *just* to make a higher commission. In many cases, even if the product is appropriate, there are likely comparable lower-cost alternatives the broker doesn't show the investor, because they pay less commission.

> **A broker is obligated to provide a suitable recommendation; there is *no* obligation to provide the lowest-cost option.**

In addition to up-front commissions and fees that reduce the value of your investment, there are also annual fees embedded in most products. Mutual funds, ETFs, variable annuities and other products all have operating costs, known as expense ratios. These fees increase costs *and* reduce return.

There are also miscellaneous fees, such as ticket charges and postage and handling fees. There are SEC and Industry taxes. There are markups and markdowns. There are debit balance charges, margin balance charges, credit balance charges, and more.

Below is a *partial* list of the Industry's major charges, fees, costs, expenses, etc.:

1. Commissions: Investors pay commissions for securities transactions, i.e. a purchase or sale. In earlier times, there were elite brokerage firms that made significant investments in owning and operating a "newfangled" ticker tape machine. When stocks first started trading, information regarding current prices and recent sales was incredibly valuable.

> **Ticker tape** was the earliest digital electronic communications medium, transmitting stock price information over telegraph lines, in use between around 1870 through 1970. It consisted of a paper strip which ran through a machine called a **stock ticker**, which printed abbreviated company names as alphabetic symbols, followed by numeric stock transaction price and volume information. The term "ticker" came from the sound made by the machine as it printed.

Paper ticker tape started to become obsolete in the 1960s, as television and computers were increasingly used to transmit financial information. The concept of the stock ticker lives on, however, in the scrolling electronic tickers seen on brokerage walls and on financial television networks.

Ticker tape stock price telegraphs were invented in 1867, by Edward A. Calahan, an employee of the American Telegraph Company – source: Wikipedia[1]

Prior to the 1970's, investors were more than willing to pay a commission to a broker, because information about stock prices was very limited. There was value in finding out the last price at which a stock traded. There was even more value in finding buyers for sellers and sellers for buyers. Commission brokers spent time and resources sourcing this information.

Those days are long gone. Today, price information and transaction execution are commodities. They should cost very little – if anything.

Instead, the value today is in strategy and product selection. There's an overwhelming amount of information. There is a dizzying array of products from which to choose. A good financial advisor will listen to an investor, identify a sensible financial strategy, and find appropriate products for that investor's strategy.

Today, intellectual capital should be valued most highly. There are income strategies, growth strategies, different types of retirement plans, various types of education savings vehicles, supplemental retirement plans, executive benefit plans, financial plans, estate plans, tax and accounting strategies, legal and structural strategies for investment ownership, etc. In addition to all the different types of financial, legal, and tax strategies, there are all the potential investment products from which to choose.

It's highly unlikely that any single advisor can know or possess all the strategy and product knowledge required to properly serve a wide range of investors over each investor's life cycle. This is the reality for financial advisors who dedicate full-time careers to the Industry. Armchair investors beware.

As for what makes a commission reasonable, there's no definite answer. FINRA created a rule that states: "Commissions must be fair and just…" and provided guidance that 5% on the investment was probably high enough. This sums up the problem right there. FINRA creates rules and provides guidance, but firms make up their *own* policies. It's back to that circular bullshit the Industry has gotten away with for years. The Industry governs itself; the fox guards the hen house. And the Industry wants to know why investors don't trust it?

Here's an idea: create and publish a standardized pricing guide that's fair and transparent. Firms can compete for business on pricing and service, like every other business in the world.

In addition to discount brokers, there are full service brokers that will work for negotiated, discounted fees. There are also discount investment advisors.

You can get a Fee Review by visiting: http://www.investorprotector.com/solutions-center/.

2. <u>Advisory Fees:</u> Investors pay asset-based fees for certain products and services. Investment advisory accounts are for investors who believe a fee-based arrangement will remove "conflicts-of-interest," or who think commissions are evil. The bottom line is, if an investor wants to buy and hold a few investments – such as bonds or a couple of stocks – then a commission arrangement probably makes more sense. If an investor wants ongoing active management of an account, a fee-based arrangement generally makes sense.

Neither pricing arrangement – commission versus fee-based – is inherently superior. The investor's preference matters; other factors that matter include the number of positions, the style of management, and the frequency and cost of trading. In total, the costs of either the commissions or the fees must be considered.

> **WARNING: One highly questionable practice is charging an advisory fee to manage the subaccount investments inside a variable annuity. Variable annuities generally cost 1.35% to 1.65% per year for internal product fees (mortality and expense charges). In addition, the subaccounts (basically mutual funds) can cost an additional 1.00% (more or less) in annual fees. If you have a typical death benefit or income benefit rider, you can add another 1.00% (more or less). The total cost, at this point, would be 3.35% to 3.65% annually. Charging an additional advisory fee simply adds more cost and further reduces return. If you were incurring 4.65% per annum, while everyone else would be guaranteed to get paid, your return would have to be very high for you to actually ever earn any *real* return – after all these fees.**
>
> **Even worse, for variable annuities with Living Benefits, the imposition of an advisory fee can destroy the very benefits the annuity was purchased to provide. For most investors – particularly income-oriented investors – paying advisory fees for the "management" of variable annuity subaccounts is generally inappropriate and unsuitable.**

You can get an Annuity Review by visiting: http://www.investorprotector.com/solutions-center/.

3. Cash Balances: Firms make money off clients' cash in two ways:

   a. Cash in brokerage and advisory accounts generally sweeps into a money market fund/product/vehicle that pays a low rate of interest to the investor, because the fund pays the brokerage/advisory/custodian firm for steering investor cash into it. Somewhere in a new account agreement is a lengthy, unintelligible disclosure document informing you that the default cash investment vehicle pays your broker and their firm for steering your cash into a low-yielding product. Often, your broker and their firm may make considerably more on your cash than you do. If you're lucky, you may have the right to request a different investment for your cash.

You can get an Account Review by visiting: http://www.investorprotector.com/solutions-center/ .

b. "Free-credit balance" is a fancy term for either cash used (required to pay for an investment due to a purchase) or for cash created (proceeds pending settlement from a sale). You generally don't earn any interest on free-credit balances, since this cash is "in-transit" between a purchase or a sale. In reality, it's free cash to the firm and costly cash to you, since it's tied up and not earning anything.

4. Margin Loans: If you are credit-worthy, the Industry will lend you money, collateralized by your own investments, so you can invest/risk more money (leverage) at very high rates of interest. The first problem with margin is who makes the decision whether you actually *are* "credit-worthy." The brokerage firm that wants to sell you more stock makes the decision as to your credit-worthiness.

> **WARNING: Margin adds cost and risk. You'll need to earn higher rates of return simply to pay your borrowing costs. In addition – with margin – you might control $10,000 worth of stock by only putting up $5,000. If the stock goes up, you can earn higher returns, because you controlled more stock by using margin. However, if $10,000 worth of stock falls by 20% – or $2,000 – you *lose* 40% of your $5,000, because you owned stock on margin.**

> **With margin, you may actually pay interest to lose money faster...**

5. Market Making: Remember the spread the Industry creates, between the lower "bid" price the Industry pays a seller of stock and the higher "ask" price the Industry charges a buyer of stock? That spread goes to Industry market makers. By enabling and allowing a two-tier pricing system, the Industry lets different firms "make markets" in stocks. An Industry market maker could theoretically buy stock from investors all day at low prices and sell stock back to investors at high prices. In reality, different firms jump in on the bid and ask, as stock prices fluctuate throughout the day.

Brainwashed Industry "veterans" will exclaim that the spread is needed, to create liquidity for certain stocks. As one of my friends from the south would say, "I call bullshit on that..." Supply and demand create liquidity. If there's no liquidity for a certain stock, perhaps that company shouldn't be publicly traded. Perhaps that company should seek capital from professional investors, rather than from general investors who get sucked in by the credibility implied by a stock that trades publicly. Buying and selling stock over the counter doesn't provide capital for a business. It doesn't finance growth. It doesn't create jobs. It simply facilitates speculation; it generates ticket charges, fees, and spreads for the Industry.

The market making spread is a completely made up mechanism to separate buyers and sellers and keep the Industry in the middle and line the Industry's pockets.

> **WARNING: Discount brokers might not be so cheap. A ticket charge is just a small portion of the price you'll pay – either to a full-service or to a discount broker. Ticket charges and market making spreads will eat away at returns – which costs you money.**

6. <u>Underwriting:</u> When a company issues shares of stock, some Industry firm (or group of firms) generally acts as the underwriter, structuring the offering, valuing the stock, and helping sell the company stock to investors. Companies charge fees for their services. These fees are primarily embedded in the stock being issued. In other words, the company issues stock to the underwriter at a price that's less than what the investor will ultimately pay. The price of stock to the underwriter is less than or "under" the soon-to-be public offering price. Kind of like a sale. Except – it's a legal way to discount a stock to the Industry, which can then mark *up* the stock to investors. By the way, if a broker wanted to offer the discount to the investor, it wouldn't be allowed and the broker could lose his or her license for sharing a commission with an investor.

7. <u>Investment Banking:</u> A business that needs capital can turn to investment bankers who specialize in raising funds via various structures, i.e. debt, equity, etc. These "masters of the universe" get paid massive fees for their time and work on structuring deals, raising money, finding merger and acquisition candidates, and so forth. They eat at expensive restaurants and drink a ton of expensive wine (generally red – and mostly at dinner meetings). Out of investment banking departments come "special deals" that a firm has determined will be particularly attractive to investors. Brokers are provided with "tear" sheets, pitch books, and bullet points, so they can sell these deals to investors.

Once upon a time, it was noble to introduce investors with capital to entrepreneurs with ideas. It is very risky to back new ventures and highly uncertain if an investor will ever see either a return on or return of his or her capital. Over time, entrepreneurs have consistently blown themselves up and lost investor's money – more often than not. The only certainty in investment banking is that the banker will get paid on each and every transaction.

> **WARNING: For investors who have capital to invest _and_ a willingness to take risk, there is a right way and a wrong way to invest – particularly in private placements which**

> **have no liquidity and cannot be readily cashed in or easily sold. First, the investor must be accredited – meaning you have a high enough income and net worth to withstand the total loss of your investment. Second – and the biggest mistake made by most – is to NOT allocate funds to multiple deals. Each and every private placement has a high risk of failure. Only by making several bets can you hope one will work out well. The greatest mistake made by most private placement investors is they invest too much money into one single deal.**

8. Proprietary Products: Just as the auto Industry has car makers (manufacturers) and car dealers (distributors), the Industry has manufacturers of investments and distributors of those investments. Insurance companies, mutual fund companies, and bankers generally manufacture investment products. Brokers and agents distribute the products. Since both the manufacturer and distributor each wants to make a profit, there's a profit margin built in for both. An investor will pay this profit margin to both the manufacturer and to the distributor – whether they're together (the same firm) or separate (at different firms). Some cynics will tell you never to buy a proprietary product. It's kind of like saying if the ACME Company created an ACME mutual fund, don't buy it from an ACME broker. That's just stupid. If the ACME fund is a good fund, the ACME broker *should* offer it to clients – where appropriate. If however, the ACME fund sucks and the ACME broker only offers it because it pays a higher commission, then it's all wrong. Other firms, like some major discount brokerage firms, will promote their lack of proprietary products as a benefit. While the firm might not manufacture the product, it's likely still getting paid for distributing the product These "supplemental" payments for distributing non-proprietary products (described below) should be disclosed – but you might need to read hundreds of pages of fine print to find out the truth.

9. <u>Supplemental Revenue Sharing Arrangements:</u> This is the best part of the Industry – from the Industry's perspective, that is. Some companies, in order to increase distribution of their products, will create supplemental or extra compensation arrangements with firms that agree to aggressively promote and distribute higher quantities of the firm's product.

Perhaps you've seen "No Transaction Fee Mutual Funds" or "Focus/Spotlight Vendors"? These companies may not have been selected for being top performers. They may not have been subjected to any rigorous due diligence process. Many of these funds are being promoted because they are paying extra fees for greater access, visibility, and *distribution*. Mutual funds, in particular, pay 12b-1 distribution fees to firms and brokers as ongoing revenue, to support sales, marketing, and service.

There has been an increasing amount of regulatory scrutiny concerning 12b-1 payments. Accordingly, many mutual fund companies have re-named or re-categorized 12b-1 fees and now call them "shareholder servicing fees." They're *still* fees. Many mutual fund companies pay up-front annual fees to firms to join a "No-Transaction Fee Network." Fund companies also pay recurring annual fees based on assets, to retain the favorable "No-Transaction Fee" status. A firm should disclose if they receive *any* supplemental revenue from *any* vendor, prior to making a recommendation, since there's clearly a conflict of interest caused by the higher compensation. In many cases, that higher compensation isn't even shared with the actual broker who makes the recommendation. Often, supplemental revenue sharing arrangements are private agreements between a vendor and a firm that have nothing to do with the individual broker.

In the stock-selling business, the supplemental payments were so bad even the Industry realized it had to do something about them. Now you'll see that analysts must disclose if they or their family owns the stock they discuss, or if their firm has accepted money, done business, or has any relationship with the company whose stock the analyst recommends. I know – it's hard to believe a broker might recommend buying a stock because the broker's firm took the company public, or got paid to produce a positive research report.

10. <u>Miscellaneous Charges:</u> In the independent broker-dealer channel, the firm often adds charges to the branches and brokers. For example, brokers are generally charged fees for technology, email, trading systems, and so on. All these charges create expenses that each broker must cover each month by generating commissions and fees from clients. In that sense, while these charges are paid by the broker, they get passed through to investors.

Branches that house brokers generally have a deal – or economic arrangement – with the firm. This deal covers the branch payout, fees, and expenses, such as ticket charges and postage and handling. For example, a firm might charge a branch a $15 ticket charge for each stock trade. The branch might charge the brokers that work in that branch a $25 ticket charge for each stock trade. With this structure, the branch makes $10 every time the broker trades for an investor, regardless of whether the client makes money or not. In addition, the branch and broker might also add a "postage & handling" charge. This is just another charge to the client. In addition to the ticket charge and postage and handling charge, there's a small fee per transaction that goes to the SEC. The broker also will charge a commission. So, basically, on each and every trade, the Industry gets paid; the firm gets paid; and the broker gets paid. All this is paid, whether the client ever makes money or not.

> **FEE SCORECARD:**
>
> **Find out how much you actually pay in annual product fees by visiting:** http://www.investorprotector.com/solutions-center/.

2. Taxes

Paying lower taxes is like earning higher returns. Income taxes range from 20% to 40% or more. If you earn 6% and pay 30% in taxes, you just lost 1.8% of your return. If you pay taxes on top of fees and commissions, you could lose 50% or more of your returns annually.

If you can keep more of what you earn, you can accumulate more. If you can accumulate more, you may be able to take less risk. If you can take less risk, you can avoid potential losses.

Taxes play a significant role in developing and implementing a sensible investment strategy. Investors might pay local, city, state, and federal taxes. There are income, estate, and gift taxes. There are short-term and long-term capital gains taxes. There are taxable bonds and tax-free bonds. There are accounts that enable pre-tax contributions. There are certain products (annuities) and account types (IRAs, 401k plans, 529 plans) that provide tax deferral. There are tax consequences and penalties for taking income too soon from certain products and there are penalties for not taking income after a certain age, from other accounts. Yet, most brokers and advisors can't and won't provide tax advice.

Without tax advice, no investment strategy is complete. Taxes create a slow, significant cause of loss to investors, each and every year.

The three most basic tax strategies investors should consider are:

1) making pre-tax contributions to a retirement plan
2) seeking tax-efficient management, to minimize tax loss over time on taxable investments
3) investing surplus long-term funds in additional vehicles that provide tax-deferred compounding

Consider pre-tax contributions. In an IRA or 401k, you can save your own money *before* you pay taxes. If you're in a 25% tax bracket, $5,000 of taxable income only leaves $3,750 to invest, after taxes. Alternatively, you would have to earn $6,666, *before* taxes, to invest $5,000 after taxes. With pre-tax contributions to a retirement plan, a $5,000 contribution on a pre-tax basis directly reduces your current taxable income, (saves you the $1,250 in taxes) and maximizes your retirement savings contribution – all $5,000 goes into your account.

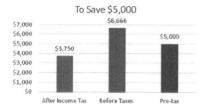

- You save less with after-tax dollars

- It takes more to save with pre-tax dollars

Keep this simple: would you pay a fee or commission of 25% on your money, if you could avoid it? Definitely *not*!

Pre-tax contributions enable you to pay less current taxes and save more money.

With tax-deferral, the funds you save can be invested to grow on a tax-deferred basis. Ultimately, you'll pay taxes when you withdraw the money, but the math is clear: you can save more and accumulate significantly more when you save on a pre-tax basis and invest on a tax deferred basis.

In the below example, you can accumulate over $100,000 more in a tax-deferred account.

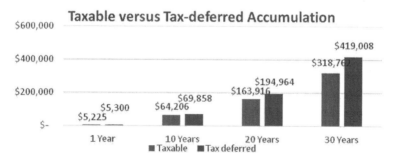

Assumes $5,000 annual savings earning 6% in a 25% tax bracket

In between taxable and tax-deferred investing is tax-efficient investing. For taxable money, tax-efficient investing can significantly reduce the amount of return lost to taxes. Municipal bonds and treasuries have different tax treatment. Careful selection can substantially increase after-tax income. For equities, ETFs, mutual funds, and other investments, there's a significant difference between the long-term versus short-term capital gains rate. Consequently, the timing of a decision to sell should consider the potential tax costs.

On an ongoing basis, certain investments create taxable income each year. Investors can lose anywhere from 15% to 40% or more of their return to taxes each and every year. Mutual funds that have high turnover (a lot of internal purchases and sales of securities), and which are tax-inefficient, could lose even more to taxes. Over time, compounding only increases this loss:

> "In the ten-year period ending June 30, 2005, mutual funds on an average returned 9.6% a year. Assuming a 35% tax rate, this annual return was reduced to 7.8%. In examining the Morningstar data...mutual fund investors in the 35% tax bracket lost an average of 1.84 percentage points per year to taxes over the last ten years. ...A study by Peterson et al. [2002] found U.S. equity fund investors in high tax brackets lost an average of about 2.2 percentage points annually to taxes in the 1981–1998 time period.

> Consideration of after-tax results is important because, in the long run, taxes have a compounding effect on reducing portfolio returns. For example, consider one dollar invested for twenty years at an annualized return of 10%; if taxes reduce return by 2% per year it will be worth $4.95, after taxes. But, if the investor is more tax-efficient and taxes reduce annual return by only 1% per year, the dollar is worth $6.04 – a full 22% more."[7]

Tax efficient investing can counter tax loss and improve overall performance. Reducing the amount of return lost to taxes can have a

---

[7] The Value of Tax Efficient Investments: An Analysis of After-Tax Mutual Fund and Index Returns, by Geoff Longmeier and Gordon Wotherspoon, published in THE JOURNAL OF WEALTH MANAGEMENT. Summer 2006

meaningful impact. If you invested $100,000 for 30 years and your after-tax compounded return is 6%, your money would grow to $574,349; if the net return were tax-managed to be just 1% higher – or 7% – the same invested amount would be worth $761,225. That's 39.4% more profit on your investment.

At InvestorProtector.com, there are free tools to help you analyze the potential tax loss of your current mutual fund investments:

Tax Analysis

	1-Mo	3-Mo	6-Mo	YTD	1-Yr	3-Yr	5-Yr	10-Yr	15-Yr	Since Inception
Pretax Return										
ABCDE Fund	1.75	6.34	13.25	16.78	16.78	7.89	14.05	6.63	9.13	11.54
Tax-adjusted Return *										
ABCDE Fund	-5.71	-1.46	4.95	8.22	8.22	4.62	11.61	4.91	7.43	9.32
% Rank in Category	95	92	75	86	86	92	52	48	3	—
Tax Cost Ratio										
ABCDE Fund	—	—	—	—	2.71	1.45	1.18	1.13	1.23	—
Potential Cap Gains Exposure										
ABCDE Fund	18.70									

(12/31/2013)

Source: InvestorProtector®, Morningstar®

In the above example, this fund cost the investor approximately 2.71% of the amount invested in tax costs over the past year. On $10,000 invested, the investor would have lost $271 to taxes; that could add up to $2,710 over 10 years. Instead of losing this money to taxes, it could be in your account.

That's the *easy* part about taxes. The next issues are a little more subtle. According to Morningstar, during one year, at least 14 funds that lost money *still* generated taxable events for investors, ranging from 12% to nearly 28% of their net asset value.

Imagine losing money and *still* having to pay taxes!

Mutual funds are excellent vehicles for diversification and professional money management. However, as common pools, they're not particularly well-suited to manage taxable events for individual investors. For investors in a high tax bracket, this drawback can be very costly, particularly when alternatives exist.

Other investments that pay dividends – such as stocks, closed-end funds, unit investment trusts, and others – can also create tax problems. Investors who buy right before a dividend is declared will be buying into the tax bill for that dividend. Since security prices generally change, leading into and following the payment of a dividend, it's possible to pay a higher price *before* a dividend is paid, receive the dividend, see your investment drop in price, and then get a tax bill. Paying taxes and realizing a price drop is a loss that *can* be avoided.

Missed deductions are another big source of tax losses for many investors. According to a report issued by the Treasury Inspector General for Tax Administration, of the 60.5 million tax returns received through March 4, 2011, there were 52.6 million tax refunds issued, totaling approximately $161.3 billion.[8]

About 87% of tax payers received a refund. If you weren't one of them, it's likely you either missed deductions or didn't file a tax return.

While it's a crime to not pay taxes, many consider it a crime to overpay taxes. In any event, money overpaid or refunds not received are funds lost to the investor. You have up to three years to review and file amended returns. There are many services that will review your last three years of tax returns, to find any deductions you might have missed and any refunds to which you might be entitled.

For most, income taxes will be the single greatest expense over a lifetime. For the wealthy, estate taxes might create the single biggest loss of all – but the bill has to be paid by the surviving beneficiaries. For all, there is the opportunity to be protected from some Estate Taxes. Every individual is entitled to pass on a certain amount of assets without any tax bill.

---

[8] TREASURY INSPECTOR GENERAL FOR TAX ADMINISTRATION: Interim Results of the 2011 Filing Season
http://www.treasury.gov/tigta/auditreports/2011reports/201140032fr.pdf

Individuals can gift assets without a tax bill, on an annual basis and over their lifetime – subject to certain limits.

In order to maximize the amount of money you can gift without any taxes, you need good tax advice. In order to maximize the amount of assets you can pass on tax-free when you pass away, you also need good tax and legal advice. Within nine months of your death, estate taxes will be due.

In short, investors can minimize losses due to income, gift, and estate taxes by utilizing various trusts, financial, tax, and legal strategies.

At www.investorprotector.com, there are tools that can help you analyze, understand, and act on this information, to help protect you from unnecessary tax loss. Our salaried staff can help.

We don't sell any investments. In fact, we're bound by a "no sales, no solicitation" policy.

You can sign up for free at: www.investorprotector.com.

3. Financial Literacy & Investor Behavior

"An investment in knowledge pays the best interest."
—Benjamin Franklin

Financial illiteracy causes loss. Not knowing how to spot and avoid fraud, trusting a rogue broker, picking bad investments, or paying excessive fees can cause dramatic and significant losses. Not knowing how to maximize pre-tax savings, leverage tax-deferred accumulation, budget cash flow to minimize debt and maximize equity, decrease fees, reduce taxes, and other factors can cause losses.

> **Financial literacy, information, and education about investing can solve *many* investor problems.**

Benjamin Franklin is also credited with saying, "If you fail to plan, you are planning to fail!" Shockingly, many investors don't have a written investment plan to guide their saving, investing, accumulation, and disposition of wealth. While most of us wouldn't attempt to drive across the country without a map and directions, when it comes to something as important as saving for retirement or as complex as investing, many don't have a written investment or financial plan.

According to the National Association of Personal Financial Advisors:[9]

- 56% of U.S. adults lack a budget
- 50% of Americans with children do not have a will
- 40% of U.S. adults are saving less than in 2011
- 39% of U.S. adults have *zero* non-retirement savings
- 39% of U.S. adults carry credit card debt from month to month
- 25 million people are underinsured

Investor behavior – particularly the behavior of those with less financial knowledge – can be *very* costly. A recent paper for the National Bureau of Economic Research quantified how low levels of consumer financial literacy lead to many money-losing decisions:[10]

1. Those who are more financially literate are more likely to undertake retirement planning.
2. Those who plan also accumulate more wealth.
3. Learning the concept of compound interest increases pension contributions.
4. Not refinancing mortgages during a period of falling interest rates can cost an overall $50 billion to $100 billion a year in higher mortgage interest payments nationwide.
5. Those unable to correctly calculate interest rates borrow more and accumulate less wealth.

---

[9] http://www.napfa.org/consumer/WhyFinancialPlanningisImportant.asp

[10] http://money.msn.com/personal-finance/15-ways-financial-decisions-cost-us

6. The least financially literate are more likely to pay higher investment fees and expenses.

7. The average credit-card fees paid by those with low knowledge are 50 percent higher than those paid by the average cardholder.

8. **Financial literacy can explain more than half the wealth inequality observed in U.S. data.**

Last, but not least, the failure to plan can be very costly to investors with children or higher levels of assets and investments. According to LexisNexis, approximately 55% of American adults don't have a will or other estate plan in place.

The following story explains the problems this can create:

Real-estate developer Roman Blum wasn't famous during his lifetime. But, when the 97-year-old died in 2012, he quickly became famous for something he failed to do during his lifetime: write a will. Or, if he did write one, he neglected to leave it where someone could find it.

Blum, a Holocaust survivor with no living family members, passed away with an estate worth nearly $40 million. It is the largest unclaimed estate in the history of the state of New York, and unless the court-overseen administrator of his assets finds relatives through a genealogist search, every penny could end up going to the state government.

Legacies Left in Limbo

Millions of people don't have wills, never considering the consequences of their actions on the family members and friends who survive them.[11]

---

[11] The Consequences of Dying Without a Will – DailyFinance by Dan Caplinger May 9th 2013 http://www.dailyfinance.com/2013/05/09/dying-without-a-will-intestate/

Failing to plan costs time and money. If you die without a Will, state law will determine how your assets are distributed. If your family can't find your Will – or if they can't find the most current version of your Will – your wealth distribution plans may not be honored. If you have children and die without a Will, state law may determine how you children are cared for after you're gone. Lack of planning, the lack of communication about plans, and family disagreements, can all lead to legal battles which cost time, money, and hardship.

Even when you die with a Will, the probate process can still cost you time and money. Probate takes time. A complicated Will can take years to probate; simple Wills can still take months. Most states have minimum periods of time for creditors to respond to a plan of asset distribution. During this time, estate assets are essentially frozen.

Improving financial literacy – simply helping individuals become more knowledgeable investors – is clearly one message of *The Financial "Fix"*. To support this message, I've established www.investorprotector.com, to provide educational tools and resources.

These resources are available to help you care for your financial well-being. You can access the information you want, with self-help expert videos. You can call and ask for help. Our salaried staff can guide you – we do *not* sell any products or services!

At the end of this chapter, you can see some of the information, tools, and videos that are available at www.investorprotector.com.

Besides financial literacy or illiteracy, other investor behavior causes loss. Specifically, market timing or emotional reactions to global, political, or other events can result in a significant loss of return. For example, studies have revealed that investors in mutual funds earn lower returns than the mutual funds in which they are invested:

> Morningstar analysts studied the performance of mutual funds and their investors and found that in all 17 fund categories they examined, the returns earned by investors were *below* the returns of the funds themselves. For example, among large-cap growth funds, the 10-year annualized dollar-weighted [investor] return

was 3.4% less than the time-weighted [mutual fund] return. For mid- and small-cap growth funds, the underperformance was 2.5% and 3.0%. Investors in sector funds fared worse, with tech investors producing particularly disastrous results, underperforming the very funds they invested in by 14% per year.[12]

The loss of return is easier to understand if you consider the difference between time and timing. Mutual fund performance is measured over time, i.e. the start of the year to the end of the year. Investor performance is measured over the timing of the investor's investment in a fund – from their purchase date to their withdrawal date.

A calendar has no emotions; investors do. Investors react to market events, world events, political events, life events, etc. Rarely does an investor invest on January 2 and withdraw their investment on December 31. The result of market timing – and the consequence of emotional investor behavior – is a loss of return.

Various investor behaviors can cause loss. From emotionally buying and selling investments, to a lack of proper planning, to the total failure to plan – the losses can be *massive*.

You can always get a second opinion and double-check that your broker/advisor is doing the right thing with the right product and service for your financial well-being.

In addition to helping protect your life savings, InvestorProtector™ provides information to help you plan your financial future. You can review this information on your own, or with our salaried staff.

---

[12] Mutual Fund Returns: Worse Than You Thought. By Larry Swedroe published on BNET.com 1/18/2011

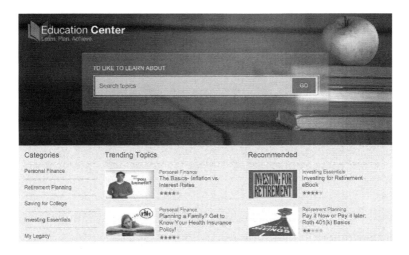

"An investment in knowledge pays the best interest."
—Benjamin Franklin

4. Scams, Scammers, & Scoundrels

The most obvious and sudden cause of loss is fraud. Each and every year, investors get conned, scammed, duped, and otherwise ripped off. The pattern of fraud is remarkably similar; yet investors continue to get victimized.

The most common scam is a Ponzi scheme. Ponzi schemes come in many shapes and sizes. The perpetrators are generally similar – a friendly salesman (predominantly male) with a good story. The investors who become victims are generally similar – they wanted more returns and trusted too much. The difference is generally in the "too-good-to-be-true" story that's told, believed – and sold.

If Charles Ponzi knew how popular his schemes would become, he could have trademarked the name and retired comfortably on royalties. Instead, he defrauded investors and went to jail.

Carlo Pietro Giovanni Guglielmo Tebaldo Ponzi, commonly known as Charles Ponzi, was an Italian businessman and con artist in the U.S. and Canada. His aliases included Charles Ponei, Charles P. Bianchi, Carl and Carlo. Wikipedia

1910 police mug shot of Charles Ponzi

A Ponzi scheme is a fraudulent investment operation that pays returns to its investors from their own money, or from the money paid by subsequent investors – rather than from profits earned by the individual or organization running the operation. The Ponzi scheme usually entices new investors by offering higher returns than other investments, in the form of short-term returns that are either abnormally high or unusually consistent. Perpetuation of the high returns requires an ever-increasing flow of money from new investors to keep the scheme going.[1] Wikipedia

Before Charles Ponzi, in 1899 William "520 Percent" Miller opened for business as the "Franklin Syndicate," in Brooklyn, New York. Miller promised 10% a week interest and exploited some of the main themes of Ponzi schemes, such as customers reinvesting the interest they made. He defrauded buyers out of $1 million and was sentenced to jail for 10 years. After he was pardoned, he opened a grocery store on Long Island. During the Ponzi investigation, Miller was interviewed by the Boston Post, to compare his scheme to Ponzi's – the interviewer found them remarkably similar, but Ponzi's became more famous for taking in seven times as much money.[1] Wikipedia

The promise of high returns with safety is at the heart of every Ponzi scheme. That alone is the first red flag that should make investors suspicious. Higher returns ALWAYS come with higher risks. The "private" nature of the "investment," and the fact that a local advisor has such a good deal for the average investor, is the next red flag. There are billion-dollar institutions that get the first crack at the best deals – sorry, none of us individual investors are that special or fortunate that some local schmuck happens to bring us the investment of a lifetime. If the check or payment isn't made to a major institution, or if the investment can't be held by a well-known bank or brokerage firm, then you have the *next* red flag.

Keep it simple. There is *no* risk without reward. There are *no* "special" investments. There *is* fraud, loss, and, then, victims.

But – let's not overlook or forget the many, many other types of scams perpetrated on investors each and every day. Below are descriptions of some different types of fraud and fraudsters:

As defined by the U.S. Supreme Court a **Bucket shop** is "[a]n establishment, nominally for the transaction of a stock exchange business, or business of similar character, but really for the registration of bets, or wagers, usually for small amounts, on the rise or fall of the prices of stocks, grain, oil, etc., there being no transfer or delivery of the stock or commodities nominally dealt in."[1] Wikipedia

A **Boiler room** has been defined as a place where high-pressure salespeople use banks of telephones to call lists of potential investors (known as "sucker lists"), in order to peddle speculative, even fraudulent, securities. People often mistakenly interchange the words bucket shop and boiler room, but there is actually a significant difference. However, with a bucket shop, it could be better thought of as a place where people go to make "side bets" – similar to a bookie. Wikipedia

Bucket Shops and Boiler Rooms are terms now applied to any fraudulent stock-selling operation that has an undisclosed relationship with the company being promoted or undisclosed profit from the sale of house stock being promoted. These operations promote (via telephone or email) thinly-traded or even fraudulent investments, generally known House Stock. Wikipedia

A **House Stock Scam** generally refers to the use of high pressure sales tactics to sell fake stock in a fake company or real stock in a fake company or fake stock in a real company or any investment in which the brokers are paid excessive commissions to make a sale, the employing firm controls the investment being sold, and the investors will eventually be left with a worthless investment.

"**Pump and dump**" is a form of microcap stock fraud that involves artificially inflating the price of an owned stock through false and misleading positive statements, in order to sell the cheaply purchased stock at a higher price. Once the operators of the scheme "dump" their overvalued shares, the price falls and investors lose their money. Stocks that are the subject of pump-and-dump schemes are sometimes called "chop stocks".[1] Wikipedia

The "night singer of shares" sold stock on the streets during the South Sea Bubble. Amsterdam, 1720.

While fraudsters in the past relied on cold calls, the Internet now offers a cheaper and easier way of reaching large numbers of potential investors.[1]

A variant of the pump-and-dump scam, the "**short and distort,**" works in the opposite manner. Instead of first buying the stock and then artificially raising its price before selling, in a "short and distort," the scammer first short-sells the stock, and then artificially *lowers* the price, using the same techniques as the pump-and-dump, but using criticism or negative predictions regarding the stock. The scammer then buys back the stock at the lower price.[16] Wikipedia

A **get-rich-quick scheme** is a plan to acquire high rates of return for a small investment. The term "get rich quick" has been used to describe shady investments since at least the early 1900s.[1][2] Wikipedia

Most such schemes promise that participants can obtain this high rate of return with little risk, and with little skill, effort, or time. Get rich quick schemes often assert that wealth can be obtained by working at home. Legal and quasi-legal get-rich-quick schemes are frequently advertised on infomercials and in magazines and newspapers. Illegal schemes or scams are often advertised through spam or cold calling. Some forms of advertising for these schemes market books or compact discs about getting rich quick, rather than asking participants to invest directly in a concrete scheme.

It is clearly possible to get rich quickly if one is prepared to accept very high levels of risk – this is the premise of the gambling industry. However, gambling offers the near-certainty of completely losing the original stake over the long term, even if it offers regular wins along the way. Wikipedia

A **pyramid scheme** is a non-sustainable business model that involves promising participants payment or services, primarily for enrolling other people into the scheme, rather than supplying any real investment or sale of products or services to the public.[1][2] Wikipedia

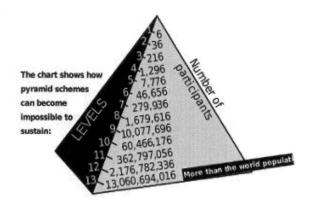

The chart shows how pyramid schemes can become impossible to sustain:

LEVELS — Number of participants

2	6
3	36
	216
4	1,296
5	7,776
6	46,656
7	279,936
8	1,679,616
9	10,077,696
10	60,466,176
11	362,797,056
12	2,176,782,336
13	13,060,694,016

More than the world populat

These types of schemes have existed for at least a century, some with variations to hide their true nature. Many people consider all multilevel marketing plans to also be pyramid schemes.[26][27][28][29]

Among the problems with these schemes is that, after a few levels, you can quickly exceed the entire population of your family, friends, neighborhood, city, state, country, and even the world. Rather unrealistic. Clearly unsustainable!

GunnAllen's broker, Frank Bluestein, ran a Ponzi scheme in Michigan for years. His scheme worked because of certain local factors. First, Michigan had been in economic decline for years. The auto Industry, in particular, had been closing plants and laying off workers in waves. This dynamic created financial hardship among a large pool of good hard-working people – many of whom were relatively unsophisticated investors. These employees frequently got severance checks and had retirement plan balances to roll over. They had money they *needed* to invest. They had no job and no income. They were susceptible to a pitch that promised to replace their lost income with a high-yielding investment.

There was also a *lot* of multi-level marketing going on in Bluestein's community. In fact, several of Bluestein's victims actually served as "marketing agents" *for* Bluestein. The need to roll over severance checks, combined with the need to generate income, combined with ability to get paid to refer other investors, had disastrous consequences. Bluestein's investors went out and found other investors for Bluestein's scam. Frequently, these other investors were friends, family, and neighbors.

They *all* became victims.

Scams and confidence tricks Wikipedia	
Terminology	
• Confidence trick • Error account • List of confidence tricks	• Shill • Sucker list • Conman
Notable scams and confidence tricks	
• 2G spectrum scam • Advance fee fraud • Art student scam • Badger game • Bait-and-switch • Black money scam • Bogus escrow	• Hustling • Indian mining scam • Miracle cars scam • Mock auction • Patent safe • Pig in a poke • **Ponzi scheme**

• Boiler room	• Pump and dump
• Charity fraud	• Pyramid scheme
• Clip joint	• Reloading scam
• Commonwealth games scandal	• Shell game
• Coin rolling scams	• Sick baby hoax
• Drop swindle	• Slavery reparations scam
• Embarrassing cheque	• Spanish Prisoner
• Employment scams	• Strip search prank call scam
• Fiddle game	• Swampland in Florida
• Fine print	• Telemarketing fraud
• Fodder scam	• Thai gem scam
• Foreclosure rescue scheme	• Thai tailor scam
• Forex scam	• Thai zig zag scam
• Fortune telling fraud	• Three-card Monte
• Get-rich-quick scheme	• Trojan horse
• Green goods scam	

Pyramid and Ponzi schemes	
• Dona Branca	• MMM
• Caritas	• Make Money Fast
• Bernard Cornfeld	• Petters Group Worldwide
• Foundation for New Era Philanthropy	• Pyramid schemes in Albania
• High-yield investment program	• Reed Slatkin
• Investors Overseas Service	• Scott W. Rothstein
• Bernard Madoff	• Stanford Financial Group

TOP SCAMMERS

GunnAllen brokers were unfortunately involved, directly or indirectly, in four separate Ponzi schemes. I'll present how they happened and show how to avoid them in the future.

By now, many investors have heard of the following:

en.wikipedia.org

Name: Bernard Madoff
Location: New York
Stolen: $65 billion
Crime: Massive Ponzi Scheme, securities fraud, investment advisor fraud

(Reuters) – Bernard Madoff was sentenced on Monday to 150 years in prison—the maximum penalty the judge could give him for "extraordinarily evil" crimes in Wall Street's biggest and most brazen investment fraud. Mon Jun 29, 2009 7:20pm EDT

en.wikipedia.org

Name: Allen Stanford
Location: Texas
Stolen: $9 billion
Crime: Ponzi Scheme, fraud, conspiracy, obstruction

(Reuters) – Former billionaire Allen Stanford was sentenced to 110 years in prison on Thursday for running a $7 billion scheme in which he stole money from his investors to finance an extravagant lifestyle in the Caribbean. Thu Jun 14, 2012 5:22pm EDT

Names: Provident; Paul Melbye, Brendan Coughlin, Henry Harrison
Location: Texas
Allegedly Stolen: $485 million
Alleged Crime: Ponzi Scheme

Name: Frank Bluestein

Location: Michigan
Allegedly Stolen: $250 million
Alleged Crime: Ponzi Scheme

WHY ARE PONZI SCHEMES SO COMMON?

When need meets greed, investors become victims. Investors generally want to earn higher returns. Scammers promise high returns with low risk – with *no* regard for the truth. With a good story and a cloak of credibility, Ponzi schemes attract investors who then refer friends, family, neighbors, and other contacts. With a big up-front commission, brokers will gladly sell a good-sounding high-returning investment to clients.

All Ponzi schemes seem like great ideas at the time. The collapse usually is caused either because a market/bubble bursts, or current cash inflows from new investors can't support the cash outflows falsely promised to prior investors. Rarely has a Ponzi scheme been exposed because of great due diligence or keen critical analysis, or because alert Industry regulators detected it.

Unfortunately, the collapse occurs when payments stop. Typically, newer investors find out most of their money went to support the lavish lifestyle of a charming thief – and only a little money went to repay prior investors.

WHY DO INVESTORS "FALL" FOR PONZI SCHEMES?

Generally, Ponzi schemes seduce investors with:

1. the promise of a high(er) rate of return (relative to comparable "investments),
2. a good "investment" story,
3. a smooth sales pitch, and
4. some external or third-party implied credibility factor, such as, "...our lawyers and accountants are highly respected..." or, "...our client list includes..." or, "...we do business with the following

major companies..." All these implied endorsements or claims of approvals are used to create a false sense of credibility and/or legitimacy.

GunnAllen was involved with Provident, which claimed it was buying land in areas known to contain oil and gas and which were already under exploration by credible oil and gas Industry firms. Provident claimed it would make money either by leasing the land for exploration or from royalties earned from any oil and gas discovered on their land. Provident created offering documents that were filed with Industry regulators. Federal and state securities regulators, and more than 50 other broker-dealers, and GunnAllen failed to identify Provident as a Ponzi scheme before the scheme collapsed.

Frank Bluestein had been running a Ponzi scheme for years before he joined GunnAllen. Working with another criminal, named Ed May, Bluestein sold investments that claimed to finance the purchase and installation of telephone equipment in hotels around Las Vegas. Ed May claimed to earn royalties from the exorbitant prices charged by these hotels for phone calls. Since everyone knows how much a hotel charges for making calls, the scam made perfect sense – but it was all a lie.

The fact that no one uses a hotel phone any more, or that there never were any hotel contracts to begin with, or that Provident wasn't properly buying, leasing, or exploring for oil and gas, didn't seem to matter.

WHY DON'T PONZI SCHEMES GET DETECTED IN ADVANCE, OR STOPPED SOONER?

First of all, fraud is, by its very nature, based on deception. The Industry and most broker-dealer supervisory systems are not specifically designed to detect fraud. When a determined fraudster is intent on violating laws, ignoring legitimate business practices, and deceiving unsuspecting investors, they can and do find ways to perpetrate their deception.

As long as investors keep getting paid, no one – not the scammer or the investors – wants the money to stop. The human condition forces us to hope against hope that what we might suspect is a scam actually *isn't* a scam. Each check re-assures the investor – until the next check is due.

The cycle then repeats.

Maybe it's greed that lures in the investor. Maybe it's the fear that saying something will somehow cause the checks to stop coming. Often, I believe the embarrassment of getting scammed causes investors to remain silent. I think, in their heart of hearts, most investors – at some point in time – suspect something isn't right with their investment. But, when the check is received and the funds clear, one can't argue with cash. As long as the interest payments and/or dividend checks keep coming, the scam continues.

In other cases, it's not greed or fear that failed to stop the scam. It was simply incompetence. Madoff was a former Chairman of the NASDAQ – one of the Industry's largest stock exchanges. His credibility, according to some, was beyond reproach. The SEC audited his investment advisory firm multiple times over a 16-year period. SEC examiners *did* find certain irregularities, but SEC management chose to ignore the warnings. In an interview from jail, Madoff claimed the SEC examiners *"never asked"* for basic business records that would have exposed his scam. Remember – *nothing* Madoff says should be believed.

The SEC staff follows certain formal policies and procedures during an exam. Likewise, FINRA audited Madoff's broker-dealer over the same period and found *no* evidence of wrongdoing. So – either Madoff was a *great* scammer, or the regulatory agencies tasked with identifying scams and misconduct were incompetent. Or both.

From my own personal experience, FINRA examiners tend to understand transactional business. Yet, FINRA is understaffed. When a brokerage firm is audited, a senior examiner is generally accompanied by several junior staff members who are "in training." There are simply too many firms, too many brokers, and way too many transactions to properly supervise.

As for the SEC, it's a government bureaucracy staffed by lawyers and accountants with little real-world practical experience. During multiple SEC exams, at multiple firms, it was clear the SEC staff had no idea what they were looking at when they reviewed transactions and money flows. Even when the SEC was presented with complete files showing that accounts were opened and trades were executed for *dead people*, I saw blank stares. It's against the rules to open an account or to trade the assets of a dead person. I looked into the blank uncomprehending eyes of an SEC senior examiner after this information was presented. Hello? Is anybody home?

A simple solution is to separate rule making from enforcement. Let the lawyers and accountants at the SEC make rules and let FINRA enforce compliance. Police don't make laws; they enforce them. FINRA should act like Industry police. Congress and the SEC can pass rules and laws that FINRA should enforce.

Finally, the whole system should be paid for by taxes assessed per transaction and based on the value of accounts. Investors should pay for their own protection – *not* the Industry. Any and all fines paid by brokers and firms should go to fund a recovery pool for harmed investors – and NOT to FINRA!

It's that simple.

Protection from Ponzi Schemes

Ponzi schemes are generally misrepresented to clients as low-risk investments. The brokers who sell them also either hid their activities, or lied about the sales to the Industry firms that were supposed to supervise them.

If an investor called the broker's firm or asked their own lawyer or accountant before investing, most losses to scams could be avoided.

> **Before making *any* large investment, get a second opinion.**

Specific Product Problems: Legitimate Products; Illegitimate Sales Practices

The following sections explain investment products, reveal common problems, and provide strategies to help you protect yourself. Each section is designed to demonstrate both legitimate and illegitimate uses of each product.

While every effort has been made to present factual information as clearly as possible, no product or service should be judged independently from *any* individual investor's financial goals and objectives. For most products and services, there are suitable and unsuitable uses.

As you read these stories, you may find similarities to your personal situation. If you have any specific questions or concerns, InvestorProtector.com has salaried staff that can help you. There is no cost or obligation to call. We do not sell any investments and we do not permit any solicitation. We protect investments as well as investor privacy.

Also as you read, keep in mind the below list of InvestorProtector's Independent Monitoring & Automated Alert services. If you think any of these protection services could be helpful, please call for a free trial. If you have multiple accounts at multiple institutions, InvestorProtector™ provides a simple, safe, and secure way to connect and protect your life savings and investments.

Investment Alerts:

 Asset Value Change
Alert me when an asset value changes by a defined %, from one update to the next.

Liability Value Change

Alert me when a liability account value changes by a defined %, or exceeds a maximum balance, from one update to the next.

 Security Price Change

Alert me when a security's end-of-day price is more or less than a specified threshold.

 Top Holdings Change

Alert me when my top holdings change by a defined %, from one update to the next.

 Asset Allocation Threshold Change

Alert me when my current asset allocation is changed, above or below a specified threshold.

 Net Worth Change

Alert me when my net worth changes by a specified percentage.

 Margin Balance Change

Alert me when my margin balance changes by a certain specified percentage.

If you think any of these protection services could be helpful, please call or click, to try www.investorprotector.com for free. There is *no* cost. There is *no* obligation. You can enjoy the protection you need with *no* sales or solicitation of any kind. Your privacy is guaranteed.

Brokerage Accounts

Brokerage Accounts enable investors to buy and sell securities.

Brokers typically charge a commission for executing transactions for investors. Commission charges vary from firm to firm, broker to broker, and from security to security. Back in 1943, regulators determined that, for most transactions, a 5% commission would be considered "fair and reasonable." This became known as the "5% policy," which was generally considered to be the maximum allowable commission. If you paid 5% to purchase an investment and 5% to sell the investment, you would need to earn 10%, just to break even.

Recently, FINRA proposed consolidating multiple rules into FINRA Rule 2121 – Fair and Reasonable Markups, Markdowns and Commissions. This proposal would eliminate the 5% policy and replace it. Under the old rules, selling one security and buying another would count as one transaction; even though the broker could charge a transaction on the sale and another transaction on the purchase, the combined commission had to be less than 5%. Under the proposed policy, the broker can now treat *each* transaction *separately*. Consequently, under the proposed policy, brokers might actually be able to charge *more* than under the old policy.

However, in classic form, FINRA doesn't provide any specific guidelines for commission charges. Instead, FINRA has proposed using at least seven criteria, to ensure the commissions are not "excessive."

Just to be clear, the broker who is trying to generate a commission is also supposed to consider seven separate technical criteria, prior to determining a "fair and reasonable" commission to charge?

Brilliant. This is rulemaking at its finest.

Fortunately, FINRA's vague guidance and terrific rulemaking is supported by the Industry's self-regulatory system that allows it to set its own policies for itself. Each firm can create its own definition of "fair and reasonable." If a broker is charging excessive commissions, it's up to the broker's firm to first define and determine the amount of commission that is excessive. Then the firm must have adequate systems to monitor and detect excessive commissions – on each and every trade. Then the firm must determine if and how it will intervene on the investor's behalf. Now remember, the firm shares in the broker's commission. The Industry entrusts and empowers the firm that shares in each commission to determine the fairness of a commission. To me, that's simply unfair and unreasonable.

Since it's easier to charge a lot of small commissions than a few big ones, some brokers charge less but trade more. In this situation, the turnover of an account matters. The firm should add up the total amount of the commissions charged for all the trades. A $25 commission might not sound bad. Yet, just 10 trades per month for a year would add up to a total commission cost of $3,000. On a $25,000 account, the total commission rate would be 12%. In short, the investor would have to earn more than 12% before realizing a profit.

Whether the commissions are large or small the rules are vague, the Industry is conflicted, and investors pay the price.

Commissions arise from two main types of transactions:

1) **Agency transactions** are executed with a fully disclosed commission that's charged separately from funds used in the transaction. If an investor buys $10,000 worth of stock at $10.00 per share, the client receives 1,000 shares, pays a $250 commission, and uses $10,250.00.

2) **Principal transactions** are executed with a commission that's embedded in the price of the security involved in the transaction. If an investor buys $10,000 worth of stock that's trading at $10.00

per share, the client *could* actually pay $10.25 per share and receive approximately 975 shares. The client uses only $10,000.00, but pays a higher price and receives fewer shares. The commission was "principalized," or embedded in the price of the stock. While this may be fully disclosed on a confirmation, most clients don't see the commission cost in principal trades as clearly as in an agency trade. Because the commission is hidden in the "price" of the stock, many brokers prefer to trade on a principal basis.

THE PROBLEMS:

HOW CLIENTS LOSE MONEY IN BROKERAGE ACCOUNTS

Obviously, the most common way an investor loses money in a brokerage account is via a **market loss**. Bad news, bad earnings, a bad stock pick, or a market correction can quickly cause a loss. The loss will be realized when the investor sells the investment for less than what was paid.

Most investors don't know what to ask for and don't have the time, ability, or willingness to ask tough questions and challenge suspect answers.

It sometimes can be difficult to determine if a market loss was caused by broker negligence, investment-specific problems, or a general market correction. There are tools that can help determine the cause of a loss. In general, if the market is down and your account is down about the same amount, the answer is relatively clear. If the market is flat or up and your account is down, the situation needs to be reviewed.

For every brokerage account, an independent party should review transactions for gains, losses, commissions, fees, expenses, timing of purchases of sales, and more. The broker should be asked to explain and account for any losses. Most investors don't know what to ask for and don't have the time, ability, or willingness to ask tough questions and challenge suspect answers. After reading the next few sections, I truly hope that will change.

Aside from general market losses, the most common losses in brokerage accounts are caused by:

- Unsuitable/bad investments
- Churning
- Unauthorized trading
- Excessive fees, markups, & commissions

UNSUITABLE/BAD INVESTMENTS

When an investor opens a brokerage account, a level of trust has already been established whereby the investor reasonably believes the broker will recommend a suitable investment.

In fact, the broker is obligated to know each investor's investment objectives, risk tolerance, time horizon, liquidity needs, and other financial information. Each investment recommendation must be suitable on its own merits and in conjunction with other investments already owned by the investor.

It's not very complicated. Investments come with significant disclosures and known characteristics. Any experienced broker knows his or her obligation to each investor. Any experienced broker should absolutely understand the risks and rewards of any investment they recommend. It's that simple.

Yet – when the need to generate a commission overwhelms the obligation to do the right thing, investors become victims:

NEWS RELEASE

For **December 15, 2011**

Wells Fargo Investments, LLC Action; Alfred Chi Chen Action

FINRA Fines Wells Fargo $2 Million for Unsuitable Sales of Reverse Convertibles to Elderly Customers and Failure to Provide Breakpoints on UIT Sales

Firm Agrees to Pay Restitution to Affected Customers

WASHINGTON—The Financial Industry Regulatory Authority (FINRA) announced today that it has fined Wells Fargo Investments, LLC, $2 million for unsuitable sales of reverse convertible securities through one broker to 21 customers, and for failing to provide sales charge discounts on Unit Investment Trust (UIT) transactions to eligible customers. As part of the settlement, the firm is required to pay restitution to customers who did not receive UIT sales charge discounts and to provide restitution to certain customers found to have unsuitable reverse convertible transactions.

FINRA also filed a complaint against Alfred Chi Chen, the former Wells Fargo registered representative who recommended and sold the unsuitable reverse convertibles, and made unauthorized trades in several customer accounts, including accounts of deceased customers.

In this example, a broker sold a complex derivative investment to elderly customers. The investment basically provided income – unless a stock went down. If the stock went down far enough, the investor lost the income and, instead, got the stock at a low price and with a principal loss. This product is totally unsuitable for income-oriented investors who don't want principal risk. Any experienced broker knows this. Most investors don't.

Not only did the broker sell these unsuitable investments to investors, he also sold other investments which offered commission discounts. Except the broker didn't pass through the commission discount. The investment may or may not have been suitable, but the sales practice was definitely *not* suitable.

Lastly, the same broker executed trades without speaking to clients. We know this, because some of the clients were deceased. There is absolutely no ability for a broker to fulfill his or her obligation to recommend suitable investments when they trade without authorization in a dead person's account.

CHURNING

When a broker executes many transactions and an investor's account is not increasing in value (or is decreasing), an investor is at risk of **churning**. Churning occurs when a broker generates excessive commissions via numerous transactions – many of which are unnecessary and unjustified.

Unfortunately, it's generally in a firm's or broker's best interest to trade frequently, as firms and brokers generate revenue from commissions, ticket charges, postage and handling fees, and other transaction-related charges paid by investors.

Whether the investor has a gain or loss, transactions make money for the firm and the broker. Keep in mind, in addition to commissions, ticket charges and postage and handling fees may not sound like a commission – but they are. All additional charges must be included, along with the actual commission that's charged, to determine if the total commission was fair and reasonable.

The SEC defines churning as follows:

> **Churning occurs when a broker engages in excessive buying and selling of securities in a customer's account chiefly to generate commissions that benefit the broker.**
>
> **Churning is illegal and unethical. It can violate SEC Rule 15c1-7 and other securities laws.**

Just in case you thought the Industry got something right and made it simple for investors to understand and act against churning, the SEC adds the following:

> **For churning to occur, the broker must exercise control over the investment decisions in the customer's account, such as through a formal written discretionary agreement.**

The above arguments are technical legal bullshit to minimize unwanted actions by harmed investors. Churning most often occurs without any form of broker control or written discretionary agreement. Most times, an investor is uninformed and sometimes unaware of the excessive number of transactions and the exorbitant amount of commissions.

Churning can occur in good or bad markets. It's sometimes easier to hide churning in a down market, as losses can be blamed on the "bad" market and not on excessive commissions.

In my opinion, churning is nothing more than stealing. The broker is removing money from an investor's account and placing it in his or her own pocket. The broker converts the investor's assets into the broker's income by charging excessive commissions. A broker who churns an account is simply a thief.

The following is a true story. Since many think churning applies only to stocks, I've highlighted an example where a broker churned bonds.

The following story is real. I couldn't make this up if I had to.

In April of 2010, the SEC initiated administrative proceedings against stockbroker Paul George Chironis, alleging that he churned two accounts owned by the Sisters of Charity—one account with money for the care of nuns in assisted-living facilities, and a second account to support the nuns' charitable endeavors.

SEC ADMINISTRATIVE PROCEEDING File No. 3-13869

Summary

1. While a registered representative at Capital Growth Financial, Inc. ("Capital Growth"), a now-defunct broker-dealer, respondent Paul Chironis defrauded the Sisters of Charity of New York ("Sisters of Charity" or "Congregation") through abusive trading in their accounts. The Sisters of Charity maintained two accounts at Capital Growth (the "Accounts"), both of which contained predominantly mortgage-backed securities, including securities issued or guaranteed by the Federal Home Loan Mortgage Corporation (Freddie Mac), the Federal National Mortgage Association (Fannie Mae), the Government National Mortgage Association (Ginnie Mae), and the Federal Housing Administration ("FHA") (collectively, "MBS"). Chironis was the registered representative on both accounts.

The broker charged excessive commissions and executed a ridiculous number of trades.

2. During the period January 1, 2007 through January 31, 2008 (the "Relevant Period"), Chironis engaged in a pattern of abusive trading and charged undisclosed excessive markups and markdowns. In addition, Chironis churned the accounts by virtue of his de facto control, excessive trading, and reckless disregard for the customer's interests. Specifically, during the relevant period, Chironis purchased 46 bonds for the accounts, predominantly long-term MBS. Of the 46 bonds purchased, he sold 38 within the same period. The average holding period for bonds acquired and sold during the relevant period was only 4.3 months. Chironis frequently sold one bond and replaced it with a bond issued by a similar issuer and offering a similar yield over a similar duration. Similarly, Chironis made 35 purchases of closed-end bond funds, selling 12 of these positions during the relevant period. The average holding period for the closed-end bond funds purchased and sold during the relevant period was 4.8 months. The impact of

Chironis' frequent trading of securities in the accounts was exacerbated by the excessive transaction fees – in the form of markups and markdowns – that Chironis charged.

3. **Chironis' trading had a devastating impact on the Accounts, while enriching Chironis.** In 2007, the accounts had an average combined balance of approximately $8.3 million. During the relevant period, the accounts purchased approximately $20.1 million and sold $18 million worth of securities. The trades cost the Accounts $959,027 – over 10.8% of their value – in 13 months.

http://www.sec.gov/litigation/admin/2011/33-9170.pdf

The broker defrauded a bunch of nuns by churning bonds!!

This guy actually stole from a bunch of elderly nuns – some of whom were in assisted living facilities. Instead of providing safety and generating income for the nuns, the broker created over $1,170,000 in losses and generated more than $950,000 in commissions for himself. On bonds that paid about 6% to the investor, the broker made over 10.8% for himself. These bonds, that should have been held for years (or to maturity), were traded roughly every 4.3 months.

Neither the broker's firm that was responsible for supervising the broker nor the Industry regulators who were responsible for supervising the broker's firm did anything to prevent this misconduct.

Was there any way to protect against these losses and this misconduct? Let's see:

1. In November, 2005, Merrill Lynch rescinded Chironis' offer of employment, due to customer complaints against him – including complaints of excessive trading.

2. In 2005, prior to joining Capital Growth, seven customer complaints were filed against Chironis – including allegations of churning and unsuitability.

3. In January, 2006, the Michigan Securities Division required that Chironis be placed on heightened supervision.

4. In March of 2006, the Vermont Securities Division prohibited Chironis from soliciting investors in Vermont.

IF THE INDUSTRY DID ITS JOB, OR IF THE BROKER-DEALER DID ITS JOB, THIS SHOULD <u>NEVER</u> EVER HAVE HAPPENED!

CHURNING WAS AND IS BOTH DETECTABLE & PREVENTABLE!

Paying excessive commissions to lose a lot of money does <u>not</u> have to happen.

UNAUTHORIZED TRADING

Hand-in-hand with churning is a practice known as unauthorized trading – or "UT," as it's known in the Industry. UT occurs when a broker buys or sells a security without an investor's authorization. Often, a UT occurs without an investor's knowledge. In general, a broker must discuss each recommendation with an investor, prior to execution. The broker must have a reason for making a buy or sell recommendation; the recommendation must be suitable and appropriate for the client's objectives and risk tolerance; the broker must communicate the price, number of shares, funds required and amount of commission. Once all that's done, the client must then authorize the trade. The broker must enter the order, date-and-time-stamp the order, and submit the trade for execution. Correspondence and trade blotters must be retained – for each and every trade.

That's a *lot* of work. Some brokers simply don't like to work that hard. If a broker has bills to pay and an investor who doesn't pay attention, the broker might generate commissions by trading the investor's account without authorization.

Unauthorized trading should be easy to detect. Every time there's a transaction, a confirmation is also sent to the client. Every month for which there are trades in an account, an investor gets a statement. The statement will show *all* positions and activity in the account for the month.

> UNTIL NOW, THERE WAS NO
> INDEPENDENT SYSTEM OF
> DETECTION AND PREVENTION IN
> THE INDUSTRY THAT WAS
> OFFERED DIRECTLY TO INVESTORS

In reality, unauthorized trading can be extremely difficult to detect. In general, an investor wouldn't entrust their money to a broker or advisor without some degree of trust. Many investors have the mistaken belief that their broker is the expert – and that's why they hired them. The investor doesn't think they should have to watch over their money.

Wrong! Many investors just don't know what to look for. Investments and statements and purchases and sales can be confusing and overwhelming.

But, if the investor isn't paying attention, many unauthorized trades can take place over an extended period of time. Unless there's a major change in the pattern of transactions, or in the types of transactions, and unless there are highly-specialized supervisory systems in place to detect pattern changes, it's extremely difficult for a firm, or for the Industry, to detect or prevent unauthorized trades.

TIP: A general rule of thumb is that:

- **Brokerage accounts are collaborative; the investor must authorize each and every trade.**
- **Advisory accounts can be discretionary; the advisor can be authorized to trade without asking the investor for permission.**

Unauthorized trading usually goes unnoticed during rising markets or when an account value stays relatively flat. Some investors have the mistaken belief that receiving confirms in the mail (or email) and seeing activity on an account statement means the broker is doing his or her job.

In reality, the broker may be doing a job converting client funds into brokerage commissions via unauthorized trades.

TIP:

- **Check account values frequently – at least monthly – for changes.**
- **Check activity – make sure all transactions were discussed and authorized.**
- **Check the commissions/fees for each transaction – lots of little trades with small fees can add up to *big* commissions for your broker and losses for your account.**

So – unless the investor is paying attention, unauthorized trading can go undetected. This is particularly true if trades are done in the account of a dead person!

FINANCIAL INDUSTRY REGULATORY AUTHORITY
OFFICE OF HEARING OFFICERS

DEPARTMENT OF ENFORCEMENT,	Disciplinary Proceeding
Complainant,	No. 2008015382001
	Hearing Officer - SNB
v.	
ERIC ANTHONY FOSTER,	**ORDER ACCEPTING OFFER OF SETTLEMENT**
CRD No. 3267556,	
	Date: February 9, 2012
Respondent.	

INTRODUCTION

Disciplinary Proceeding No. 2008015382001 was filed on December 19, 2011, by the

Department of Enforcement of the Financial Industry Regulatory Authority (FINRA)

(Complainant). Respondent Eric Anthony Foster (CRD No. 3267556) submitted an Offer of

Settlement (Offer) to Complainant dated January 23, 2012. Pursuant to FINRA Rule 9270(e),

On December 21, 2011, the State of Illinois Securities Department entered a Consent

Order where Foster consented to findings that he violated sections 12.A, 12.F, 12.G and 12.I of

the Illinois Securities Law of 1953. Specifically, the Order contains findings that "Foster took

advantage of the age and trading experience of [two customers, a husband and wife] to earn

excessive income for himself and Maxim, all the while reducing [the customers'] account

balance to zero."

FINDINGS AND CONCLUSIONS

It has been determined that the Offer be accepted and that findings be made as follows:

SUMMARY

1. During the period from February 28, 2006 through June 6, 2006, Foster effected six
   unauthorized purchase and sale transactions in the Maxim Group LLC (BD No.
   120708) ("Maxim") account of deceased customer LS. Customer LS had died on
   January 12, 2006, prior to the transactions.

CAUSE OF ACTION
(Unauthorized Trading)
(Violation of NASD Conduct Rule 2110)

In this disciplinary action, the broker took advantage of some clients and churned the account. The magnitude of the commissions and the extent of the losses wiped out the client's account. Additionally, the broker generated even more commissions by executing numerous trades in the account of a dead person.

To remedy the broker's violations of executing unauthorized trades in the dead person's account, FINRA ordered restitution of $2,500 to the client's estate. In addition, FINRA imposed a fine of $10,000 for itself!

Records also show Foster was involved in other customer disputes that settled from 2010 to 2011 for a whopping total of $1.24 million.

Unauthorized trading is usually a recurring event. Once a broker crosses the line, or thinks he or she knows better, or that they're doing the client a favor, or just doesn't care about the consequences, the broker takes on a false license to trade – generally across multiple client accounts – without client permission and without regard to the rules. A little effort in looking at account statements can solve this problem.

EXCESSIVE MARKUPS & MARKDOWNS

Most commissions in brokerage accounts are fully disclosed. The amount of the commission is clearly indicated on a transaction confirmation that accompanies each trade. However, there are ways for brokers to "embed" or, frankly, to hide the commission in the price of the trade. For example, in what is called a principal transaction, a stock that trades for $15.00 might be sold to an investor for $15.50. In this example, the extra $0.50 is actually a brokerage commission. It's technically legal for a broker to effectively change the price of a security by marking up the price of the security by the amount of the commission. Conversely, on a sale, the broker can also mark down the price of security. By using markups and markdowns, brokers can generate commissions that often aren't seen by the client.

Though it's technically legal, even the Industry has limits on the amount of markups and markdowns it will allow. In rare cases, the Industry even goes after brokers that really abuse the already abusive practice of marking up and marking down securities.

SEC Charges Four Brokers with Defrauding Customers in $18.7 Million Scheme

FOR IMMEDIATE RELEASE -- 2012-207

Washington, D.C., Oct. 5, 2012 – The Securities and Exchange Commission today charged four brokers who formerly worked on the cash desk at a New York-based broker-dealer with illegally overcharging customers $18.7 million by using hidden markups and markdowns and secretly keeping portions of profitable customer trades.

The SEC alleges that the brokers purported to charge customers very low commission fees that were typically pennies or fractions of pennies per transaction, but in reality they were reporting false prices when executing the orders to purchase and sell securities on behalf of their customers. The brokers made their scheme especially difficult to detect because they deceptively charged the markups and markdowns during times of market volatility in order to conceal the fraudulent nature of the prices they were reporting to their customers. The surreptitiously embedded markups and markdowns ranged from a few dollars to $228,000 and involved more than 36,000 transactions during a four-year period. Some fees were altered by more than 1000 percent of what was being told to customers.

http://www.sec.gov/litigation/complaints/2012/comp-pr2012-207.pdf

UNAUTHORIZED TRADING, CHURNING, & FRAUD

By now you should understand how bad it is when brokers execute trades without authorization, or churn accounts, or use hidden markups and markdowns to generate excessive commissions. However, when a broker does all three of the above, the harm to investors can be *massive*.

The case below represents a worst-case scenario for victimized investors. Massive commissions were charged while clients incurred massive losses. All the while, the broker sent out fake statements, to hide the losses.

In this case, the broker charged over $1.8 million in commissions while investors lost over $1.5 million!

Richard Allan Finger Jr. (CRD #4432634, Registered Representative, Bellevue, Washington)

...submitted a Letter of Acceptance, Waiver and Consent in which he was barred from association with any FINRA member in any capacity. Without admitting or denying the findings, Finger consented to the described sanction and to the entry of findings that as a result of his trading activity in his customers' accounts, some of his customers incurred approximately $1,594,947 in losses in accounts at his employer firm, and that the customers were charged approximately $1,842,031 in commissions in those accounts.

The findings stated that Finger concealed the losses incurred in those accounts by sending fabricated account statements to the customers via email. The fabricated statements overstated the net asset values by amounts ranging from approximately $6,742 to approximately $1,540,719. Some of those statements also understated the amounts of commissions that had been charged in those accounts by amounts ranging from approximately $2,417 to $430,000. (FINRA Case #2011029005802)

This broker was able to create massive losses and cover them up over an extended period of time by creating false statements.

> **With independent monitoring via a service such as www.investorprotector.com, these losses would have triggered automated alerts that would have been sent directly to the investors.**

THE PROTECTION:

For brokerage accounts, always:

1. Hang up on a telephone investment pitch!
2. Never open an account over the phone!
3. Request a commission schedule in writing.
4. Check confirmations (sent after each trade) to verify:
    a. price paid to buy, or price received on a sale
    b. capacity (agency or principal)
    c. the commission charged is consistent with the commission schedule and with what was agreed

5. Check monthly statements for:

    a. all transactions (they all must have been approved and authorized by you)

    b. changes in value (any large gains or losses need to be explained)

6. Periodically call the compliance department, to request a copy of a statement.

    a. Make sure compliance sends a statement, independently from the broker.

    b. Compare the compliance copy to the broker copy, to ensure accuracy.

7. Review the account to ensure investments are:

    a. allocated to a suitable amount of stocks, bonds, and cash

    b. diversified across many different types of stocks (growth, value, large, small, etc.)

    c. not concentrated to any sector or single position

8. Utilize stop loss orders, to ensure you have pre-arranged protection triggering the sale of stocks when they fall below certain prices (in case there is a major correction).

    a. This is more work for your broker; too damn bad.

    b. Be sure to ask what the commission will be if a stop loss order is executed, since it can default to a maximum charge that can be negotiated down.

If you would like help or assistance, InvestorProtector.com provides independent monitoring and automated alerts that will notify you when account value changes need to be reviewed. Our salaried staff can help you understand why values changed. An ounce of protection is worth a pound of cure.

InvestorProtector.com also provides easy-to-use tools that help you see your account progress and performance. You can easily review accounts and investments against various benchmarks.

Growth of $10,000

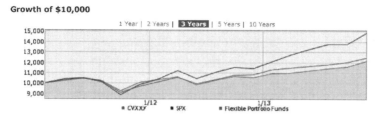

In the preceding situations, the amount of commissions and the significant losses would have triggered multiple warnings and alerts from InvestorProtector.com!

Advisory/Managed Accounts

The Securities and Exchange Commission (SEC) admitted in April 2010 that it has never examined some 3,000 registered U.S. investment advisers, *Investment News* reported.

THE PRODUCT:

The rise of advice. The mounting distrust and growing hatred of full service commission-based brokers has driven investors to discount brokerage firms and to fee-based investment advisors.

Investment advisors provide continuous portfolio management for a fee, based on a percentage of the assets under management. Investment advisors with assets under management of less than $30 million dollars are generally registered with their home state regulator, whereas investment advisors with $30+ million under management are registered directly with the SEC.

Advisors legally have a higher standard of care to investors than brokers, who simply execute transactions. To put it plainly, an investment advisor has a fiduciary obligation to act in an investor's best interests. A broker is simply an agent who acts on behalf of a buyer or a seller. An investment advisor must ensure each and every investment is suitable the entire time it's owned by an investor. A broker generally needs to ensure that an investment is appropriate at the time it's bought or sold. An advisor generally only charges asset-based fees – they want to gain and retain clients and grow assets over time; a broker generates commissions per transaction – they want to buy and sell securities.

An advisor who manages an account should never also serve as the custodian. In other words, the advisor can trade securities within an account, but they can't access money or cause money to be moved into or out of an account. A custodian holds the money and can move/disburse money, based on proper client instructions. An advisor should *never* be empowered to disburse or access client funds, other than to initiate appropriate securities transactions (buy or sell investments) on the client's behalf. An advisor often has discretion to execute transactions without first consulting an investor. A broker almost never has discretion.

Lastly – and most important – advisors typically deliver a performance report, on a quarterly basis. A performance report states the gain or loss of an account, in both dollars and percentages. It's critical that an investor receive separate and independent account statements from their custodian, in addition to any performance report from their advisor. In 90%+ of fraud cases, advisors created fake statements and/or fake performance reports, to keep a scam alive. Had clients also received and reviewed independent account statements directly from a legitimate custodian, most cases of fraud would have be exposed and prevented.

THE PROBLEMS:

The first and generally most troubling problem with investment advisory accounts is the recurring annual fee. What's it for? If an advisor is simply allocating your assets and picking mutual funds, you should not pay an advisory fee of much more than 1%. Even *that* may be too much.

You should also understand the difference between an advisor and a money manager. The difference is simple: an advisor is a gatherer of clients and accounts; a manager is, as the name implies, the manager of assets. While some advisors do act as managers, most advisors generally allocate assets and pick mutual funds and/or money managers or some combination of both. Money managers actually do the work of researching, buying, and selling individual stocks, bonds, and exchange traded funds.

The advisor's job is to make sure your asset allocation is suitable and that each selected mutual fund and/or money manager delivers appropriate performance. In general, an advisor can hire and fire money managers. The advisor should meet with you periodically to make sure your allocation remains suitable and that your account is progressing according to your plan. In some cases, the advisor may also be the money manager. However, the trend has been for advisors to get registered so they can charge additional recurring fees to allocate assets and place investor assets for actual management with a separate money manager.

As for the fee, you are generally paying for the advisor, and the money manager, and then for any transaction charges and custodial fees. There can be layers of fees. These fees reduce return and cost you money.

I'm not saying an advisor shouldn't get paid, but – in my opinion – the amount of fees paid to the advisor should not be as high as the amount of fees paid to the actual money manager. An advisor can serve an important role. For those who want and need help allocating assets, an advisor can provide a valuable service. That service should be at the right price.

Going forward, just as discount brokerage firms gathered significant assets from traditional full-service firms, there will be a wave of discount advisors that compete with full-service advisors. You can and will be able to access a network of low-fee (discount) advisors just like you can execute low cost (discount) securities transactions. However, discount broker and discount advisors may not provide all the financial planning, legal, tax, insurance and other services that a well-served investor needs.

If you already have an advisory account, it's probably time to review your current fees, performance, and services. While a trusted advisory relationship has value, that value should be priced appropriately.

In my experience, too many advisors are sitting back collecting plenty of recurring fees while managers do all the work. Investors who trust too much or who get too busy with life may be paying a high price for advice. Each and every year, the recurring fees add up. Especially variable annuity investors who also pay advisory fees.

So – how do some of the more unscrupulous advisors victimize investors?

1. Falsification of performance

Since most advisors are hired based on past performance, unscrupulous advisors will create and market falsified performance reports. The falsification of performance generally occurs on two levels:

- Past performance is inflated, in order to acquire new investors under false pretenses, and
- Current performance is inflated or simply falsified, in order to cover up underperformance, hide losses, or conceal a scam

Advertising by investment advisers is subject to general prohibitions on fraud contained in the federal securities laws. Most specifically, Section 206(4) of the Advisers Act broadly prohibits an investment adviser (whether registered or not) from engaging in "fraudulent, deceptive, or manipulative" activities.

Advertising or communicating any misrepresentation or falsification of performance is, simply, fraud.

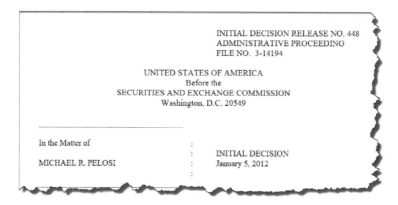

```
                                INITIAL DECISION RELEASE NO. 448
                                ADMINISTRATIVE PROCEEDING
                                FILE NO. 3-14194

                  UNITED STATES OF AMERICA
                          Before the
            SECURITIES AND EXCHANGE COMMISSION
                    Washington, D.C. 20549


   In the Matter of                :
                                    :        INITIAL DECISION
   MICHAEL R. PELOSI                :        January 5, 2012
                                    :
```

In the above case, Michael R. Pelosi, a credentialed advisor with a CFA designation, MBA degree, and 15 years of experience, was caught sending erroneous performance reports. In letters to client, Pelosi claimed to deliver performance that was markedly different than what his firm's actual performance reports calculated.

When the discrepancy was discovered, instead of firing Pelosi, his firm allowed him to resign. Firing Pelosi would have placed a derogatory mark on his license and drawn attention to his employer's failure to properly supervise his activities.

Upon investigation by the SEC, the two wrongs were discovered, which resulted in an enforcement action against the employer and a regulatory mark against Pelosi.

When an advisor has the presumption of a higher standard of care, the advisor must provide honest and accurate information to clients – including performance reports. Overstating investment values is simply lying. Charging higher fees as a result of overstating investment values is simply stealing.

2. Fiduciary Obligation means NO CONFLICTS OF INTEREST!!!

An advisor has a fiduciary *obligation* to each client. This means the client's best interest *must* come first. When an advisor has the discretion to trade on behalf of clients, there's an obligation to seek out "best" prices and to execute trades with lowest costs. When an advisor has discretion, it's illegal for that advisor to make all kinds of trades, simply to generate additional commissions or fees.

In any advisory relationship, if the advisor can earn additional revenue per transaction or per product, the client is exposed to a conflict of interest and a high potential for misconduct.

SEC Penalizes Investment Advisers for Compliance Failures

FOR IMMEDIATE RELEASE
2011-248

Washington, D.C., Nov. 28, 2011 — The Securities and Exchange Commission today charged three investment advisers for failing to put in place compliance procedures designed to prevent securities law violations.

Feltl & Company, Inc.

… Feltl engaged in hundreds of principal transactions with its advisory clients' accounts without informing them or obtaining their consent as required by law. Feltl also improperly charged undisclosed commissions on certain transactions in clients' wrap fee accounts.

Under the settlement, Feltl & Company agreed to pay a penalty of $50,000 and return more than $142,000 to certain advisory clients. Additionally, the firm will hire an independent consultant to review its compliance operations annually for two years, provide a copy of the SEC's order to past, present, and future clients, and prominently post a summary of the order on its Website.

This advisor abused the trust bestowed upon it by investors. In addition to charging an asset-based advisory fee, the advisor also generated commission revenues for itself by trading in client accounts. The commissions would have shown up on confirmations and should have been detected.

3. Overcharging

In the next example, Merrill Lynch overcharged 95,000 accounts more than $32.2 million in fees. These amounts are simply staggering. The explanation is laughable – the firm lacked proper systems to make sure investors were billed: **"…in accordance with their contracts and disclosure documents."** Somehow, saying "oops – my bad" doesn't cut it. http://www.finra.org/web/groups/industry/@ip/@enf/@ad/documents/industry/p127128.pdf

BofA Fined $2.8 Million for Overbilling 95,000 Accounts

By Laura J. Keller - Jun 21, 2012 12:47 PM ET -- Bank of America Corp.'s Merrill Lynch wealth-management unit was fined $2.8 million by the Financial Industry Regulatory Authority for overbilling customers by $32.2 million over an eight-year period.

Merrill Lynch charged the fees to about 95,000 accounts between April 2003 and December 2011, FINRA said in a statement today. New York-based Merrill Lynch, which was acquired by Bank of America in 2009, lacked an adequate supervisory system to ensure that customers were billed in accordance with their contracts and disclosure documents, the regulator said.

"Investors must be able to trust that the fees charged by their securities firm are, in fact, correct," Brad Bennett, FINRA's chief of enforcement, said in the statement. "When this is not the case, investor confidence is threatened."

Bill Halldin, a spokesman for Charlotte, North Carolina-based Bank of America, said the charges were largely "the result of improper coding of accounts," which the firm discovered on its own. "We have improved our systems to address these issues and we have reimbursed affected clients," he said in a telephone interview.

FINRA also faulted Merrill Lynch for failing over a four- year period to send 10.6 million trade confirmations to 230,000 customers.

The fact that these errors went undetected for more than eight years is simply *astonishing*! With all the systems and all the employees reviewing all these accounts, it's hard to imagine this misconduct went on for almost a decade. Over that time, I'm certain the firm was also audited by federal and state regulators. It looks like everyone simply missed the problem. Makes you wonder how many *other* problems have occurred...or are still are occurring...?

Also noteworthy is the last statement..."FINRA also faulted Merrill Lynch for failing over a four-year period to send 10.6 million trade confirmations to 230,000 customers." The firm that holds and controls the client's funds failed to send confirmations regarding over 10 million trades? The firm simply *forgot* to send 230,000 customers the details regarding account activity, such as purchase price, sale price, fees, commissions, etc.? Imagine if your bank failed to send you statements. Would that be acceptable? No way!

But – rest assured, if it happened, your bank might get "faulted," too.

Industry protection at it's finest.

4. Reverse Churning

Reverse churning occurs when a firm charges fees for doing nothing. There is no account activity. There are no transactions. Investors are paying fees, but not receiving any actual services. Charging excessive fees is bad. Charging hidden fees is worse. Charging fees for doing nothing is *the worst*.

NEWS RELEASE

For Release: Wednesday, February 18, 2009
Contacts: Nancy Condon (202) 728-8379, Herb Perone (202) 728-8464

FINRA Fines Robert W. Baird & Co. $500,000 for Fee-Based Account, Breakpoint Violations
Firm to Return More Than $434,000 in Fees, Plus Interest, To Customers

Washington, DC.—The Financial Industry Regulatory Authority (FINRA) announced today that it has fined Robert W. Baird & Co. $500,000 for supervisory violations relating to its fee-based brokerage business. FINRA also ordered Baird to return $434,510 in fees, plus interest, to 154 customers. Those customers either paid fees in fee-based accounts without generating activity or paid fees higher than those indicated on the Baird fee schedule.

FINRA fined Robert W. Baird & Co. $500,000 for supervisory violations relating to its fee-based brokerage accounts and ordered the company to return $434,510 in fees to 154 customers. FINRA found that customers were charged fees in accounts that were not generating any activity, otherwise known as "reverse churning." FINRA also found clients were charged excessive fees.

According to FINRA, Baird failed to adequately review or supervise these accounts. The firm's failure to supervise allowed customers to get billed fees even though there were no trades for at least eight consecutive quarters. These accounts paid over $269,000 in fees during the inactive quarters to a firm that did nothing; they didn't manage the accounts; they didn't even supervise their brokers.

Additional actions involving reverse churning occurred at firms such as AXA Advisors, Morgan Stanley, SunTrust Investment and Wachovia Securities. The fines for these firms ranged from $700,000 to $6.1 million.

If you went to a restaurant that didn't serve you any food – would you still pay?

I didn't think so.

THE PROTECTION:

1. Choose your advisor carefully.
2. Hire a fee-only planner to whom you can pay a flat fee to develop a written plan with financial strategies and recommendations free from any commissions or conflicts of interest.
3. Hire an investment advisor for ongoing active account management under the following conditions:

    a. Negotiate fees – there are *always* discounts

    b. Ask for a "flat fee" arrangement or maximum charge

4. Get a services agreement *in writing.*

5. Know your custodian (the actual holder of your funds) is legitimate.

6. Ask for *and actually review* copies of all fee invoices, at least quarterly.

7. Review statements and performance reports.

8. Establish a specific benchmark against which to measure performance.

9. Use more than one advisor.

    a. Competition for your business is healthy and other eyes may see things you might miss.

10. **MEASURE PERFORMANCE – Independently**

    a. Get independent reports and statements – most fraud occurs when managers create fake and/or false statements and performance reports.

    b. Your advisor should be really nice and trustworthy; they should also be competent!

Growth of $10,000

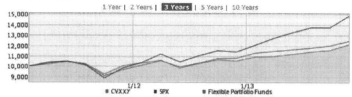

Along with independent monitoring and automated alerts,
InvestorProtector.com *provides on-demand performance reports, so you can track the progress and performance of your life savings.*

In general, ongoing portfolio management can add value by establishing an appropriate investment strategy (asset allocation policy with appropriate benchmarks, to measure performance), buying and selling securities, adapting a strategy in response to life changes, and maintaining a strategy in response to market events.

Most import, I believe there's a right way to invest. In general, get passive indexed management with low fees and high tax efficiency for a portfolio's core, and active management, to add incremental value with sector rotation and opportunistic investments around the portfolio's core.

For additional information, visit: www.investorprotector.com.

Mutual Funds

The U.S. mutual fund market—with $13 trillion in assets under management at year-end 2012—remained the largest in the world, accounting for 49 percent of the $26.8 trillion in mutual fund assets worldwide.[13]

THE PRODUCT:

Mutual funds are generally considered to be convenient investment vehicles that provide professional management and broad diversification. With just a few dollars, an investor can buy shares of a fund and gain access to a diversified portfolio of securities owned by the fund.

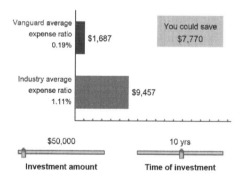

See how much you can save

This hypothetical illustration assumes an annual 6% return for both examples. This illustration does not represent any particular investment nor does it account for inflation. There may be other material differences between investment products that must be considered prior to investing.

Sources: Vanguard and Lipper, a Thomson Reuters Company, as of December 31, 2012.

---

[13] http://www.icifactbook.org/fb_ch2.html

Each mutual fund has one common pool of money. That money is used to buy and sell various investments. The mutual fund issues shares of the fund to investors. When investors buy shares of a fund, they add money and the fund buys more underlying investments. When investors sell shares of a fund, they redeem money, so the fund sells underlying investments. Accordingly, investors don't directly own the fund's underlying investments. The investor owns shares of the fund, which entitles the investor to share in the profits and losses of the fund, during the time the investor owns the shares.

Each fund has a prospectus that provides extremely detailed descriptions of the fund's investment objective, strategy, fees, risk, etc. Unfortunately, there are thousands of funds to choose from and the average prospectus can be over 100 pages long. Apart from doing a spectacular job of bombarding you with advertising and excessive disclosure information, investors get hurt investing in mutual funds primarily due to bad broker sales practices, excessive fees, and commissions.

THE PROBLEMS:

Fees:

There are actively managed funds that charge approximately 1.11% per year and there are passively managed indexed funds that charge an average of 0.19% per year.

This difference in fees could cost you an additional $7,770 in fees over 10 years on a $50,000 investment.

But that's just the tip of the iceberg...

According to John Bogle, the founder of Vanguard – the world's largest mutual fund company with about $2 trillion in assets under managers, "In investing, you get what you don't pay for."

After adding up all the fees of actively managed mutual funds, investor returns are practically wiped out.

- Expense Ratio: 1.12%
- Turnover, Loads, Broker/Advisor Fees: 1.15%
- Taxes: 0.75%
- Cost of Investor Behavior: <u>1.20%</u>

  Total Annual Cost: **4.22%**

Now Assume:

- Average Market Return: 7.00%
- Average Inflation Rate: 2.50%

  Total Real Return: **4.50%**

  Net Investor Return: **0.28%**

Bogle concludes: **"All-in" fund costs would confiscate 94% of the stock market's annual real return.**[14]

Consequently, Vanguard's no-load (commission free) mutual fund expense ratios are approximately 83% lower than the Industry average.

> **Understanding mutual fund fees is the first step to avoiding fees and bad broker sales practices.**

The mutual fund world generally can be divided into two universes: Load funds versus no-load funds. Essentially, load funds pay commissions to broker-dealers for selling funds to investors. Load funds raise assets by paying brokers a commission to sell funds.

No-load funds generally are selected either directly by investors or by fee-based advisors who are compensated directly by investors. No-load funds raise assets by advertising or by paying fees to fund "supermarkets," to attract funds from self-directed investors.

[14] **The Arithmetic of "All-In" Fund Expenses.** *(Financial Analysts Journal,* January/February 2014)

The nature of paid sales via the commission/fee structure of load mutual funds has been particularly problematic for individual investors. It becomes easy to understand bad-broker sales practices when you realize there can be three or more prices for the exact same fund.

The mutual fund Industry often creates different classes of shares of the same fund. Even though the underlying fund is exactly the same, each different share class has a different fee structure. According to the mutual fund Industry, these different share classes are created to best meet the needs, goals, and objectives of different types of investors. Think of an airline that sells first class, business class, and coach class tickets. The plane represents the fund; the different seats represent the different share classes of a fund. The different seats are all on the exact same plane (fund). However, the different seats (share classes) have dramatically different prices.

In general, there are two main components that make up the "price" of each mutual fund's share class: 1) commissions and 2) annual expenses.

For example, some share classes pay commissions up-front. Other share classes pay the commissions in arrears, upon withdrawals. Other share classes pay commissions annually. Yet, other share classes don't pay any commissions at all. Again, this is just the commission component for different share classes of the exact same fund.

For mutual funds that pay commissions – also known as loads, or sales charges, or contingent-deferred sales charges – there are different amounts and methods of charging commissions:

- Class A shares: Front-end sales charge that declines as the investment amount increases. Lower annual fund expenses apply.
- Class B shares: Back-end sales charge that declines over time, assessed on withdrawals. Higher annual fund expenses apply.
- Class C shares: Recurring annual sales charge assessed on total balances. Higher annual fund expenses apply.

- Class-I shares: No sales charge. Offered only to institutions and/or through participating fee-based programs. Lower annual fund expenses apply.

Based on the commission structure, the annual fee charged by each share class also can vary. A typical mutual fund has the following annual fees associated with the various share classes:

Annual Fees				
Share Class	A	B	C	I
Management Fees	0.24%	0.24%	0.24%	0.24%
Distribution (12b-1) and/or Service Fees	0.24%	1.00%	1.00%	None
Other Expenses	0.14%	0.14%	0.18%	0.14%
Total Annual Fund Operating Expenses	*0.62%*	*1.38%*	*1.42%*	*0.38%*

A-shares, which charge an up-front commission, generally have the lowest operating expenses (annual fees). Since B shares only charge a commission upon a withdrawal, many investors choose this option, since 100% of their money gets invested and they don't see the commission. However, these share classes have higher annual fees that cost the investor more over time than A-shares. Many brokerage firms and many fund companies have stopped offering B shares since brokers frequently misrepresented them as having "no commissions" when, in fact, they do.

In conclusion, the main differences between share classes are:

1. the amount and manner of the commission/load (one time charge)
2. the distribution (12b-1) or shareholder services fee (ongoing annual charge)

Otherwise, the different share classes are simply different prices for the exact same fund with the exact same investments. So – what goes wrong? With A shares, investors are entitled to commission discounts if they invest more money in a specific fund or in multiple funds offered by the same mutual fund company. This commission discount is called a "breakpoint." The commission discount received by the investor directly reduces the commission paid to the broker.

Accordingly, for A-shares which have up-front commissions, brokers have been known to try to:

1. split up purchases, to avoid breakpoints that reduce the commission, or

2. spread investments across different fund companies, to avoid breakpoints, or

3. switch funds frequently, to generate new commissions

For B and C shares, which have higher annual costs to the investor and pay higher recurring annual fees to the broker, brokers have been known to:

1. recommend large dollar investments in B and C shares, when A-shares cost less, and

2. falsely represent that there are "no commissions" on B and C shares

Examples of abuses are cited below:

> **Registered Representative Suspended and Fined for Recommending Unsuitable Class B & Class C Mutual Fund Share Purchases to Customers** – NASD settled a matter involving a registered representative who recommended to customers the purchases of Class B & Class C mutual fund shares without having a reasonable basis for believing that the recommendations were suitable. NASD found that the recommendations were not suitable because the customers' accounts were economically disadvantaged by the costs associated with the purchases of Class B & Class C shares. NASD found that the customers would have incurred fewer costs if the representative had recommended that they purchase Class A shares of the same mutual funds.

In the above situation, the broker sold B & C share classes which had higher annual fees than A shares. This cost the investor more money.

Registered Representative Suspended and Ordered to Pay Restitution to Customer for Recommending Unsuitable Mutual Fund Switches – NASD settled a matter involving a registered representative who recommended that an elderly retired client engage in a pattern of mutual fund switching in two different accounts. The switching involved both open-end (Class A and B shares) and closed-end funds and unit investment trust shares. NASD found that the representative's recommendations were unsuitable in view of the frequency of the transactions, the types of investments recommended, and the customer's financial situation and investment objectives. The customer lost approximately $70,000 in both accounts and incurred other added expenses, such as unnecessary contingent deferred sales charges, additional and unnecessary sales loads and commissions, and higher 12b-1 fees. The representative also ignored the customer's option of utilizing repurchase rights, which would have enabled the customer to avoid additional expenses. NASD found that the representative's actions violated NASD's rules, suspended the representative in all capacities for six months, and ordered that the representative pay restitution of more than $22,000 to the customer.

In this situation, the broker basically churned mutual funds. Note that the investor lost $70,000, but the broker only paid restitution of about $22,000.

Despite the existence of a prospectus with information for the investor, the broker still chose to recommend the share class of the product that would pay the broker more, instead of offering a different share class of the same product that would cost the client less. These situations were deliberate, inappropriate acts of misconduct by individual brokers.

However, there have been deliberate, inappropriate acts of misconduct by individual firms: 15 firms, to be exact.

NASD Charges 15 Firms with Directed Brokerage Violations, Imposes Fines Totaling More than $34 Million

Washington, DC—NASD announced today that it has imposed fines totaling more than $34 million on 15 broker-dealers in connection with the receipt of directed brokerage in exchange for preferential treatment for certain mutual fund companies.

Today's cases, part of NASD's efforts to eliminate conflicts of interest in the sale of mutual funds, focus on brokerage firms involved in selling mutual funds to retail investors, as well as one mutual fund distributor. All of the cases involve violations of NASD's Anti-Reciprocal Rule, which prohibits firms from favoring the sale of shares of particular mutual funds on the basis of brokerage commissions received by the firm. Among other things, a firm may not recommend specific funds to sales personnel or establish preferred lists of funds in exchange for directed brokerage.

Firms and brokers promoted these funds over others because they got paid more. Investors want objective advice – not recommendations that are bought and paid for by the industry.

NASD found that the 14 retail firms, most of which sold funds offered by hundreds of different mutual fund complexes, operated "preferred partner" or "shelf space" programs that provided certain benefits to a relatively small number of mutual fund complexes in return for directed brokerage. The benefits to mutual fund complexes of these quid pro quo arrangements included, in various cases, higher visibility on the firms' internal Websites, increased access to the firms' sales forces, participation in "top producer" or training meetings, and promotion of their funds on a broader basis than was available for other funds.

In addition to the already high commission that would be paid to a broker, insurance companies agreed to pay extra fees to the brokerage firms. Investors were not told about these fees. The product recommendations were bought and paid for by the industry.

"When recommending mutual fund investments, firms must act on the basis of the merits of the funds and the investment objectives of the customers and not because of other benefits the brokerage firm will receive," said NASD Vice Chairman Mary L. Schapiro. "NASD's prohibition on the receipt of directed brokerage is designed to eliminate these conflicts of interest."

The mutual fund complexes that participated in these programs paid extra fees for enhanced visibility. The additional fees were typically based on a combination of sales and/or assets under management by the brokerage firm. Some of the complexes participating in the preferred partner programs paid part or all of the revenue sharing fees by the use of directed brokerage – that is, by directing a portion of the trades in the portfolios they managed to the trading desks of the firms participating in the program.

For firms that did not have the capacity to provide trade execution, trades were sent to designated third parties, which then remitted a portion of the trading commissions to the retail firms – although they provided no services in connection with the trade. These commissions were sufficiently large to pay for the benefits received by the funds as well as the costs of trade execution.

The retail firms generally monitored the amount of directed brokerage received to ensure that the fund complexes were satisfying their revenue sharing obligations. The use of directed brokerage allowed the fund complexes to use assets of the mutual funds instead of their own money to meet their revenue sharing obligations.

Mutual funds used fund assets to meet "revenue sharing obligations." This means the additional fees were actually paid by directly by investors. Investors had no way of knowing about the conflicts of interest and higher fees.

NASD also censured and fined one mutual fund distributor, AllianceBernstein Investment Research and Management, Inc. AllianceBernstein paid for some of its shelf space obligations by having its affiliated investment adviser direct portfolio transactions to or for the benefit of firms to which the distributor owed revenue sharing fees.

The fifteen firms and their respective fines are as follows (firms noted with asterisks are wholly owned subsidiaries of AIG Advisor Group, Inc.):

Royal Alliance Associates, Inc.*	$6,600,000	New York, NY
H.D. Vest Investment Services	$4,015,000	Irving, TX
AllianceBernstein Investment Research and Management, Inc.	$3,984,087	New York, NY
Linsco/Private Ledger Corp.	$3,602,398	Boston, MA
Wells Fargo Investments, LLC	$2,970,000	San Francisco, CA
SunAmerica Securities, Inc.*	$2,500,000	Phoenix, AZ
FSC Securities Corp.*	$2,400,000	Atlanta, GA
Securities America, Inc.	$2,400,000	Omaha, NE

RBC Dain Rauscher, Inc.	$1,700,000	Minneapolis, MN
McDonald Investments Inc.	$1,500,000	Cleveland, OH
AXA Advisors, LLC	$900,000	New York, NY
Sentra Securities Corporation* and Spelman & Co., Inc.* (joint fine)	$780,000	Phoenix, AZ
Advantage Capital Corp.*	$450,000	Atlanta, GA
Advest, Inc.	$286,415	Hartford, CT

The fines imposed on eight of the firms – Royal Alliance Associates, SunAmerica Securities, FSC Securities Corp., Advantage Capital Corp., Sentra Securities Corp., Spelman & Co., RBC Dain Rauscher, and McDonald Investments – included charges relating to their failure to retain emails as required by the federal securities laws and NASD rules.

The fine imposed on H.D. Vest Investment Services included charges related to violations of NASD rules relating to non-cash compensation. H.D. Vest reimbursed brokers' expenses incurred in connection with certain firm training and educational conferences based, in part, on the brokers' sales of funds that participated in its preferred partner program – instead of giving equal weight to the sales of all mutual funds, as required by NASD rules.

H.D. Vest Investment Services, RBC Dain Rauscher, and McDonald Investments were also charged with violations of NASD's supervisory systems and procedures rule.

In settling these matters, the firms involved neither admitted nor denied the charges, but consented to the entry of NASD's findings.

NASD has brought five previous actions for similar violations, including a complaint that is still pending against American Fund Distributors and settlements with Quick & Reilly, Inc., Piper Jaffray & Co., Edward D. Jones & Co. L.P. and Morgan Stanley DW Inc.

In conclusion, mutual funds offer many benefits for individual investors, i.e. diversification, professional management, and others. The mutual fund vehicle is *not* the problem. Bad brokers and bad sales practices *are* generally to blame for mutual fund problems.

THE PROTECTION:

To protect themselves, investors need to:

1. Know the time frame over which you plan to hold the investment.
2. Understand the costs of the prospective mutual fund investment:
   a. Up front costs – load versus no-load:
      i. For load funds,
         1. Understand if the commission is paid:
            a. Up-front (one-time)
            b. Upon withdrawal structure (declining schedule over time)
            c. On an annual recurring basis
         2. Determine if there are commission breakpoints/discounts for:
            a. Investing a certain amount up-front, or
            b. Committing to invest a certain amount over time
   b. Annual fees (expense ratio):
      i. How much does it cost to own the investment each and every year?
   c. Ask if there are alternative, lower-cost share classes of the exact same fund.
      i. You shouldn't have to ask – a broker is actually obligated to disclose this to you.

There are public Websites and tools that can help investors protect themselves:

FINRA Mutual Fund Links & Tools:

http://www.finra.org/Investors/ToolsCalculators/P117435

InvestorProtector.com provides tools that can help you easily evaluate whether you're paying reasonable fees for the performance returned by mutual funds you own or are considering buying:

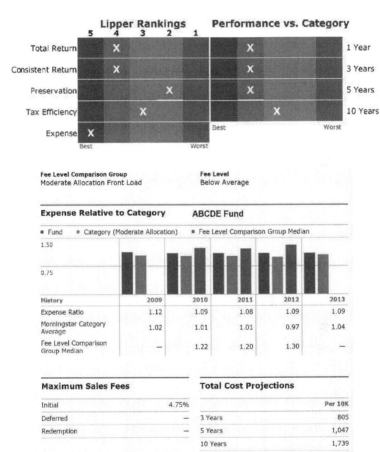

Source: InvestorProtector®, Lipper®, Morningstar®.

In addition to helping you minimize your ongoing mutual fund fees, InvestorProtector.com can also help you avoid paying sales loads and commissions.

Exchange-Traded Funds

In 2013, the US exchange-traded funds (ETF) market reached $1.3 trillion in assets and more than 3.4 million Americans now own ETFs.

THE PRODUCT:

ETFs took the concept of a mutual fund and improved upon it. While mutual funds remain the most prominent investment vehicle in retirement plans, ETFs are rapidly gaining market share.

The most common type of ETF replicates the return of a specific stock market Index, such as the S&P 500. This is similar to an index mutual fund. However, a mutual fund investor owns shares in a fund that only trades one time per day at one price; an ETF investor owns a basket of securities that trades throughout the day, at market prices. The ability to buy and sell ETFs intra-day is a major difference between mutual funds and ETFs.

Another major difference is cost: mutual fund expense ratios are generally higher than ETF expense ratios – so there are cost advantages to ETFs. For taxable accounts, ETFs provide another advantage over mutual funds. When a mutual fund investor cashes out, the underlying shares must be sold, in order to raise cash. Since every investor in a mutual fund owns a little piece of every holding, one investor's redemption can trigger taxable capital gains across all other investors. ETFs, on the other hand, don't generally spread capital gains across investors.

With intra-day trading, low operating expenses, and tax advantages, ETF investments have become very popular among investors, brokers, planners, and advisors.

THE PROBLEMS:

The rapid growth and incredible popularity of ETFs has also been accompanied by rapidly increasing sales practice complaints regarding certain complex ETF products. Specifically, a portion of the ETF universe is comprised of leveraged ETFs.

Leveraged ETFs deliberately seek to magnify return and, consequently, risk. They can be two or three times more volatile to both market advances and corrections than the index to which they're linked. Alternatively, there are also inverse ETFs. Inverse ETFs trade in the *opposite* direction of the index to which they're linked. There are also leveraged inverse ETFs.

The complexity and volatility of leveraged and inverse ETFs resulted in the issuance of a warning by FINRA to the Industry:

July 2009 FINRA ETF Notice

As described in "Non-Traditional ETFs: FINRA Reminds Firms of Sales Practice Obligations Relating to Leveraged and Inverse Exchange-Traded Funds" (FINRA Regulatory Notice 09-31)

Leveraged ETFs seek to deliver multiples of the performance of the index or benchmark they track. Some Non-Traditional ETFs are "inverse" or "short" funds (or combinations of both), meaning that they seek to deliver the opposite of the performance of the index or benchmark they track. Such objectives are achieved through the use swaps, futures contracts and other derivative instruments.

Therefore, inverse and leveraged ETFs that are reset daily typically are unsuitable for retail investors who plan to hold them for longer than one trading session, particularly in volatile markets.

When the Industry actually has to warn brokers – who are purported to be educated financial professionals – about the risks, volatility, and complexity of these vehicles, it's *not* a good sign for individual investors. Especially when individual investors are depending on their broker to accurately represent the products they sell. Clearly, within the Industry, there was concern that brokers didn't understand the products they were selling to unsuspecting investors.

The warning was too late. It was issued in 2009, after the S&P 500 was down 37% in 2008. Once again, the losses had already occurred. Only then did the Industry issue a warning, to help cover its own self-regulated ass. Yet, the Industry also found another way to profit at investors' expense:

NEWS RELEASE

For Release: May 1, 2012
Contacts: Michelle Ong (202)728-8464, Nancy Condon (202)728-8379

Citigroup Global Markets, Inc Action
Morgan Stanley & Co., LLC Action
UBS Financial Services, Inc Action
Wells Fargo Advisors, LLC Action

FINRA Sanctions Four Firms $9.1 Million for Sales of Leveraged and Inverse Exchange-Traded Funds

For failing to supervise, educate and train its brokers, and for their unsuitable recommendations:
• $604,584 to harmed investors
• $1,750,000 to FINRA
The firms allowed these sales.

WASHINGTON – The Financial Industry Regulatory Authority (FINRA) today announced that it has sanctioned Citigroup Global Markets, Inc; Morgan Stanley & Co., LLC; UBS Financial Services; and Wells Fargo Advisors, LLC a total of more than $9.1 million for selling leveraged and inverse exchange-traded funds (ETFs) without reasonable supervision and for not having a reasonable basis for recommending the securities. The firms were fined more than $7.3 million and are required to pay a total of $1.8 million in restitution to certain customers who made unsuitable leveraged and inverse ETF purchases.

FINRA sanctioned the following firms:

- Wells Fargo – $2.1 million fine and $641,489 in restitution
- Citigroup – $2 million fine and $146,431 in restitution
- Morgan Stanley – $1.75 million fine and $604,584 in restitution
- UBS – $1.5 million fine and $431,488 in restitution

Look at the amounts of fines versus restitution.

- $1.8 million in restitution to harmed investors
- $7.3 million in fines to FINRA

Once again, FINRA profited while investors lost.

Unlike traditional ETFs, which offer intra-day trading, low costs, and tax efficiency, the complex leveraged and inverse ETFs offered risk and unpredictability. The unexpectedly volatile product performance was bad enough. The misuse of these highly risky leveraged products with senior citizens was even worse.

Morgan Stanley to Pay Nearly $2.4 Million ETF Fine and Restitution

For the purpose of proposing a settlement of rule violations alleged by the Financial Industry Regulatory Authority ("FINRA"), without admitting or denying the findings, prior to a regulatory hearing, and without an adjudication of any issue, Morgan Stanley & Co. LLC submitted a Letter of Acceptance, Waiver and Consent ("AWC"), which FINRA accepted. In the Matter of Morgan Stanley & Co. LLC, *Respondent* (AWC 20090181611, May 1, 2012).

A product that was supposed to deliver twice the return of an index that was up 2% actually declined by -6%. The product that was supposed to deliver twice the inverse (opposite) of 2% declined by -26%!

The AWC asserts that Non-Traditional ETFs generally "reset" daily, and such a factor can have significant ramifications that distort the performance of the subject ETF and its underlying index or benchmark. For example, the AWC notes that the Dow Jones U.S. Oil & Gas Index, between December 1, 2008 and April 30, 2009, gained two percent, while an ETF seeking to deliver twice the index's daily return fell six percent, and the related ETF seeking to deliver twice the inverse of the index's daily return fell 26 percent.

Despite the risks associated with holding Non-Traditional ETFs for longer periods, the AWC alleges that certain Morgan Stanley customers held Non-Traditional ETFs for extended time periods during the relevant period of January 2008 through June 2009. In fact, certain Morgan Stanley customers with a primary investment objective of income held Non-Traditional ETFs for periods of several months. The AWC offers these examples:

Elderly clients seeking income were sold concentrated positions in highly risk equity investments!

The firms allowed these sales.

- A 74-year old customer with a primary investment objective of income and a net worth under $300,000 allocated over 25% of the account to a single Non-Traditional ETF that was purchased on a solicited basis and held for 128 trading days, sustaining losses of over $13,000; and

- An 89-year old customer with a primary investment objective of income and a net worth under $200,000 allocated over 59% of the account to a single Non-Traditional ETF that was purchased on a solicited basis and held for 39 trading days, sustaining losses of over $10,000.

During the relevant period from January 2008 through June 2009, FINRA alleged that Morgan Stanley failed to establish and maintain a supervisory system, including written procedures, reasonably designed to achieve compliance with applicable NASD and/or FINRA rules in connection with the sale of leveraged, inverse, and inverse-leveraged Exchange-Traded Funds ("Non-Traditional ETFs"). The AWC alleges that Morgan Stanley supervised Non-Traditional ETFs the same way it supervised traditional ETFs. Thus, Morgan Stanley failed to establish a reasonable supervisory system and written procedures to monitor the sale of Non-Traditional ETFs.

The AWC further alleges that Morgan Stanley also failed to establish adequate formal training regarding Non-Traditional ETFs during the Relevant Period.

In addition, certain Morgan Stanley registered representatives allegedly did not have an adequate understanding of Non-Traditional ETFs before recommending these products to retail brokerage customers. Certain Morgan Stanley registered representatives also made unsuitable recommendations of Non-Traditional ETFs to certain customers with a primary investment objective of income.

As such, the AWC alleged that Morgan Stanley violated NASD Rules 3010, 2310, and 2110 and FINRA Rule 2010, and, according to the terms of the AWC, FINRA imposed sanctions of a Censure, a $1.75 million fine, and $604,584 in restitution.

http://www.finra.org/web/groups/industry/@ip/@enf/@ad/docume nts/industry/p126127.pdf

With low costs, tax efficiency, and intra-day trading, ETFs can play a significant role in a portfolio. That said, leveraged and inverse ETFs have limited application and are best used by sophisticated investors, speculators, or portfolio managers to hedge short-term risk. Once again, the ETF vehicle is not the problem. Bad brokers and bad sales practices are generally to blame for problems with most ETFs.

THE PROTECTION:

To protect themselves, investors need to:

1) Understand if they are investing in traditional ETFs versus leveraged or inverse ETFs.

   a. Avoid leveraged and inverse ETFs

   b. Do not hold leveraged and inverse ETFs for long time frames (more than a few days)

2) Allocate investments to several ETFs.

3) Diversify the types of ETFs that are owned.

4) Track the ETF performance against a benchmark, to ensure performance accuracy.

ETFs can play a significant role in a portfolio – specifically, by providing exposure to equities in a low-cost tax-efficient manner.

According to Morningstar, Inc., the average of the most recent total operating expenses (or prospectus net expense ratio) among active U.S. mutual funds, excluding load-waive share classes and active U.S. Exchange Traded Funds (ETFs) are:

Category	Average Total Operating Expenses	
	Mutual Funds	ETFs
STOCK/EQUITY FUNDS		
US Large-Cap Stock	1.31%	0.47%
US Mid-Cap Stock	1.45%	0.56%
US Small-Cap Stock	1.53%	0.52%
International Stock	1.57%	0.56%
BOND FUNDS		
Taxable Bond	1.07%	0.30%
Municipal Bond	1.06%	0.23%

Many professional advisors are now properly using ETFs to construct portfolios. Surrounding a core of ETFs with actively managed mutual funds and/or sector ETFs (more specific and potentially volatile) can deliver lower costs and greater tax efficiency than traditional mutual fund only portfolios.

At www.investorprotector.com, you can find resources that track the performance of ETFs against appropriate benchmarks:

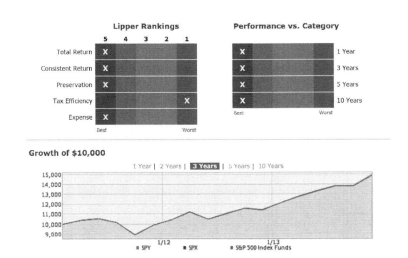

At www.investorprotector.com, you can also find tools to compare the mutual funds you own with ETF alternatives, to identify opportunities to lower fees, reduce tax loss, and thereby improve returns.

For example, the following two investments are similar – but the ETF has significantly lower costs, which can save you money over time.

SPDR S&P 500: SPY

Expense Ratio:	0.09%

American Funds Growth Fund of America: AGTHX

Net Expense Ratio:	0.70%
Expense Difference	0.61%
10-Year Cost Savings per $10,000 Invested	$610.00

Paying lower fees is just like earning higher returns – without any additional risk!

For a complimentary analysis, click, call, or chat at www.investorprotector.com.

Variable Annuities

Variable annuities are insurance contracts with investment options. They enable investors to seek growth potential by investing in equities while simultaneously creating income and death benefits that provide protection against market declines. The combination of potential growth with protected income and death benefits makes variable annuities attractive for investors to own and for brokers to sell.

Contracts have an accumulation phase and an annuitization phase. In the accumulation phase, investors can allocate funds to a variety of investment sub-accounts and seek variable (market driven) rates of return (hence the product name). Contributions (premiums or purchase payments) create an account value – which moves up and down with the market. These contributions also can create living and death benefits. A living benefit is a value against which an investor can receive lifetime income or guaranteed withdrawal benefits. With lifetime Income, payments can continue for as long as the investor lives. With guaranteed withdrawal benefits, payments continue until the client receives all of his or her original investment back. More on these later. There is also a death benefit, which can return all contributions (less any withdrawals) upon death.

That said, in general, there are three major and distinct components within a variable annuity:

1. Account Value	2. Living Benefit	3. Death Benefit

The account value is a tax-deferred investment account that experiences gains or losses, based on investments within the product. The account is funded by contributions which are considered premium payments. The value can go up and down with the market, like an elevator. This is a cash value that can be withdrawn, subject to various terms, conditions, tax issues, and surrender charges.	The living benefit value is used to create either lifetime income payments or guaranteed withdrawals. The benefit value is set by the contributions. It generally increases annually by a minimum crediting factor, like an escalator. Market declines don't reduce this value. The benefit is accessed either by periodic income or withdrawal payments; it isn't cash and can't be taken in a lump sum.	The death benefit value is used to create a return of premium payments (less withdrawals) upon death. Contributions to variable annuities are considered premium payments. The benefit value is set by these premium payments. It can increase by a minimum annual crediting factor, like an escalator. Market declines don't reduce this value; it is available at death.

Variable annuities are complex investments. Contracts have an owner who funds the contract and an annuitant, who receives the living and death benefits. The owner and annuitant can be the same person or different people (husband and wife, trust, and income beneficiary, etc.).

Variable annuities have multiple features and benefits. Some of the benefits are optional, i.e. income/withdrawal benefits and death benefits. These benefits are called riders. Investors can select different riders, based on their needs and goals. Each rider comes with certain terms and conditions, along with specific fees and expenses. There can be multiple riders per product and these riders can be used in various combinations.

If you already stopped reading, I don't blame you. If you continue reading, consider how complex each product is and multiply that by the number of riders per product, then multiply *that* by the number of products per company, and then by the number of different companies. There's an enormous amount of information about multiple products. After adding all the technical details, terms, and conditions of all the optional riders, the amount of information is simply overwhelming.

All these details can materially impact a variable annuity investment's performance, features, and benefits – for better or worse. It's incredibly difficult for a broker to understand all the different products, features, benefits, fees, and expenses. It's virtually impossible for an investor.

That said, with equity upside potential, principal protection benefits, lifetime income benefits, and death benefits, variable annuities can provide a solution for many investors' goals.

THE PROBLEMS:

Two of the biggest problems with variable annuities are:

1. Fees (as in commissions, annual expenses, surrender charges, etc.)
2. Misrepresentation

In 2004, the North American Securities Administrators' Association ("NASAA") ranked the sale of variable annuities – "often pitched to seniors" – as one of the "Top Ten" investment scams affecting the investment public – and particularly senior citizens.

On March 29, 2006, Patricia D. Struck, the President of NASAA, in her testimony before the Special Committee on Aging of the United States Senate, stated:

"A perennial fixture on NASAA's annual list of top scams involve the sale of variable annuities to investors with little regard to whether or not the product is suitable. While these are legitimate

and suitable investments for some, regulators are concerned that many investors aren't being told about high surrender charges for early withdrawals, the potential of exposure to market risk, and the steep sales commissions agents often earn when they move investors into variable annuities. Often pitched to seniors through investment seminars, these products are unsuitable for many retirees."

While there is clearly an appropriate role for variable annuities, the devil is in the details. Many seniors can benefit from a lifetime income guarantee or a guaranteed withdrawal benefit. Many seniors and other investors want to invest in equities with the knowledge that, even if their cash value declines, their cash flow via income payments is stable and protected. Many seniors and other investors want to know they can't outlive their money. Many seniors and other investors also want to know that, even if the market declines, they can get "all" their money back. Many seniors and other investors simply want to know that their beneficiaries can get back all of their original investment (less any withdrawals), even if the market declines.

However, there's a steep price to be paid for these products and all the benefits they can provide. Many variable annuity contracts pay very high commissions – as in 7% to 8.5% of the amount invested. While all the investor's money may get invested right away, if an investor wanted or needed money back, there could be very high surrender charges. These charges could consume 8% or more of the amount withdrawn. This would be in addition to any taxes and market losses.

Similar to mutual funds that have multiple share classes (or different prices) for the same product, variable annuities also have different share classes with different prices. Keep in mind that the product is the same. The different prices generally only impact the amount paid (a lot or a little) and the method of payment (up-front or annual) to your broker.

However, unlike mutual funds, in which fee discounts are built in, variable annuities have escaped the drive to reduce costs. For example, mutual funds offer commission discounts when larger amounts are invested. A commission discount for larger investment amounts is called a breakpoint. Investors in mutual funds can get breakpoints by investing larger amounts of money, or by agreeing to invest more over time, or by investing with family and friends. Variable annuities generally don't provide any such commission discounts or breakpoints.

Where a $100,000 investment in a mutual fund might only pay a broker 3% (reduced from 4.75%) – or $3,000 – the same $100,000 invested in a variable annuity would pay 7%, or a $7,000 commission. There may be different commissions for different variable annuity contracts, but there are generally no commission discounts for variable annuity investors.

> **Due to the higher commissions generally paid by variable annuities over other products, investors must really understand if the product is being pitched because it adds value for the investor or simply because it maximizes the commission for the broker.**

The commissions and fees are the simplest problem with variable annuities. Unfortunately, along with many potential benefits, there are also many contractual restrictions for each variable annuity rider. In particular, the living and death benefit riders that can be added to each contract involve complex and very specific terms and conditions. While these riders can create significant income and death benefits, these benefits can also easily be reduced or voided by withdrawals and simple mistakes that violate any contractual restriction.

> **Lifetime income, guaranteed withdrawal benefits, and death benefits come with strict contractual terms that limit the amount of withdrawals in any given year. If an investor withdraws too much – on purpose or by accident – the guarantees can be lost or significantly reduced.**

Two of the biggest misrepresentations/misunderstandings surrounding variable annuities involve living benefits and crediting factors.

1. A living benefit generally comes in one of two forms:
   a. Lifetime income benefit (payments for life)
   b. Guaranteed withdrawal benefit (return of 100% of the original investment)
2. A crediting factor is a minimum guaranteed increase to the above living benefit.
   a. It is *not* an interest rate – it's a rate of increase to a base value.

Living benefits, like Minimum Guaranteed Income and Minimum Guaranteed Withdrawal benefits are both figures; they're not real cash values. If an investor invests $100,000, the account value will contain $100,000 in cash and the living benefit value will also be $100,000. If the market were to decline by 20%, the account value would be $80,000 and the living benefit value would still be $100,000. However, the investor can't access the living benefit as if it were cash. It's only accessible via cash flow payments, with very specific terms – and restrictions.

For example, with a lifetime income benefit, the investor might receive 5% of the $100,000, or $5,000, for life, even if those payments add up to more than $100,000 over time. Alternatively, with a guaranteed withdrawal benefit, even though the investor's cash is only worth $80,000, due to the market decline, he or she can still take annual withdrawals that add up to the original $100,000. However, these withdrawals may be limited by some formula (usually up to 7% or $7,000 per year, in this example).

With a crediting factor, the living benefit is "guaranteed" to increase – usually annually. However the crediting factor is *not* an interest rate; it's a rate of increase. To make this clear, if the living benefit base value is $100,000, and the crediting factor is 5%, after 1 year the living benefit would be $105,000. However, unlike an interest rate, which provides real cash, the crediting factor is simply the amount by which the living benefit base value is increased. Neither the living benefit base value nor the crediting factor are cash values. They can't be accessed like cash. The insurance company that issued the variable annuity will simply use $105,000 as the new living benefit value.

For lifetime income benefits with a crediting factor of 5%, if the benefit value increased from $100,000 to $105,000, the new annual lifetime income payment would increase, from $5,000 to $5,250. For guaranteed withdrawal benefits, the new annual withdrawal amount would increase, from $7,000 to $7,350. Remember, the lower lifetime income benefit payment will last as long as the investor lives – even if the payments exceed $105,000. With the higher guaranteed withdrawal benefit, the payments will stop when the total amount withdrawn equals $105,000. Either way, the insurance company uses your own money to pay you. Only after your money is gone will the insurance company have to use any of its money.

This is a typical pattern of a broker lying:
• to investors about a product
• to the firm that supervises him to gain approval of bad sales

Lastly, many variable annuities feature a death benefit that will return all premium payments (contributions) less any withdrawals at death. Market declines will not reduce a Death Benefit. Unfortunately, some brokers market this as a principal guarantee. In reality, the investor has to die to for the death benefit to be paid. Accordingly, the principal is not guaranteed to the investor. It may be guaranteed to their beneficiary; but it is a death benefit and NOT a principal guarantee.

• Never, ever sign blank forms.
• Request copies of all account documents and applications
• Review forms to make sure income, net worth, risk tolerance, investment objective are correct.

Unfortunately, many brokers simply confuse or misrepresent the different Living benefits, the crediting factor, and the death benefit features and benefits. Not all living benefits provide lifetime income; a crediting factor is *not* interest; a death benefit isn't the same as a principal guarantee. With a 7% or 8% commission on the line, some unscrupulous brokers will easily be motivated to tell investors what they think the investor wants to hear, instead of the truth.

In the Industry, lying is fraud.

Darrell G. Frazier (Frazier) was recently barred from the securities industry by the Financial Industry Regulatory Authority (FINRA) over allegations that Frazier made fraudulent statements in the sales of variable annuities. Frazier is also alleged to have made unsuitable variable annuity sale recommendations to customers.

Frazier first became registered with a FINRA member firm in March 1988. Frazier was registered with Park Avenue Securities LLC from July 2002 through June 2010. From August 2010 through May 2011, Frazier was associated with MML Investors Services, LLC.

FINRA alleged that from 2004 to at least 2009, Frazier made materially false and misleading statements in connection with recommending customers purchase variable annuity products...Frazier has been accused of falsely representing to customers that:

- the annuities guaranteed returns of at least seven percent per year;
- principal invested was guaranteed against loss;
- no annual fees would be charged for purchasing the annuities; and
- Frazier would only make money on the annuity sale if the customer made money.

FINRA alleged that Frazier actively continued to conceal his fraud after selling the variable annuities. When customers complained that their annuities were not performing as promised, Frazier made false statements regarding the annuity's performance.

Frazier was also accused of misstating customer information on account records. It was alleged that Frazier over-stated customers' net worth and income and inaccurately stated customers' risk tolerances on variable annuity applications. Frazier is also alleged to have had customers sign blank, undated forms that Frazier would later complete.[15]

Problems with the sale of variable annuities have been so widespread the Industry published warnings (Notice to Members) in 1996, and again in 1999, and again in 2000:

> **Because variable annuities and variable life insurance are complex products, the NASD has issued additional guidance in assessing the suitability of recommendations of variable products in Notices to Members ("NTM") 96-86, 99-35, and 00-44.**
>
> In addition to existing securities laws and rules governing suitability, the National Association of Insurance Commissioners ("NAIC") has expressed concern regarding the sale of variable annuities to seniors. As a result of these concerns, on September 14, 2003 the NAIC adopted a Model Regulation entitled Senior Protection in Annuity Transactions.

That's a lot of guidance and a lot of concern over many years. Misrepresentation and sales practice violations were so severe that the SEC and NASD (now called FINRA) conducted joint studies, to "solve the problem":

---

[15] http://www.securitieslawyersblog.com/2013/09/28/darrell-frazier-accused-selling-variable-annuities-misleading-customers/

Home | Previous Page

U.S. Securities and Exchange Commission

JOINT SEC/NASD REPORT
ON EXAMINATION FINDINGS REGARDING BROKER-DEALER
SALES OF VARIABLE INSURANCE PRODUCTS

Office of Compliance Inspections and Examinations United States
Securities and Exchange Commission

I. EXECUTIVE SUMMARY

Variable annuity and variable life insurance products (collectively, "variable
insurance products" or "variable products") are being marketed and sold to a large
number of investors. While variable insurance products may be appropriate
investments for some investors, concerns have been raised about the sale of these
products. This prompted the staffs of the Securities and Exchange Commission
("SEC" or "Commission") and NASD ("Staff") to conduct examinations of broker-
dealers that sell variable insurance products. This report summarizes the findings
of those examinations.

Variable insurance products are hybrid investments containing both securities and
insurance features. The insurance features of variable annuities permit the investor
to receive a series of periodic payments from the investment over time and provide
a death benefit to the beneficiary should the investor die during the accumulation
phase. Variable life policies are a form of life insurance. The insurance features of
both products provide tax-deferred treatment of any accumulated earnings. In
both variable annuity and variable life products, the securities feature provides the
investor with an opportunity to participate in potential capital appreciation and
income through investments in the securities markets, but also subjects the

Despite the unprecedented Industry collaboration, the initiative to solve
fraudulent sales of variable annuities was a dismal failure. Investors
continued to get sold unsuitable products, unnecessarily switched
between products, and misled about product features, benefits, fees, and
expenses. Industry firms continued to fail in their responsibilities to
properly supervise the salespeople. Finally, the Industry had to get tough:

*The SEC and NASD have recently brought a number of enforcement actions involving the sale of variable
annuities. These actions involved excessive switching, misleading marketing, failure to disclose material
facts, unsuitable sales, inadequate written supervisory procedures, failure to maintain adequate
documentation, and/or failure to supervise variable product transactions.*

A summary describing recent enforcement cases brought by the SEC and
the Commission is available on the NASD Website at
http://www.nasdr.com/white_paper_0600804_apen.asp.

With more enforcement and greater supervision, the Industry thought it
was making progress in the war against unsuitable variable annuity sales.
Yet, investors continued to get killed. So, once again – this time in 2004 –

the Industry regulators proudly touted additional efforts to protect investors:

> "Variable annuities are complex products that are difficult for many investors to fully understand," said Mary L. Schapiro, NASD Vice Chairman and President of Regulatory Policy and Oversight. "The vast majority of our enforcement actions in this area involve suitability, disclosure and supervision issues, which is why we are proposing tougher rules specifically governing variable annuity sales."

www.nasdr.com/news/pr2004/release_04_027.html

Unfortunately, the truth was revealed. The battle over inappropriate variable annuity sales wasn't over. It had just begun. The problems weren't isolated to a few rogue brokers at some no-name firms.

In the following example, a Merrill Lynch broker sold over $32 million in variables annuities to a very wealthy client. The broker claimed there were no commissions or sales charges. In fact, the broker generated over $2,240,000 in commissions for their firm and themselves.

Merrill Lynch sued over variable annuity sales

InvestmentNews
The Leading Information Source for Financial Advisers

... But bad news rolls on: $11M bite in 2 lost cases

By Bruce Kelly | November 19, 2007 - 12:01 am EST

Merrill Lynch & Co. Inc., ... has lost two legal cases centering on the firm's management of wealthy clients' portfolios.

In the jury trial in Florida's Palm Beach County, the firm and one of its brokers, Karen McKinley, were hit with a $6 million verdict for taking advantage of a well-known builder turned philanthropist, George Rothman. At the start of this month, the jury awarded his two daughters, the plaintiffs in the case, an additional $1.75 million in punitive damages.

In 1995, Ms. McKinley began selling Mr. Rothman what would eventually mount to $32 million worth of annuities. The total damages, which included excessive fees and taxes, and loss of use of money, were about $7 million.

However, in three memos describing their investments to Mr. Rothman and his wife, Ms. McKinley said the product had no fees. Under the heading "Retirement Plus Annuity" in a note from July 1997, Ms. McKinley said: "You enjoy the benefits of performance, diversification and monthly income, as well as no commission or sales charges. As always, consider the annuity to be a seven-year investment."

Both Mr. Rothman and his wife were declared incompetent in 1999, and Mr. Rothman died in 2004 at the age of 86.

http://www.investmentnews.com/article/20071119/REG/711190341

Variable annuities are long-term investments. The benefits of tax-deferral and compounding are realized over long periods of time. Since retirement accounts already provide tax-deferral, variable annuities provide no additional tax benefit for IRAs, 401ks, or other retirement plans.

There are many potential benefits to variable annuities. These benefits are not always outweighed by the high fees and complex terms. Unfortunately, the seduction of high commissions for brokers and confusion caused by complex terms for investors continues to create a high potential for abusive sales practices.

THE PROTECTION:

To protect themselves, investors need to request a lot of information. There are services that can provide a side-by-side analysis of different products. Investors should compare the fees, features, and benefits against other leading products. If a broker/advisor isn't willing to provide this information or spend the time to review it thoroughly, their conduct may be 1) illegal and 2) unworthy of your business. Following are some key elements to understand:

1. **Fees**: *Sales Charges (Commissions)* – variable annuities have many ways to pay brokers for selling products to investors. Just as mutual funds have multiple share classes, so too do variable annuities. The name of the share class may vary from product to product, but these examples are simply different prices for the same product:

    a. Front load: pays an upfront sales charge and has a high multi-year (7 or more) declining surrender charge schedule – generally has the lowest annual recurring product fees.

    b. Level load: pays a recurring annual sales charge and often has a multi-year declining surrender charge – generally has a high annual recurring product fees.

c. Bonus class: pays an upfront sales charge and has a high multi-year (7 or more) declining surrender charge schedule with an additional annual fee for the bonus – generally has the highest annual recurring product fees.

There are many other share classes with different combinations of up-front broker commissions and varying surrender charge schedules.

2. **More Fees:** *Annual Expenses* – each and every year, variable annuities charge recurring fees that can cost anywhere from almost 3% to over 6% annually. Of course, there are variable annuities with lower fees – but brokers generally don't sell those.

Annual Fees

Annual Fees	Minimum	Maximum
Mortality & Expense Risk	1.15%	1.95%
Administrative Charge	0.15%	0.35%
Living Benefit	1.00%	1.00%
Enhanced Death Benefit	0.00%	1.00%
Subaccount Fees	0.53%	2.59%
TOTAL	**2.83%**	**6.89%**

An investor has to earn more than the annual expenses in order to see any increase in account value. Additionally, many variable annuities charge more fees for the living and death benefit riders. This high fee is deducted from the investor's account value – further reducing the real money in the variable annuity contract. If these benefit values increase, but market declines or withdrawals have reduced the account value, the variable annuity company charges a large fee for the higher benefit value to the already reduced cash value.

In order to get more sales, variable annuity companies have conveniently combined large up-front commissions with "low" annual fee share classes. This way, a broker can tell an investor that the highest commission share class has the lowest recurring annual fees.

3. **Even More Fees:** *External Advisory Fees* – After you're sold a variable annuity, many advisors will offer to provide "additional services," such as managing the sub-account investments within the product. While this might seem "nice," it likely adds no value and will certainly increase costs. Most variable annuities include professional asset allocation strategies, institutional money managers, and automatic rebalancing – for no additional fee. The initial selection of sub-accounts is a service that should be included with the initial investment. It's a required part of the account application process. It's *not* a favor or value-added service. In addition, most variable annuity contracts pay an initial commission and, after some period of time, also pay the broker ongoing service fees, to provide continual services. Unless a broker or advisor is using a no-load, low-cost variable annuity and has no other form of compensation, the imposition of an external advisory fee will definitely add cost and may be unnecessary, unethical, and unscrupulous.

4. **Liquidity**: *Surrender Charges* – Most variable annuities limit annual withdrawals to 10% of the invested amount without the imposition of surrender charges, as follows:

Year	Charge
1	8.50%
2	7.50%
3	6.50%
4	5.50%
5	5.00%
6	4.00%
7	2.00%

These surrender charges directly reduce the amount of money you receive when taking withdrawals greater than 10% of your original contribution. In addition to the surrender charge, there may be taxes on some or all of the withdrawal. For any investor who takes a taxable withdrawal before the age of 59½, there can be an additional 10% early withdrawal penalty tax.

5. **Liquidity**: *Contractual Benefits* – For most investors, the single greatest reason to invest in a variable annuity is to gain a lifetime income or guaranteed withdrawal benefit. These benefits come with very specific terms as to:

   a. When they can be accessed, e.g. ten years from the contract start date

   b. How they can be accessed, i.e. via annuitization or via withdrawal

   c. How much can be accessed, i.e. 5% per year maximum

   d. Who can access, i.e. husband and wife, joint or individual

If the investor violates any of the above terms, the benefits can be reduced or forfeited. Not knowing the details can be *very* costly at a time when the investor can least afford to lose the benefit.

A few last words about Income Payments & Annuities

Most annuities offer to provide lifetime income, with or without annuitization. If you annuitize and elect lifetime payments, you essentially give your money to the insurance company, in exchange for guaranteed payments. You surrender control over your money and wipe out any death benefit. Basically, the annuity company uses up your money first then uses its money, if you live long enough. The good thing about annuitization is that payments can continue for as long as you live – even long after you would have depleted all your own money. If you die before all your money is used, the annuity company will return any remaining balance to your beneficiaries.

Alternatively, if you elect lifetime payments without annuitization, you retain control over your money and you keep the annuity's death benefit intact; but you need to know the "payout factors" and the impact withdrawals will have on the account value, death benefit value, and future income payments.

Remember, there are three distinct values within most annuities: a cash account, a living benefit value, and a death benefit value. For example, if you invested $100,000, and your account value immediately declined to $50,000, your living benefit and death benefit value would still be $100,000. That, however, is only the first part.

The critical part is knowing the living benefit payout factor. Simply put, the living benefit value that you hopefully grow and increase over time is multiplied by a payout factor, to determine your lifetime income payment (or a guaranteed withdrawal amount).

If, at age 65, the payout factor for a single life is 4%, then your lifetime income payment is guaranteed to be 4% * $100,000 – or $4,000 per year – for as long as you live. If, at age 66, the payout factor is 4.5%, then your lifetime income payment would be $4,500 per year – so you might be better off waiting one more year, before turning on your lifetime income. If you need cash sooner, you might be able to withdraw money before, instead of "turning" on your income benefit. However, you need to understand the impact any withdrawals will have on the benefit values and future income payments.

Next, you need to know how withdrawals and income payments affect the account value and benefit values (living & death). In most annuities, both the account value and benefit values will be reduced by withdrawals. In most cases, the reduction will be on a dollar-for-dollar basis. In some cases – often when withdrawals exceed permitted contractual limits – withdrawals reduce benefit values on a pro-rata basis, which means benefit values are reduced by more than $1 for each $1 withdrawn. Cash is always reduced on a dollar-for-dollar basis.

Ultimately, over time, withdrawals and/or market declines might wipe out your cash value. In that case, some contracts enable you to annuitize the remaining living benefit value and "turn on" a lifetime income rider (living benefit) which obligates the insurance company to make guaranteed payments for as long as you live (and sometimes to your spouse, if married when you die).

Living benefits, with or without annuitization, protect you against longevity risk – outliving your money. You can only get the contractually agreed-to income payment amount – so you need to budget accordingly. In addition, if the markets enter a protracted period of declines or experience a sharp sudden decline (which typically happens every ten years), your income is protected – even if your account value is at risk. Accordingly, annuities protect cash flow from market declines.

The final point to remember: know what your options will be in the future. If you're offered a high up-front bonus to invest in a product, or the crediting rate or participation rate or cap rates are all high and attractive, *ask what the payout factors will be at different ages.*

If you create a really high living benefit value and multiply it by a low payout, you'll get lower guaranteed income payments than you would from a product with lower crediting rates, lower participation rates, and lower caps – but with a higher payout factor.

If $50,000 created a $100,000 benefit value in two different annuities, the higher payout factor wins:

Product:	Benefit Value:	Payout Factor:	Lifetime Payment
Annuity A	$100,000	3.00%	$3,000 per year
Annuity B	$100,000	4.50%	$4,500 per year

Even if annuity A offers a higher up-front bonus, higher participation rates, and higher caps, annuity B will likely provide more guaranteed lifetime income, because it provides a higher payout factor. The combination of all the details can have a material impact on your future financial well-being. Annuities are complex products. They can resolve concerns over longevity risk and market risk.

Without expert guidance, you can make costly mistakes in:

1. The selection of an annuity
2. The maximization of a currently owned annuity's benefits

Finally, beware the pitch to switch. By changing products, you can forfeit benefits, restart surrender periods, and increase fees – without adding any additional features or guaranteed benefits.

At www.investorprotector.com, we don't sell any products. We *do* provide complimentary information, analytics, and explanations of current, proposed, and alternative products:

ANNUITY INTELLIGENCE
REPORT

Contract Name Carrier	Series VA MetLife Investors USA Insurance Company	Premier Retirement B Series Pruco Life Insurance Company	Perspective II (7-year CDSC) Jackson National Life Insurance Company
Available Benefits			
Living Benefits			
GMIB	Optional	Not Available	Not Available
GMAB	Optional	Optional	Optional
GMWB	Optional	Not Available	Optional
Lifetime GMWB	Optional	Optional	Optional
Death Benefits			
Return of Principal	Standard	Standard	Standard
Highest Anniversary Value	Optional	Optional	Optional
Fixed Percentage Increase	Optional	Optional	Optional
Earnings Enhancement	Optional	Not Available	Optional
Contract Information			
Contract Type	B	B	B
Prospectus Date	5/1/2010	5/1/2010	10/11/2010
Supplemental Date	7/19/2010	n/a	n/a
Date Last Updated	7/27/2010	6/11/2010	10/19/2010
AM Best Rating	A+(as of 2/9/2010)	A+(as of 6/4/2010)	A+(as of 6/29/2010)
Website	www.metlifeinvestors.com	www.prudential.com	www.jackson.com
Phone Number	(888) 776-6710	(800) 513-0805	(800) 873-5654
Notes	Available in all states except GU, NY, PR & VI. Check with carrier for current state availability.	Available in all states	Available in all states except NY. Optional 2-5% bonus available on first year payments (subject to recapture). If the 5% bonus option is elected payments will not be accepted after the first year.
Surrender Schedule			
Years of CDSC's	7	7	7
Surrender Schedule	7,6,6,5,4,3,2	7,7,6,6,5,5,5	8½,7½,6½,5½,5,4,2"
Expenses & Fees			
Mortality & Expense Risk Charge	1.050%	1.150%	1.100%
Administration Charge	0.250%	0.150%	0.150%
Distribution Charge	-	-	-
Total Annual Expense	1.300%	1.300%	1.250%
Annual Policy Fee	$30	$50	$35
Annual Policy Fee Waived If Anniversary Value is Equal To Or Greater Than	$50000	$100000	$50000

Make sure you understand the terms and conditions of your contract benefits, so you don't lose them.

For a complimentary analysis, click, call, or chat:
www.investorprotector.com.

Fixed-Indexed & Equity-Indexed Annuities

THE PRODUCT:

An annuity is an insurance contract in which an insurance company makes payments to an annuitant for the term of the contract, usually until the annuitant dies. The insurance company guarantees both principal and interest. There are immediate annuities, which start payments right away, and there are deferred annuities, which credit interest for a period of time, until the product matures, the investor cashes out, or the investor annuitizes the contract. When an investor annuitizes a contract, they essentially "give" their money to the insurance company, in return for guaranteed payments. The decision to annuitize is irrevocable.

Fixed annuities provide tax-deferral and generally pay higher interest rates than treasuries and certificates of deposit. With fixed annuities, there's a stated interest rate, similar to a CD. Since interest rates have been so low and, since fixed annuities don't offer the upside potential of equities, the insurance Industry created fixed-indexed and equity-indexed annuities. With indexed annuities, the interest rate isn't fixed. Instead, it's linked to the performance of a stock market index, such as the S&P 500. If the market were to rise by 5%, the fixed-indexed and equity index annuity would convert the market return into an interest rate and pay 5% interest to the investor.

However, unlike equity investments, there's no risk to cash if the market declines when the index annuity is held to maturity. Alternatively, there are limits – called cap rates – to the maximum amount of "interest" an investor might receive in a rising market. For example, if an index annuity has a cap rate of 6% and the stock market is up by 20%, the investor will only receive 6%.

Another limit on the potential interest that can be earned is the participation rate. For example, if an index annuity has a participation rate of 50% and the stock market is up by 20%, the investor will only receive 10%.

Most index annuities have some combination of cap rates and participation rates that limit the "interest rate" an investor can receive. The trade-off, for this upside potential with no downside risk, is a limit to the upside via either caps, participation rates, or both. Remember, there's no risk to cash when held to maturity – and these are still technically supposed to be conservative fixed annuities.

In addition to a cash account with an indexed interest rate, index annuities generally offer a guaranteed minimum interest rate.

Many index annuities also offer living benefit riders such as variable annuities. At maturity, an investor can choose to take their cash value plus the interest. Alternatively, during the term of the contract, or at maturity, the investor can elect to receive lifetime income payments, based on the living benefit value.

Should the investor want to access his or her cash value, prior to maturity, or to take withdrawals greater than their lifetime income benefit payments, there may be substantial penalties, a significant reduction in benefits, and a loss of the principal protection guarantee.

Index Annuity Pros & Cons:

Pros	Cons
Principal is guaranteed	The guarantee is valid only when held to maturity
Guaranteed minimum interest rate	The guaranteed rate is usually very low
Equity indexing creates the opportunity to earn a potentially higher interest rate	The participation in the index return: • may be less than 100% • may be subject to a cap • may not include dividends, which can be

	a meaningful portion of the equity index return
No "up-front" fees/commission	Contracts may have: • high surrender charges of 10%, 15%, or more • long-term surrender periods of 10 or 15+ years • low participation rates • low caps All the above create fees for the insurer and commissions for the agent
Living benefits/Lifetime income	Withdrawals will: • use investor cash first • void the principal guarantee, if taken before maturity • reduce or eliminate the lifetime income benefit, if any annual or periodic withdrawal is too high
Interest crediting options	Equity-linked interest returns may be: • Point-to-point, from the start of a period to the end, which means a large decline at the end could wipe out all gains • Averaged over the period, which evens out gains and losses (may lead to lower returns) • Simple interest eliminates compounding and reduces total return • Credited at maturity, which eliminates compounding and may be forfeited, if the contract is surrendered early
Participation Rates give you equity upside	Most Participation Rates are less than 100%, and: • Participation rates can change • Don't get sucked in today with a high participation rate that can be lowered • Make sure there's a contractual minimum
Cap rates are in exchange for principal	Cap rates limit return:

protection	• Cap rates can change • Don't get sucked in today with a high Cap rate that can be lowered • Make sure there's a contractual minimum
Payout factors provide lifetime income	Know the payout factor: • A low payout factor can destroy the highest participation rates, best caps, etc.

Ultimately, a product that's marketed as providing principal protection (safety) with stock market upside (high potential returns) is bound to be misunderstood and abused.

THE PROBLEMS:

Fixed index annuities and equity indexed annuities refer to the same product, but neither is a fixed annuity. That's where the confusion begins.

The insurance Industry will inform you that a fixed index annuity is an insurance product and not a security. The securities Industry will inform you that an equity index annuity implies an equity investment – like a stock or bond – and, therefore, *is* a security.

You know a product must be confusing when the insurance Industry files a lawsuit against the Security and Exchange Commission, in a fight over who gets to regulate the product:

Coalition Sues SEC Over New Annuities Regulation
February 2009

A coalition of insurance companies and independent marketing organizations has filed suit in federal court to overturn Rule 151A, the newly published rule by the Securities and Exchange Commission that classifies indexed annuities as securities...

http://insurancenewsnetmagazine.com/article/coalition-sues-sec-over-new-annuities-regulation-1579

Not to be outdone by a loose confederation of sales organizations, the National Association of Insurance Commissioners (NAIC) and the National Conference of Insurance Legislators (NCOIL) also filed suit against the SEC to block Rule 151A.
http://insurancenewsnet.org/html/HealthInsurance/2009/0306/NAIC--NCOIL-Petition-to-block-SEC-indexed-annuity-rule.html

If the securities Industry and the insurance Industry can't determine what a product is and, therefore, who should regulate it – how much chance do investors have of understanding it?

Since indexed annuities offer principal protection with stock market upside, the attraction for investors is clear. Unfortunately, so is the confusion. Brokers and insurance agents tend to emphasize the benefits of these complex products without clearly explaining all the potential risks – such as high commissions, long surrender charges, a lack of liquidity, uncertain returns, and more. Consequently, FINRA issued an investor alert, to warn prospective investors about the complexity of index annuities.

Equity-Indexed Annuities—A Complex Choice

Why an Alert on Equity-Indexed Annuities?

Sales of **equity-indexed annuities (EIAs)** — also known as "fixed-indexed insurance products" and "indexed annuities"—have grown considerably in recent years. Although one insurance company at one time included the word "simple" in the name of its product, EIAs are anything but easy to understand. One of the most confusing features of an EIA is the method used to calculate the gain in the index to which the annuity is linked. To make matters worse, there is not one, but several different indexing methods. Because of the variety and complexity of the methods used to credit interest, investors will find it difficult to compare one EIA to another.

With the SEC engaged in a lawsuit filed by the insurance Industry, and with FINRA – the primary broker-dealer regulator – issuing guidance to brokers and providing alerts to investors, it's clear there are major concerns with index annuities.

Many of those concerns were elegantly summarized by an article in Reuters, titled: Beware the pitch for indexed annuities. The first paragraph explains the allure of the pitch:

> "Wouldn't it be nice to earn competitive returns without getting slammed by the stock market?"

With claims of principal protection, market participation, and lifetime income, it is easy to see why there have been record sales of indexed annuities. Yet, the article goes on to succinctly summarize the problems:

> "What brings out the critics is their view that any safety net these annuities may offer is vastly overshadowed by high costs and complex terms."

The article details the following problems that have led to multiple index annuity complaints:

> "—Hidden fees and commissions. Commissions typically run between 5 percent and 10 percent of the contract amount, but can sometimes be more. These and other expenses are taken out of returns, so it's hard for buyers to determine exactly how much they're paying.

> "—Complex formulas and changing terms. The formulas used to determine how much annuity owners earn are so complex that even sales people have a hard time understanding them, and they can change during the life of the contract.

> "—Limited access to funds. Buyers who try to cash out early will incur a surrender charge that typically starts at 10 percent and decreases gradually each year until it stops after a decade or more.

> "—Limited upside. An annuity's 'participation rate' specifies how much of the increase in the index is counted for index-linked interest. For example, if the change in the index is 8 percent, an annuity with a 70 percent participation rate could earn 5.6 percent. However, many annuities place upside caps on the index-linked

interest, which limits returns in strong bull markets. If the market rose 15 percent, for example, an annuity with a cap rate of 6 percent would only be credited with that amount."

Index Annuity Problems:
• Hidden fees & commissions
• Complex terms
• Limited access to cash (illiquid)
• Limited return
• High surrender charges
• Long surrender time frames

With a sales pitch like "you can't lose," or "it can make more money than just leaving it in the bank," or "your principal is guaranteed," or "you can invest in stocks without any risk," there has been a wave of fraudulent sales practices involving indexed-annuities.

In a recent case that "shocked" the Industry, an insurance agent was actually sentenced to jail for theft and embezzlement of an elder:

What's most shocking to me about the above case isn't that Neasham was criminally charged and sentenced to jail. What's shocking is that Neasham was able to commit the crime in the first place.

Every insurance agent undergoes licensing exams, general training, product-specific training, continuing education, senior suitability training, etc. Brokers and agents simply aren't that stupid. Some *are* just that greedy. Others are ignorant and arrogant and truly believe they know better than all the warnings, education, and training. In any event, there's an explicit obligation on the writing agent/broker to assess suitability and recommend an appropriate product.

Since a broker or agent who stands to make a huge commission might be conflicted in performing his or her explicit obligation to do the right thing for an investor, there *are* checks and balances. After the agent/broker "writes up the sale," the investor's application is supposed to be reviewed by the agent's/broker's supervisor, for approval. Clearly, Glenn Neasham's supervisor also failed in this job. I don't see any mention of consequences for the failure to properly and adequately supervise the agent/broker and transaction. This supervision is not a "loosy-goosy" process. There are very specific policies, procedures, rules, and regulations that are applied to ensure each transaction is suitable for the specific investor. There was a failure to properly supervisor Neasham.

In addition to the failure by Neasham's direct supervisor, there is an additional review by the insurance company that's the issuer of the product. In this case, the insurance company *also* failed to prevent a transaction with an 83-year-old.

On multiple levels, the Industry failed to protect this investor. Before an insurance product can be sold, the agent who wants to sell the product must first be insurance licensed in the state where the agent lives *and* where the client lives – if different. Next, the selling agent must be "appointed" with the insurance company. This means the agent must submit an application that asks questions about the agent's criminal, regulatory/Industry, and credit history. These applications are designed to provide the insurance company with considerable information about the agent's personal and professional background. Many agents are denied appointment with certain insurance companies because of derogatory information – i.e. bad credit, customer complaints, criminal convictions, etc.

I don't know if there was any derogatory information in Glenn Neasham's background. I *do* know:

1. He had to be insurance licensed to sell the product
2. He had to be appointed with the insurance company, whose product he sold
3. He was obligated to determine suitability before he sold the product

4. The transaction had to be reviewed and accepted by his agency or broker-dealer

5. The transaction had to be reviewed and accepted by the insurance company

The last two steps, above, are designed to prevent inappropriate, unsuitable, and fraudulent product sales. Once again, the system failed. Suitability and appropriateness are grey areas. They're subject to interpretation. When that interpretation is left in the hands of a self-regulatory system that polices its own, repeated failures occur.

That *is* the financial "Fix."

A few last words about Income Payments & Annuities:

Most annuities offer to provide lifetime income, with or without annuitization. If you annuitize and elect lifetime payments, you essentially give your money to the insurance company, in exchange for guaranteed payments. You surrender control over your money and wipe out any death benefit. Basically, the annuity company uses up your money first then uses its money if you live long enough. The good thing about annuitization is that payments can continue for as long as you live – even long after you would have depleted all your own money. If you die before all your money is used, the annuity company will return any remaining balance to your beneficiaries.

For additional information on income payments and annuities, please refer to the same content in the chapter about variable annuities.

THE PROTECTION:

If you have a very long time horizon before you need access to your funds, you have sufficient additional savings in other liquid accounts, you want to seek higher potential returns than you can get from a bank, you're willing to annuitize your money and give up control over your cash, and accept a guaranteed payment you can't outlive, then – and only then – might an index annuity make sense for some small portion (less than 30%) of your investable funds.

If anyone is pushing index annuities as your "best" solution, however – run like hell.

That said, before purchasing *any* insurance product, here are some ways to protect yourself:

1. Check that your agent is licensed in his or her home state, and in your state of residence.
2. Check if your agent is registered with an insurance agency and/or broker-dealer.
3. Ask the agent to present more than one product and explain the differences.
4. Get product illustrations, in writing, via mail, or via email.
   a. You shouldn't have to ask – an illustration is required.
5. Ask for a product prospectus
   a. For securities products, like a variable annuity, a prospectus delivery is required.
   b. For fixed and indexed annuities – there is no prospectus.
6. Read the illustrations and review the prospectus.
7. Here's some of what you're looking for and need to ask:
   a. What is the commission?
   b. Do the different products pay different commissions?
   c. What are the product fees, specifically the *total* annual cost of ownership?
   d. When can you access your money?
   e. Are there any fees or surrender charges to access your money?
   i. If so, how much and for how long do they apply?
   f. Are there limits on the amount of withdrawals you can take?
   g. How will withdrawals impact your account and benefit values?

    h. What is the participation rate?

        i. Can the participation rate change and is there a guaranteed minimum?

    i. What is the cap rate?

        i. Can the cap rate change and is there a guaranteed minimum?

8. What are the income options?

    a. Do you have to annuitize?

    b. Can you receive lifetime income without annuitization?

        i. If so, what are the payment options (single life, joint life, term with refund)?

        ii. Do these payments change as you get older or if you start them later?

9. Is there a death benefit?

    a. How do income payments affect the death benefit?

10. How do withdrawals affect the income and death benefit values?

If you have existing annuities and life insurance policies with cash value, at www.investorprotector.com you can get a complimentary audit. If you've ever been audited by the IRS, you might not have liked that process. This is different. We help you turn the tables: in essence, we enable *you* to audit your insurance company!

An audit will explain the features and benefits of your current product and provide independent and objective comparisons of your product's features, benefits, fees, and expenses – with alternatives. You'll receive confirmation and validation if your current product is good. You'll receive specific information that identifies opportunities to improve your current product, if possible.

If you're paying too much – you'll know.

If you could pay less and get more – you'll know.

If your product might or will have changes in costs or benefits – you'll know.

Most import, if what you own is doing what you want it to do at the right price – you'll know.

We do not and will not sell any product. We just provide analytics, information, and explanations.

Alternative Investments: Direct Participation Programs

Alternative investments is a broadly defined category that generally includes: Real Estate investment trusts ("REITs"), limited partnerships (private placements), hedge funds, and others products. In general, an Alternative Investment is a category that includes investments other than Stocks, Bonds, Options, Cash, Mutual Funds, ETFs, Annuities, Insurance, etc.

> **While there are publicly traded alternative investments, the securities to be most careful of are those that do not trade publicly. Since there's no public market for these, there's limited liquidity to buy or sell and there's no real-time price established by transactions between buyers and sellers.**

In simple terms, without a public market, you can't easily sell. Without trading volume, you won't know what price you'll receive if and when you do decide to sell. Without liquidity or publicly determined prices, it's amazing these investments are popular at all.

Yet – they are surprisingly popular...especially following a decade of negative equity returns and declining interest rates. For the ten-year period ending in Feb. 2009, the stock market, as represented by the S&P 500, delivered the second lowest average annual returns in the past century: -3.43%.[16]

---

[16] http://www.quantmonitor.com/the-bigger-picture-sp-500-rolling-10-year-annual-returns/

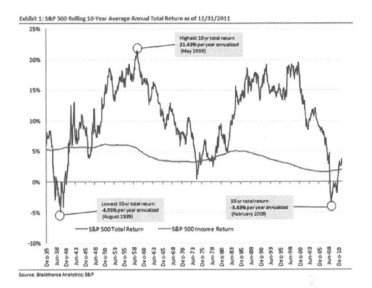

Exhibit 1: S&P 500 Rolling 10-Year Average Annual Total Return as of 12/31/2011

Source: Blackhorse Analytics; S&P

After adjusting for inflation, it actually was the worst decade on record, in terms of "real" return. Investors lost about -5.86%, on average, per year – for the ten years ending Feb. 2009. For recent investors, the 2000's were a truly a "lost decade."

Simultaneously, since the hyperinflation of the late 1970's and early 1980's, bond yields have been on a steady decline, to today's record low yields.

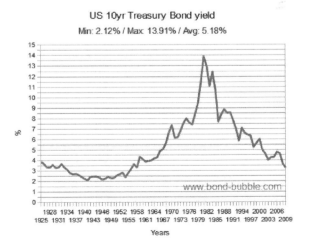

US 10yr Treasury Bond yield
Min: 2.12% / Max 13.91% / Avg: 5.18%

Years

After a decade of losing money in the stock market, and after a decade of trying to reinvest maturing certificates of deposits into ever-lower yields, investors needed – and even demanded – better alternatives. The Industry was only too happy to oblige.

In Part 1, I covered the Provident Shale Ponzi Scheme debacle. This was an oil and gas private placement that was sold as an alternative investment program. It promised investors an 18% rate of return for investing in dirt. The fracking mania sparked resurgence in US oil and gas exploration and Provident played into this hype. With hype that implied credibility, and with a ridiculously high yield, thousands of investors were lured into Provident's scam.

Provident was *not* an alternative investment. It was a fraudulent criminal Ponzi scheme that *masqueraded* as an alternative investment. Provident used the alternative investment structure and asset class and – along with other fraudsters – it poisoned the entire well of alternative investments.

There *are* reputable firms with excellent products in the alternative investment universe. There are benefits to non-publicly traded investments: one being that they're not directly correlated with the volatility of the stock market.

In addition, the abuses by fraudsters like Provident and others created greater scrutiny on the space. With more scrutiny, came increased transparency. However, the alternative investment space remains highly risky.

When markets heat up, there's a rush to create investments in the "hot" spot. When markets are bad, there's a rush to create "alternatives" to poor-performing investments. With a name like alternative investments, you have a catch-all category for the Industry's product manufacturers. These are often untested structures, untested products, and untested markets.

Nonetheless, despite a stock market gain of over 32% for the S&P 500 in 2013, record amounts of investor money still flowed into alternative investments by investors seeking yield:

The Leading News Source for Financial Advisers

Sales of nontraded REITS, other illiquid investments surge amid hunt for yield
Industry shakes off unflattering headlines of 2011, 2012 to set sales record
By **Bruce Kelly**
Jul 31, 2013 @ 2:54 pm (Updated 5:37 pm) EST

Sales of nontraded real estate investment trusts and other illiquid securities known as "direct-participation programs" are roaring, according to the Investment Program Association, a trade group, and Robert A. Stanger & Co. Inc., an investment bank.

Equity capital flows to such illiquid securities, including nontraded REITs and nontraded business development companies, hit record levels in the first half of the year, totaling more than $10.7 billion, the highest half-year total for the industry. That's an increase of 65% compared with the year-earlier period.

Sales of nonlisted securities continued their heady pace in July, topping $2.5 billion vs. $947 million for the same month in 2012, according to the IPA and Stanger

The direct-participation industry typically sells $10 billion to $11 billion in products a year, almost exclusively through independent broker-dealers. That makes this year's tabulation of sale over the first six months of 2012 that more startling.

Stanger credits a significant part of the increase in fundraising to "recycling" of funds received from investors from other REITs that have had "liquidity events", such as selling portfolios or listing on an exchange.

About $3.6 billion of such liquidity event occurred in the second half of last year, and the pace accelerating to a staggering $11 billion in liquidity events this year, according Stanger.

The boom in sales in nontraded REITs comes after a series of unflattering headlines in 2011 and 2012 that highlighted REITs' struggles after the credit crisis. Some of the largest REITs have suffered sharp devaluations, wiping out billions of dollars in shareholder equity, and regulators have began a series of investigations in broker-dealers' sales practices regarding the products.

Nontraded REITs raised more than $8.5 billion in the first half of the year, while sales of nonlisted BDCs topped $2 billion.

And while investors have been pouring cash into these illiquid programs, that cash has been focused largely on two firms. According to Stanger, two broker-dealer managers, Realty Capital Securities LLC, an affiliate of American Realty Capital, and FS Capital Partners LLC raised more than half the equity capital in the industry. Through the end of June, Realty Capital Securities, which primarily distributes REITs, raised close to $4.5 billion, while FS Capital, which distributes BDCs, raised $1.3 billion.

"Investors in today's yield-starved environment are eager for sources of above-average income and for the portfolio diversification provided by investments in hard assets and smaller companies," Kevin Hogan, chief executive of the IPA, said in a statement. "These external concerns will continue to underpin investment in the second half of 2013."

88

Investors, in the pursuit of income, basically poured record amounts of money into REITs and other alternative investments. Yet – the irony is that most of the investments featured in the above story actually don't even pay *any* yield. They provide a distribution rate that looks like "yield," but isn't.

For investors considering non-traded alternative investments, the best advice is: buyer beware!

THE PROBLEMS:

Alternative investments carry alternative risks and alternative returns that, like a great magic trick, will be revealed only at the end.

Private placements, in particular, are where major losses occur with troubling regularity. In general, firms that raise money via private placements can't raise funds from more traditional sources. These are start-up businesses. These are *risky* ventures.

That said – there is no return without risk. Some investors are willing to take more risk, in exchange for higher potential returns. Losses due to highly speculative investments, while never fun, might be acceptable. Losses due to fraud are *never* acceptable. When a product pays a very high commission to brokers, the Industry's tendency to sell first and ask questions later can be problematic.

Fraudulent private placements, like Medical Capital and Provident Royalties, masqueraded as alternative investments. Investors were victimized; individual brokers' careers were ruined; entire brokerage firms were destroyed. With the benefit of hindsight, it's easy to see today the due diligence failures that occurred in the past. Yet, at the time the investments were offered to investors, the Industry's regulators, brokerage firms, and brokers *all* missed the warning signs.

While investors bore the greatest consequence of funds lost, and while some brokerage firms closed their doors, most brokers simply moved to new firms and continued to sell new products.

As for *real* accountability, both Medical Capital and Provident Royalties were registered securities. Two of the biggest fraudulent criminal enterprises that destroyed investors and gave the Industry two black eyes submitted documents and registration statements to the SEC. These "securities" were registered with federal and state regulators. While investors became victims and brokerage firms took the blame, there has yet to be *any* accountability with any of the Industry regulators that allowed these securities to be registered for sale in the first place!

> **Unfortunately, for many alternative investments, the traditional checks and balances that can potentially detect and prevent fraud are lacking. Specifically, the lack of a public marketplace where buyers and sellers can readily transact is a problem.**

First, without a marketplace, there is no liquidity. Investors must be able to afford to invest funds knowing they won't have access to the money. If there's an emergency or change in life circumstances, the investment can't be sold.

Second, without many transactions, there is no market to establish current prices. Without current prices, an alternative method must be used to value the investment. There are layers to the valuation issue. While there may be a process to value an illiquid investment, it's not the same as having a market-determined price.

For example, consider a real estate investment trust that owns multiple large properties with multiple tenants per property. The cash flows from all the tenants will be a factor in determining the value of the property. The real estate market, in general, and recent sales of comparable properties, will also be a factor in determining the value of the property.

The property can be valued based on its cash flow and market appraisal – but that's not the same as a price. Quite simply, a price is established only when an agreement is reached between what a buyer is willing to pay and what a seller is willing to accept. For illiquid investments that can't be readily sold, you can create a value – but that's *not* the same as determining a price.

Finally, private placements require a non-traditional custodian to "hold" the investment. Many banks, trust companies, brokerage firms, and custodians (Schwab, Fidelity, TD Ameritrade, etc.) may not hold a non-registered or even a registered security that doesn't trade publicly. When a firm "holds" a security, the security can be deposited into an investor's account. This means a custodian can prepare regular statements with a value for the security.

> **For an alternative investment and/or private placement, if a well-known traditional custodian won't hold the investment, don't write a check. In fact, the odds are you should run like hell.**

So – for your average retail investor, buying an illiquid investment is inherently speculative. Along with the lack of liquidity, the investor often has to accept an arbitrary purchase price, limited visibility as to the use of funds, and an alternative method to value the investment.

Additional suitability concerns for alternative investments include:

Cash Flow Risk. When a certificate of deposit or a bond pays a yield, it's based on an interest rate the investment disclosed and agreed to pay the investor. A bond that pays 5% would return $50 per $1,000 invested. The CD or bond has a maturity date at which time principal will be returned. Until that date, the investor will receive interest payments.

With most alternative investments, there's no interest rate. There's no yield. Instead, there's a distribution rate – generally around 5% to 8%. If an alternative investment has a stated distribution rate of 7%, the investor will get $70 per $1,000.

However, a distribution isn't an interest payment. It's made from the earnings, or operations, of the investment, or by borrowing funds to make a payment – if cash flow is insufficient – or by returning the investor's own money, or by selling more shares to new investors and using those proceeds to repay old investors. With a distribution rate of 7%, it's entirely possible the investor is receiving back their own money or someone else's money.

> In effect, a distribution can be a return *of* funds and not necessarily a return *on* funds. In fact, distributions are not guaranteed and may exceed operating cash flows. If a REIT can't continue to make distributions, distribution payments may be reduced or stopped altogether. At that time, an income-oriented investor might own an illiquid investment they can't sell, which no longer even provides any "income."

No Maturity Date. Unlike most fixed income investments, such as bonds or CDs which have a maturity date, alternative investments have *no* maturity date. The risk for investors is materially different and significantly higher in alternative investments than it is in bonds or CDs. With a CD or a bond, an investor knows when the investment will mature. The investor has a known pre-determined date when they'll receive their principal back. Even if markets change, a traditional fixed income investment will return principal on its maturity.

With an alternative investment, since there's no maturity date, there's no way to know when or if the original investment will be returned. It's only after an alternative investment has a liquidity event – meaning a sale or public listing – that an investor will actually receive back some or all of his or her investment.

Unknown Return. Since the timing of a liquidity event is never known in advance, and since there's no yield, there is, in fact, no way to know the actual return of any alternative investment – at the time you invest. It's all speculation. What isn't speculation are the very high commissions these investments pay to the brokers. They also pay very high fees to the issuers. So – while brokers get paid and issuers get paid, investors have no idea if they'll get paid or what their investment will return.

Upon a liquidity event, the investor can take the sale price plus the amount of distributions they received and, with some complex formulas, figure out their total return. If, at the liquidity event, the investor receives back more than he or she invested, then all the distributions received prior to the sale add to a positive total return. If the investor receives back less than was invested, the distributions are added back, and then the investor will know if he or she actually earned any profit.

Transparency. Many alternative investments are structured as "blind pools" where money is raised to be used in a manner specified by an offering document/prospectus. For example, a REIT may raise money to go out and buy net lease commercial real estate. Unfortunately, the investor may not be able to actually *see* all the investments their funds are used to acquire. There's even *less* visibility into the cash flows and operations of each investment within their blind pool.

Valuation. For non-traded alternative investments, the Industry recently passed rules requiring investments to be independently valued after 18 months. If a REIT were buying residential apartment building complexes, factors such as occupancy, rental rates, and the sale of comparable properties all impact the value of each investment. Since valuation is inherently subjective, the best an investor can hope for is a fairly close estimate of what their investment *might* be worth – *if* the blind pool were to try to sell it around the time of the most recent valuation.

With principal risk, cash flow risk, no maturity date, unknown returns, a lack of transparency, and valuation issues, the alternative investment

Industry has been plagued by misunderstandings, omissions, and misrepresentations:

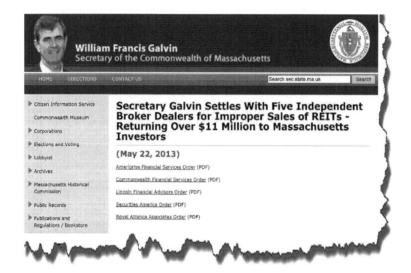

According to an article in The Boston Globe:

> "Our investigation into the sales of REITs, triggered by investor complaints, showed a pattern of impropriety in the sales of these popular but risky investments on the part of independent brokerage firms where supervision has historically been difficult to maintain," Galvin said in a statement.

THE PROTECTION:

First, alternative investments are *not* for every investor. In fact, for most, these should be limited to a very small allocation – if any.

Therein lies the first problem. When you allocate a small amount to a specific type of investment, most investors make a common mistake: they fail to diversify. Whether the investment is in stocks, private placements, or alternative investments, diversification is key. Betting too much money on any one investment is simply too risky for most investors.

For investors who decide to take the plunge into the alternative investment pool, the first order of business is to allocate a small percentage of total liquid investments that won't be needed for a long while. Invest in a broadly diversified number and type of alternatives – i.e. REITs, managed futures, currencies, commodities, oil and gas, etc. Invest in multiple deals across multiple categories.

Since REITs have been the most allocated to alternative investment lately, I'll spend some additional time on an asset class that, in my opinion, is in the middle of a dangerous level of market hype. There are essentially three types of REIT alternative investments:

1. Publicly registered, publicly traded
2. Publicly registered, non-traded
3. Non-registered, non-traded

Non-registered, non-traded:

- **Just say "No!"** Starting with #3, if a security isn't registered, it's generally not subject to the disclosure requirements of a registered security. Given all the issues specific to alternative investments, i.e. liquidity, principal risk, uncertain valuation, and so on, the lack of all required disclosure should, in my opinion, rule out non-registered securities, when comparable registered securities are available.

Registered: Traded vs. Non-traded

- **Liquidity.** For publicly registered securities, there are traded versus non-traded securities. The difference is liquidity. Publicly traded securities can be bought and sold on an exchange. Investors can look at trading volume and market prices to determine whether to buy or sell, like any traditional investment. Non-traded securities can't be easily bought; they're even more difficult to sell.
  - o To manage liquidity risk, investors need to:

- Limit their investment to a small amount of funds that won't be needed for any reason for at least five to seven years.
- Invest in several different types of REITs (commercial, residential, professional) that are geographically diversified
- Invest in multiple deals over multiple years, to minimize the impact of market cycles

- **Due Diligence.** In general, for any investment, don't invest in new products from new companies when investments already exist from established companies. For public or non-traded investments, there should be audited financials, performance histories, and disclosures regarding the professional background of key management. This process is intended to discourage fraudsters.

- **Custody.** Unless your payment is made to a well-known institution, and unless your investment can be deposited and held in a brokerage, bank, or trust account at a major institution, don't make the investment.

> **90%+ of fraud can be detected by reviewing the offering documents and checking out the custodian. At www.investorprotector.com, you can connect virtually *any* account and protect your investments with independent risk monitoring and automated change alerts. If you can't connect an account at www.investorprotector.com, there may be issues with the custodian or institution that need to be immediately resolved.**

- **Fees.** Non-traded REITs can have up-front fees of up to 15%. If the maximum fee were charged, only $0.85 of every invested $1.00 would be available to invest. Most often, the sales compensation to the broker is about 10%. The fees are detailed in a prospectus. Public REITs are also sold by prospectus at their initial public offering, but commissions are generally limited to 7%. Thereafter, public REITs are bought and sold on an exchange with a brokerage commission or transaction fee.

o   To minimize fees, investors should:

- Carefully review the prospectus to understand all fees – i.e. up-front, annual recurring charges, deferred fees, etc.

- Ask if there are commission discounts or commission waivers for purchases in fee-based accounts.

- **Returns.** Publicly traded REITs will pay dividends and, since the shares trade, provide price appreciation or depreciation. Total return will be realized from price changes and dividend yield. Non-traded REITs will pay distribution rates. These distribution rates aren't yields. They're cash flows from operations. If a REIT doesn't generate enough cash flows to pay distributions, it can lower or suspend them. If a REIT is non-traded and it suspends distributions, the investor can't sell and redeploy proceeds to an income-producing asset. The investment and the income are tied up until conditions change. With a publicly traded REIT, the investor can sell – although there will likely be a considerable loss in value.

o   To protect returns, investors should:

- Review and understand cash flows from operations (FFO), which indicate the percentage of distributions that are covered from operations. For example, if a REIT's FFO is 50% and the REIT is paying a distribution of 6%, then only 3% of the 6% is covered from operations. The remaining 3% must be covered by borrowing or by raising additional capital from new investors.

- Invest as late as possible in a non-public offering. At the start of every new offering, the investment must raise enough money before cash can be deployed to purchase a property. That will mean there are no income-producing properties on day one. This means the investor's funds (less all the commissions and operating fees) are sitting idle. Toward the end of an offering period, an investor can see the properties that have been purchased and get the FFO, so the investor knows if cash is being deployed properly for good returns. Also, investing towards the end means the investor could be closer to a potential liquidity event.

- **Valuation.** Since a non-traded REIT creates its own offering price, and since this initial offering price can remain unchanged for long periods of time – i.e. years – FINRA has proposed new rules to create greater pricing transparency.

    o To monitor the value of their investment, investors need to know:

      ▪ how their REIT is valued, and

      ▪ how often the REIT is priced

InvestmentNews
The Leading Information Source for Financial Advisers

What's a REIT worth? Finra revamps rules

Rules revised on way illiquid investments are reported

By Bruce Kelly
Apr 28, 2013 @ 12:01 am (Updated 10:09 am) EST

Finra's board of governors has put in motion a plan that has the potential to drastically change how broker-dealers report the value of illiquid investments such as nontraded real estate investment trusts on client account statements.

- -

Most nontraded REITs are sold at $10 per share and remain at that value on a client's account statement until 18 months after the REIT has stopped raising money — as required by Finra. That means that three, five or perhaps even seven years can pass before a client sees a valuation for a nontraded REIT other than $10 per share. REITs that raise money through an initial offering and then follow-on offerings have been called "zombie REITS" by some in the industry.

- -

The issue of how a nontraded REIT should be valued, and the obligation of a broker-dealer to note that valuation on clients' account statements, has been a contentious one in the years since the credit crisis. That's when some of the largest nontraded REITs suffered sharp declines in valuations quarter after quarter, after years of reporting a value of $10 per share, leaving investors and advisers struggling to understand how, why and to what degree the declines occurred.

Copyright, 2013, Crain Communications Inc. Republished under license.
http://www.investmentnews.com/article/20130428/REG/304289979

What to Do; How to Do It

When it comes to investing, many investors don't know where to start, what to do, or how to do "it." While most investors know they need to save and invest, most don't know about all the different products and services that are available, nor do they know all the financial strategies, solutions, planning techniques, and other considerations going in. So here, in my opinion, are three of the most important keys to successful long term investing:

1. **Don't Lose**

   "The first rule of investing is don't lose money; the second rule is don't forget Rule No. 1."
   —Warren Buffet, who has amassed more than $52 billion over half a century.

2. **Pay Less**

   "In investing, you get what you don't pay for."
   —John Bogle, who founded Vanguard. With $2 trillion under management, Vanguard is the world's largest mutual fund company with fund expenses that are 83% lower than the Industry average.

3. **Do More**

   "An investment in knowledge pays the best interest."
   —Benjamin Franklin, one of the Founding Fathers of the United States. A noted polymath, Franklin was a leading author, printer, political theorist, politician, postmaster, scientist, musician, inventor, satirist, civic activist, statesman, and diplomat.

Whether you work with a financial advisor or direct your own investments, there's so much information, so many investments and products, such an abundance of services and a wide range of strategies, and such a variety of solutions for investment, financial, insurance, legal, and tax issues, it simply pays to learn a little about your options.

It is also of critical importance to understand the basic differences between Saving, Investing, and Speculating.

Saving is a cash flow and budgeting exercise. Money you save should be in the bank.

Investing is when you deliberately and knowingly take some degree of risk for some expected return. In general, you can lend (buy bonds) or invest (buy stocks). You should be able to buy traditional investments without the fear of fraud or excessive commissions or fees.

Speculating is investing for higher returns with a higher degree of risk. When speculating, there is a very real possibility that you could lose most if not all of your investment. When speculating, you are betting primarily on price changes. These price changes can be uncertain, sudden, and unknown in magnitude.

So first things first: you have to accumulate some savings in order to start investing. That means you need a budget and a savings plan. At www.investorprotector.com, you can sign up for a free trial and create and manage a budget. Once you organize your finances, you can gain better control over your spending habits and start to maximize your ability to save.

If you have accumulated some savings, you may find better strategies to help save more via pre-tax contributions and/or tax deferral.

After budgeting and some basic planning, you may have funds to invest. The Internet has helped distribute information, tools, and services directly to investors, providing a virtually endless supply of self-help resources. There are a myriad of sites, blogs, and online calculators. What remains missing is a resource to help an investor navigate the overwhelming volume of information on markets, investments, products, strategies, and more. An investor often has to trust a financial advisor, some other source of information, or themselves.

When times are good, things tend to work out. When times are bad, nothing seems to work. Considering the regularity with which financial crises occur, it's likely that investors will experience at least one major market meltdown every decade.

Consequently, most investors – even those who prefer to do it themselves – at some time turn to a "financial professional," or to a professionally-guided solution that can help determine what products, services, and strategies are appropriate. Over a lifetime, it's highly likely most investors will use multiple advisors for different solutions.

The challenge is that the investor ultimately has to know:

1. what to do: which products, services, and/or strategies are necessary and appropriate
2. who to trust: which advisor will provide honest and accurate information (just like all advisors aren't perfect, neither are blogs)
3. how much to pay: what amount is a fair and reasonable commission/fee for services

Most brokers, advisors, financial planners, and insurance agents who work full-time in the Industry have some specialty or area of focus/expertise. Some are generalists. None has all the knowledge about all products, services, investments, financial strategies, tax implications, legal aspects, and more. It's just not possible for any one "financial professional" or for an individual investor to know everything about all products. There is simply an overwhelming amount of information about products, strategies, and investment choices. A little help can be enormously beneficial. A small mistake can be very costly.

In my experience, the biggest difference between professional versus do-it-yourself investing is whether the investor has a plan that considers both investment and financial (insurance, legal, and tax) issues. Having a comprehensive plan and pursuing a planned outcome separates the novice from the expert – whether the investment management is professional or do-it-yourself.

The simple answer to knowing what to do and how to do it is to have a plan, save early, and invest often. Those investors with a plan, who start saving early, who invest regularly, who enjoy the wonderful effects of compounding returns over time, simply accumulate more.

So – who can you trust to help you?

The Industry has created a bewildering array of providers and professional designations. In short, there are:

- Brokers (registered representatives), to execute transactions.
- Investment advisors, to manage your wealth on an ongoing basis.
- Insurance agents, to sell life, health, disability, and long-term care insurance.
- Planners, to review your financial picture, providing investment, insurance, and tax guidance.

Brokers, investment advisors, insurance agents, and financial planners aren't all created equally. At this time, there are over 130 different professional designations. Below are descriptions of some of the more common professional designations:

- **Registered Representative** – also called a general securities representative, a stockbroker, or an account executive, is an individual who is licensed to sell stocks, bonds, options, mutual funds, limited partnership programs, and variable annuities. Registered representatives usually work for broker/dealers licensed by the U.S. Securities and Exchange Commission (SEC) and the Self Regulatory Organizations (SRO) of the New York Stock

Exchange (NYSE) and/or Financial Industry Regulatory Authority (FINRA). To become a registered representative, one must be sponsored by a broker/dealer firm and pass the FINRA-administered Series 7 examination (known as the General Securities Representative Exam) or another Limited Representative Qualifications Exam. Some state laws and broker/dealer policies also require the Series 63 examination (known as the Uniform Securities Agent State Law Exam).

- **Registered Investment Adviser (RIA)** – is an investment adviser (IA) registered with the Securities and Exchange Commission or a state's securities agency. An IA is defined by the Securities and Exchange Commission as an individual or a firm in the business of giving advice about securities. Individuals or firms that receive compensation for giving advice on investing in securities such as stocks, bonds, mutual funds, or exchange traded funds are deemed to be investment advisers. It's also common for investment advisers to manage portfolios of securities. RIAs generally are paid in any of the following ways: a percentage of the value of the assets they manage for clients, an hourly fee, or a fixed fee.

- **CFP (Certified Financial Planner)** – a financial planner who has met the required experience and educational specifications of the Certified Financial Planner Board of Standards. Certified Financial Planners have also sworn to abide by the organization's specified codes of ethics. They've also passed a national test which is administered by the CFP Board of Standards.

- **An insurance agent** – sells, solicits, or negotiates insurance for compensation. In the United States, insurance agents are regulated by the individual states. Most states require anyone who sells, solicits, or negotiates insurance to any investor in the state to obtain an insurance agent license, with certain limited exceptions. In order to obtain an insurance license, a person typically must take pre-licensing courses and pass an examination.

An insurance agent also must submit an application (with an application fee) to the state insurance regulator in the state in which the applicant wishes to do business. The regulator determines whether the insurance agent has met all the state requirements and will also typically do a background check, to determine whether the applicant is considered trustworthy and competent.

Unfortunately, many investors fail to take action that's both necessary and beneficial. While a lack of trust or the "fear of fee" is bad, inaction is worse. There's a saying that "investors don't plan to fail; they fail to plan."

So – here's a plan to help plan your plan:

1. Use a fee-only planner to develop a plan or to check your own plan.

   a. A fee-only planner should eliminate the fear of commissions.

   b. For a small planning fee, most investors can overcome their fear of fees.

   c. The long-term value of a good plan will help make any investor understand the expression "penny-wise is pound foolish."

   d. Even do-it-yourself investors can benefit by learning what they don't know or by checking what they're doing.

   e. Don't make the mistake of sacrificing long-term results, just to eliminate a commission or one-time planning fee.

2. Any account (mutual fund, brokerage, advisory, discount) must be reviewed regularly for:

   a. Fees

      i. don't pay too much, but

      ii. don't sacrifice performance or protection just to avoid a fee

   b. Performance

    i. every account must achieve reasonable performance benchmarks – including self-directed accounts (doing it yourself means being honest with yourself, too!)

3. Use the right tool for the job:

    a. Use a Certified Financial Planner to develop an overall plan that considers:

        i. Investments

        ii. Insurance

        iii. Tax/Accounting

        iv. Legal/Structural Issues

    b. Use mutual funds or ETFs for small accounts.

    c. Use a discount broker, if you know what to buy or sell and when to buy and sell it.

    d. Use a traditional broker (commission-based) for bonds and or opportunistic growth investments: IPOs, syndicate, etc.

    e. Use a fee-based advisor to manage assets on an ongoing basis without commission concerns.

    f. Use an insurance agent for life, health, disability, long-term care, and annuities.

4. Research your planner's/broker's/advisor's/agent's credentials, and their firm's history.

5. Get references.

6. Start small.

7. Trust a little; verify often.

Working With a "Financial Professional"; Spotting a "Financial Predator"

Investors should work with someone they trust, subject to the following:

1. *Always* get a second opinion – *before* making any major investments, and

2. *Periodically* take advantage of offers for complimentary reviews, to *independently* check:

   a. financial strategy

   b. asset allocation

   c. investment selection/quality,

   d. account performance

In my opinion, the above two rules can solve 90%+ of most investor's problems.

Figuring out whom to trust can be difficult. There are many ways to look up your financial professional's credentials and background. Just beware that, in my experience, in virtually every situation in which investors became victims, the "financial predator" was a reputable, well-respected member of the community. Often, there was an affiliation with a political, religious, or charitable organization that implied credibility. There were even references and testimonials from credible sources. There may have been warning signs, but predators are masters of deception; they are experts at overcoming distrust.

In most situations, the financial predator conducts several meetings and even provides legitimate services to the investor. Then, after confidence and trust are established, the financial predator attacks.

They offer a "special" investment. They have a "personal" or "private" or "unique" investment opportunity. It might be exclusive or only available for a short time. It has little risk, but considerably more return than other traditional investment options.

The investment might not be from a well-known company or firm, so the predator suggests making a small investment – just to get a feel for this new opportunity. The predator usually states that the investment is going to close soon (or will be filled up by other investors) and may not even be available later. With that, the investor gets hooked.

The instructions to fund the "special investment" are usually different than other investments. Instead of wiring funds or depositing a check to a major well-known institution, the fraudster requests that the investor make out a check or wire funds payable to a company or some business entity. Unless the business entity is a financial institution, the scam is almost complete. If the check is written or the funds are wired, the investor has likely become a victim. It's simply a matter of time.

Unfortunately, over time, an investor can get lulled into a false sense of safety and security. They gradually increase the amount entrusted to the financial predator. It all works fine – until it doesn't. When an interest payment is late or missed, the collapse soon occurs – with sudden and traumatic effect.

In most cases, the investment is simply gone. There's little hope of any meaningful recovery.

Rogue brokers and financial fraud are hard to spot. Fortunately, there *are* clear warning signs. Unfortunately, many investors don't see the signs – in some instances, they don't *want* too.

> **Investors who want protection need to seek objective second opinions – *before* making any new or large investments.**

> **On an ongoing basis, persistent vigilance can help detect and possibly prevent fraud.**

Other than outright financial fraud, market corrections, or just bad investments, the greatest source of avoidable loss is from excessive fees, commissions, and taxes. Each and every year, fees, commissions, and taxes create a significant drag on return. In fact, even positive returns can be reduced to losses by fees, commissions, and taxes.

To minimize losses to commissions and fees, Investors need to ask questions and request that their broker or advisor openly discuss and clearly explain *all* costs for *any* investment products and ongoing services. It's up to the broker or advisor to clearly and accurately explain their compensation. It's up to the investor to pay what they believe is reasonable. Which raises the question: what *is* reasonable?

Brokers charge commissions and advisors charge fees.

Brokers get paid per transaction. They are incentivized to present new products and to recommend buying and selling investments. The commissions can add up over time. At no point should any commission be more than 5%. In fact, for most transactions in publicly traded securities, the commission per transaction should not be more than 1%. With multiple discount brokers charging less than $10 per trade, a full service broker better make good recommendations in order to earn the right to charge a higher commission. My apologies to my former broker friends! Keep in mind – a commission *can* be negotiated. There is *no* set rate.

Advisors get paid for assets under management. They are incentivized to manage your account and service your relationship over time. They need many clients and/or a lot of assets under management, to generate sufficient income to pay themselves, rent, staff, etc. However, with a fee-based advisor, you don't have to worry about a sales pitch or a bill for each call. The incentive to trade for commission has been removed. In general, if the advisor is managing your account in stocks, bonds, or ETFs, a reasonable fee should not be more than 2% of the assets under management. Frequently, the annual advisory fee is closer to 1% and there are discount advisory Websites that charge even less. Remember, if you use an advisor who places funds into mutual funds or uses separate money managers, there will be additional fees. For mutual funds and money managers, the additional fees could be 1% to 2% or more per year.

Recently, there has been a wave of new Web-based advisors who use "technology" to manage your assets for a very low fee of around 0.25%. These services may turn out to be quite good, but they're early in their life cycle and they are mass marketed, so the customization of "your" portfolio may be limited. In reality, you'll likely answer an online questionnaire that will be scored and mapped to a model portfolio. You're paying a low fee for a mass market delivery of services. Don't expect too much personalization. That said – the online questionnaire may be no different than what you answer in an advisor's office. The difference is comfort, personalization, results, and service.

If you're not comfortable and you don't trust your broker/advisor, the relationship is doomed. Keep looking for another broker/advisor.

If your broker/advisor doesn't listen to your needs and doesn't design a customized plan for your specific goals, there should be no expectation of success.

If your broker/advisor doesn't deliver measurable results over a reasonable period of time, as in performance that is in accordance with your plan's benchmarks and in reasonable alignment with markets in general, he or she should be fired. Track your performance quarterly. If your broker/advisor's performance varies significantly (5% or more) from their stated benchmark, there may be a problem. Also, never chase performance. History shows us that the "best" performing manager of today may very well be the worst performer tomorrow.

Slow and steady generally wins the asset management race.

Lastly – over time – circumstances change. You want a broker/advisor that has a team that can help guide you in response to both market *and* life events. This is your money. This is your financial future. Providing reassurance when you need it and keeping you on track is part of the job. Saying "yes" to the car and "no" to the boat is also part of the job.

So is helping you through marriage, children, education, divorce, life in general – and even death, at the end. All are responsibilities and obligations for your broker/advisor. If you re-read the first sentence of this paragraph and don't think your current financial professional can handle any of those life events, it might be time to search out a team that can and will.

Serving your financial well-being while you're alive and caring for your survivors in accordance with your wishes are the most important parts of any financial professional's job. Trust is built over time. Most important, it takes clear communication. On your part, too.

Make sure **you** take the time to help your broker/advisor get the right plan for **your** goals and objectives.

For investors, the bottom line in choosing a broker/advisor is actually very simple: it comes down to preference. Some investors have a preference for fees, or against commissions, or vice versa. There's nothing inherently wrong with commissions or fees. Commissions or fees are not evil. For good recommendation and value-added services, commissions and/or fees can be well-earned and deserved.

Not all brokers are rogue brokers. A broker or advisor who does the right thing deserves to get paid. For recommending a good product or for providing good service, the client should be willing to pay a reasonable fee.

Pay it up front or over time – but don't get too hung up on whether the compensation is in the form of a commission or a fee. Some general suggestions: for an individual transaction, pay a commission; for ongoing active management, pay a fee. Get good advice and service and pay for it. Nothing is free.

While the form of compensation (commissions or fees) may impact an investor's decision of whether to work with a broker or advisor, it should not dictate the investment solution(s) offered to an investor. An investor's goals and objectives make an investment suitable or not – not the form of compensation.

Investors must be aware that their compensation preference might have consequences on the products and services provided to them. A fee-only advisor might not recommend a variable annuity or stock transaction because of their "fee-only" bias. A broker might not recommend an insurance or bank product, if they can't get paid for their recommendation.

Lastly, the rise of do-it-yourself investing and the availability of information, products, and services over the Internet is a great thing. Yet, too much self-reliance can be dangerous. An investor's total financial well-being over a lifetime will involve investments, insurance, legal, and tax matters. Financial planning integrates all these components. Just as you use a general medical practitioner for general health checkups, but use a specialist as required, treat your financial well-being with no less care. In fact, the coordinated efforts of a team of specialists under the care of a general practitioner generally will provide the best outcome.

> **ONE OF THE SERVICES WE CREATED ENABLES INVESTORS TO RECEIVE CONTINUOUS MONITORING OF THEIR INVESTMENT ACTIVITY, TO HELP PREVENT FRAUD, TRACK PERFORMANCE, AND EXPOSE FEES, COMMISSIONS, AND ONGOING CHARGES.**

Honesty is a two-way street

An investor expects honesty. So does a broker or advisor. I've observed an interesting phenomenon in the Industry: brokers and advisors think they know everything about their clients; investors don't want their broker/advisor to know everything about their accounts and investments. There's a fickle game of cat and mouse.

Investors hold back on telling their broker/advisor all their information for many reasons. They don't want to be told or sold; they have another trusted relationship; they don't want to upset their current broker; they work with a family member; they have separate money from their spouse; they just don't trust their broker or advisor.

Yet, a broker is obligated to recommend investments and strategies that are suitable, given an investor's TOTAL financial situation. An advisor has a fiduciary obligation to do the same.

When investors hold back, they compromise their broker/advisor's ability to properly be of service. They create a false set of facts which is then used by a broker/advisor to provide recommendations.

I've seen incredibly talented financial professionals dedicate hours upon hours of time to brainstorm and create hugely beneficial financial plans and strategies for investors. I've seen investors begrudgingly dedicate just a little time and halfheartedly volunteer partial information to their broker/advisor. Garbage in; garbage out.

If you spend a lot of time planning your vacation, you'll probably enjoy it.

If you spend a lot of time planning your financial future, you'll probably enjoy that, too.

If you can't be honest with your broker, you need a new broker. If you don't want to be honest with your advisor, don't unreasonably expect your investment goals to be fulfilled.

Please don't hold the Industry's general misconduct against all financial professionals. Please don't blame all brokers and advisors for the rogue misconduct of a few.

There are some really good and really honest financial advisors out there. It's a two-way-street. If you find a really good advisor, give them *all* your information. You don't have to give them all your accounts.

But give them all your information, so they can honestly do their best to help you.

If you want independent monitoring of your current broker/advisor, or access to a network of pre-screened financial professionals, or access to a Solutions Center that lets you anonymously request proposals for services from advisors that compete for your business, please visit: www.investorprotector.com.

How Safe is Your Money?

While the Industry can't entirely prevent fraud and although the arbitration to recover losses from broker misconduct is weak and conflicted, there are some forms of protection in the event of a catastrophic event.

Brokerage Accounts

Securities Investor Protection Corporation

From Wikipedia, the free encyclopedia:

The **Securities Investor Protection Corporation** (**SIPC** /ˈsɪpɪk/) is a federally mandated, non-profit, member-funded, United States corporation created under the Securities Investor Protection Act (SIPA) of 1970.[1] It is a Self-regulatory organization (SRO) which mandates membership by most US-registered broker-dealers. "The SIPC fund, which constitutes an insurance program... is designed to protect the customers of brokers or dealers subject to the SIPA from loss in case of financial failure of the member. The fund is supported by assessments upon its members. If the fund should become inadequate, the SIPA authorizes borrowing against the U.S. Treasury. An analogy could be made to the role of the Federal Deposit Insurance Corporation (FDIC) in the banking industry."[2]

SIPC is required to report to, and be overseen by, the Securities and Exchange Commission. "Pursuant to SIPA, the Commission also has delegated authority to conduct inspections of SIPC, review SIPC annual reports, and approve SIPC's bylaws, rules, and any amendments to the bylaws and rules."[3] As the SIPC states on its website, "Though created by the Securities Investor Protection Act (15 U.S.C. § 78aaa et seq., as amended), SIPC is neither a government agency nor a regulatory authority. It is a nonprofit, membership corporation, funded by its member securities broker-dealers."[4]

The SIPC serves two primary roles in the event that a broker-dealer fails. First, the SIPC acts to organize the distribution of customer cash and securities to investors. Second, to the extent a customer's cash and/or securities are unavailable, the SIPC provides insurance coverage up to $500,000 of the customer's net equity balance, including up to $250,000 in cash.[4][9] In most cases where a brokerage firm has failed or is on the brink of failure, SIPC first seeks to transfer customer accounts to another brokerage firm. Should that process fail, the insolvent firm will be liquidated.[2] In order to state a claim, the investor is required to show that their economic loss arose because of the insolvency of their broker-dealer and not because of fraud,[10] misrepresentation,[11] or bad investment decisions. In certain circumstances, securities or cash may not exist in full based upon a customer's statement. In this case, protection is also extended to investors whose "securities may have been lost, improperly hypothecated, misappropriated, never purchased, or even stolen".[12]

While customers' cash and most types of securities – such as notes, stocks, bonds and certificates of deposit – are protected, other items such as commodity or futures contracts are not covered. Investment contracts, certificates of interest, participations in profit-sharing agreements, and oil, gas, or mineral royalties or leases are not covered unless registered with the Securities and Exchange Commission.[13]

SIPC does not protect against market fluctuations or changes in market value. It does not protect against losses in the securities markets, identity theft, or other 3rd-party fraud.[15] Unlike the FDIC, SIPC also does not provide protection where there are claims against solvent brokers or dealers.[16] It provides a form of protection for investors against losses that arise when broker-dealers, with whom they are doing business, become insolvent.[17] Claims against solvent brokers and dealers are typically managed by the securities' industry SROs: the Financial Industry Regulatory Authority (FINRA) and the Commodity Futures Trading Commission (CFTC).

Inasmuch as SIPC does not insure the underlying value of the financial asset it protects, investors bear the risk of the market. In addition, investors also bear any losses of account value that exceed the current amount of SIPC protection, namely $500,000 for securities. For example, if an investor buys 100 shares of XYZ company from a brokerage firm and the firm declares bankruptcy or merges with another, the 100 shares of XYZ still *belong* to the investor and should be recoverable. However, if the value of XYZ declines, SIPC does not insure the difference. In other words, the $500,000 limit is to protect against broker malfeasance, not poor investment decisions and changes in the market value of securities. In addition, SIPC may protect investors against unauthorized trades in their account, while the failure to execute a trade is not covered. Again, this only pertains to an insolvent broker or dealer.

1. Title 15 U.S.C. §78aaa et seq., as amended

2. "SIPA. Securities Investor Protection Act". United States Courts. Retrieved 2013-12-12.

3. SEC, "SEC's Oversight of the Securities Investor Protection Corporation's Activities" (Mar. 30, 2011), p. 4. Title 15 U.S.C. §78ccc-ggg, et seq.

4. "www.sipc.org/brochure". Sipc.org. Retrieved 2011-03-12.

5. "Richard Nixon. Statement on Signing the Securities Investor Protection Act of 1970. December 30, 1970". University of California at Santa Barbara. Retrieved 2013-12-22.

6. Thomas W. Joo, Who Watches the Watchers? The Securities Investors Protection Act, Investor Confidence, and the Subsidization of Failure, 71 S. CAL. L. REV. 1071, 1077; H.R. Rep. No. 92-1519

7. Guttman, Egon (Summer 1980). "TOWARD THE UNCERTIFICATED SECURITY: A CONGRESSIONAL LEAD FOR STATES TO FOLLOW". *WASHINGTON AND LEE LAW REVIEW.* XXXVII (3): 717–38.

8. S.Rep.No 91-1218, at 2

9. Originally SIPC protection was limited to $50,000 for securities. SIPA was amended in 1978 and raised the

securities' protection to $500,000, where it remains today. Dodd-Frank increased the cash protection to $250,000 in 2010

10. Securities' and Exchange Commission v. S.J. Salmon & Co., Inc., 375 F.Supp.867 (S.D.N.Y., 1974).

11. In re Bell & Beckwith, 124 B.R. 35 (Bankr. N.D. Ohio 1990).

12. S. Rep. No. 95-763 (1978), as reprinted in 1978 U.S.C.C.A.N. 764, 765; H.R. Rep. 95-746 at 21 (1977) |title=SIPC Chairman Owens in reports to House and Senate

13. "www.sipc.org/covers". Sipc.org. Retrieved 2011-03-12.

14. "financecareers.com". Financecareers.about.com. 2010-06-14. Retrieved 2011-03-12.

15. "Brokerage Identity Theft Warning". SIPC. 2003-12-11. Retrieved 2011-03-12.

16. "www.sipc.org/notfdic". Sipc.org. Retrieved 2011-03-12.

17. 1970 U.S.C.C.A.N. 5254, 5255 H.R. REP.No.91-1613

18. For a general discussion, see Steven Lessard, E.U. RE-HYPOTHOCATION AND LEHMAN BROTHERS BANKRUPTCY: CHANGES THAT MUST BE MADE TO THE MIFID, Appearing in Folsom, Gordon, Spangle, INTERNATIONAL BUSINESS TRANSACTIONS PRACTITIONERS TREATISE (2010 Treatise Supplement)

19. "Madoff Recovery Initiative Claims Status". Madoff Trustee/Baker & Hostetler. Retrieved 2013-10-12.

20. "www.sipc.org/q7". Sipc.org. Retrieved 2011-03-12.

Source: Wikipedia.
http://en.wikipedia.org/wiki/Securities_Investor_Protection_Corpo ration

For additional information, visit: http://www.sipc.org/

Bank Accounts

Federal Deposit Insurance Corporation

From Wikipedia, the free encyclopedia:

The **Federal Deposit Insurance Corporation (FDIC)** is a United States government corporation operating as an independent agency created by the Banking Act of 1933. As of January 2013, it provides deposit insurance guaranteeing the safety of a depositor's accounts in member banks up to $250,000 for each deposit ownership category in each insured bank. As of September 30, 2012, the FDIC insured deposits at 7,181 institutions. The FDIC also examines and supervises certain financial institutions for safety and soundness, performs certain consumer-protection functions, and manages banks in receiverships (failed banks). The FDIC receives no congressional appropriations—it is funded by premiums that banks and thrift institutions pay for deposit insurance coverage and from earnings on investments in U.S. Treasury securities.

The FDIC does not provide deposit insurance for credit unions. Most credit unions are insured by the National Credit Union Administration (NCUA); some state-chartered credit unions are privately insured.

Insured institutions are required to place signs at their place of business stating that "deposits are backed by the full faith and credit of the United States Government." Since the start of FDIC insurance on January 1, 1934, no depositor has lost any insured funds as a result of a failure.

Each ownership category of a depositor's money is insured separately up to the insurance limit, and separately at each bank. Thus a depositor with $250,000 in each of three ownership categories at each of two banks would have six different insurance limits of $250,000, for total insurance coverage of 6 × $250,000 = $1,500,000. The distinct ownership categories are:

- Single accounts (accounts not falling into any other category)
- Certain retirement accounts (including Individual Retirement Accounts (IRAs))
- Joint accounts (accounts with more than one owner with equal rights to withdraw)
- Revocable trust accounts (containing the words "Payable on death", "In trust for", etc.)
- Irrevocable trust accounts
- Employee Benefit Plan accounts (deposits of a pension plan)
- Corporation/Partnership/Unincorporated Association accounts
- Government accounts

All amounts that a particular depositor has in accounts in any particular ownership category at a particular bank are added together and are insured up to $250,000.

For joint accounts, each co-owner is assumed (unless the account specifically states otherwise) to own the same fraction of the account as does each other co-owner (even though each co-owner may be eligible to withdraw all funds from the account). Thus if three people jointly own a $750,000 account, the entire account balance is insured because each depositor's $250,000 share of the account is insured.

The owner of a revocable trust account is generally insured up to $250,000 for each unique beneficiary (subject to special rules if there are more than five of them). Thus if there is a single owner of an account that is specified as in trust for (payable on death to, etc.) three different beneficiaries, the funds in the account are insured up to $750,000.

For additional information, visit: http://www.fdic.gov/

Insurance Policies & Annuities

National Organization of Life and Health Insurance Guaranty Associations

From Wikipedia, the free encyclopedia:

The **National Organization of Life and Health Insurance Guaranty Associations**[1] (often abbreviated NOLHGA) is a voluntary, U.S. association made up of the life and health insurance guaranty associations of all 50 states and the District of Columbia. NOLHGA was founded in 1983 to coordinate the efforts of state guaranty associations to provide protection to policyholders when their multi-state life or health insurance company becomes insolvent.[2] The organization is based in Herndon, Virginia.

When an insurance company reports to its state insurance regulator that it is in financial trouble, the state will first attempt to assist the company back toward financial stability. If the state insurance department determines the company cannot be saved, then the insurance commissioner asks the state court to order the liquidation of the company.[3] Once the order to liquidate a company that operates in multiple states is handed down, NOLHGA, on behalf of affected member state guaranty associations, assembles a task force of affected guaranty associations to analyze the company's commitments to policyholders. Each affected state guaranty association pays out claims to the insurance company's policyholders in the state; in some instances, the associations arrange for policies to be transferred to a financially sound insurer.[2] Each state guaranty association is governed by state law; most associations cover up to at least $300,000 for life insurance death benefits, $100,000 in cash surrender value for life insurance, $250,000 in withdrawal and cash values for annuities, and $100,000 in health insurance policy benefits.[4][5]

1. NOLHGA web site, retrieved September 16, 2008

2. "About Us". Herndon, VA: National Organization of Life and Health Insurance Guaranty Associations. Retrieved 2009-11-16.

3. "Policyholder Information". National Organization of Life and Health Insurance Guaranty Associations. Retrieved 2009-11-16.

4. "The Insolvency Process". National Organization of Life and Health Insurance Guaranty Associations. Retrieved 2009-11-16.

5. Chizoba, Morah. "Investopedia Q&A". Investopedia.com. Retrieved 2009-11-16.

For additional information, visit:

http://www.nolhga.com/aboutnolhga/main.cfm/location/whatisnolhga

Fixing the Failed System

The system fails because the Industry's system of self-regulation, oversight, and supervision is flawed and conflicted. Broker-dealers are tasked with supervising the brokers that make them money. Money conflicts and corrupts the system.

It's not that the Industry is unregulated. It's one of the most highly regulated businesses in existence. It's my contention that this highly regulated Industry is structurally flawed and horribly mismanaged. Many rules don't make any sense while others are completely reasonable. In my opinion, the system breaks down because:

1. Regulators don't issue clear rules with specific guidelines – instead, they issue general rules and leave it up to each firm to develop policies to comply with each rule, and

2. Self-regulation leaves administration, application, and enforcement of the rules and regulations up to a private conflicted police force that works for the Industry and not for investors.

Yet, fixing the "Fix" is simple. The Industry should issue specific rules with clear guidance and supervisory requirements. All firms should be required to apply rules and regulations on a uniform basis. Firms should no longer be permitted or required to develop their own policies. While a firm may elect to adopt policies that are stricter than any published rule or regulation, there must be a baseline set of clear rules and regulations that apply uniformly for all firms. The Industry can't define its own policies and pick and choose how to interpret or when to enforce any policy, rule, or regulation.

For example, the Industry should create a standardized commission system that contemplates various transactions in different securities. There should be a clearly defined maximum allowable commission per transaction and/or fee per account. The Industry should remove subjectivity. It should not be up to a broker or a firm to determine "fair and reasonable." Firms and brokers can compete by offering lower commissions and/or better services. However, any charge in excess of the Industry regulated maximum would be a clear violation – with consequences.

As for sales practices, when each sale is subject to a subjective determination of individual suitability, you will continue to have massive problems. There are too many products, too many clients, too many transactions to perform subjective suitability tests honestly and accurately. There must be a systematic basis that evaluates sales for suitability.

For example, when a security is filed and registered with the SEC, the Industry should require the issuer to define – using a numeric score system:

1. Appropriate investor types
    a. Institutions versus individuals
        i. Different categories of investors should be defined
        ii. Specific scores should indicate appropriate investors for a given product, i.e. a 1 indicates a product is appropriate for any retail investor whereas a 5 indicates a product is only appropriate for a large sophisticated institution.
2. Suitability based on risk and liquidity
    a. Risk: define the expected volatility of each product and indicate the prospective range of returns (positive and negative) over various time frames, i.e. 1, 3, 5 and 10 year periods
    b. Liquidity: Clearly delineate liquid versus illiquid, and rank the various of degrees of liquidity in between, i.e. stocks with high trading volumes have a liquidity score of 1 whereas a variable

annuity has a score of 3 and an illiquid alternative investment has a score of 5.

For product sales and account types that utilize appropriately scored products with appropriate investors, there would be a presumption of suitability. While this might shock the Industry and remove the "romance" from a broker's job of picking the right product for each investor, the reality is that less confusion and more clarity for investors will restore trust and faith in the Industry.

There will always be some subjective use of certain products with certain investors. These transactions can be better monitored once they are distinguished from systematically defined suitable transactions with appropriate investors.

Another major change would be to transition from self-regulation to self-supervision – with mandatory reporting. Each firm should be required to supervise all business activity, according to specific criteria, with mandatory reporting to the regulators of any violations of clearly defined Industry rules. While the Industry has determined that a supervisor can't review or approve his or her own business, regulators have somehow determined that a firm *can* supervise the brokers that make the firm money. This conflict *must* be eliminated. The resolution *must* be systematic supervision with automated reporting.

The Industry has deployed massive servers and supercomputers, to take advantage of the smallest pricing errors. High-frequency traders use incredible system resources to trade enormous values and volumes of securities for the smallest price differentials. The Industry needs to dedicate the same resources to investor protection as it does for private profit.

If the Industry clearly defines maximum commission schedules, numerically scores securities based on risk and liquidity, and promulgates appropriate investor types for various security scores, there would be a quantifiable, measurable framework for Industry supervision. The

Industry could require each firm to systematically and regularly review transactions and accounts and require mandatory reporting of any exceptions. Remove subjectivity and the inherent internal conflicts of interests.

Finally, the Industry's fundamental financial conflicts of interest have to be resolved. Regulation and enforcement have to be separated from funding and finances. Supervision has to be applied uniformly. If a broker generates $1 dollar or $1,000,000 of revenue, the same rules and regulations apply. Yet, a firm will go out of its way to protect a $1,000,000 broker. The Industry will go out of its way to protect a multi-billion-a-year firm that pays dues, fines, and elects Industry members. Money corrupts the regulatory structure, along with the creation and enforcement of rules and regulations.

All Industry funding should come from transaction and account fees paid by investors who should expect proper protection that they pay for, based on the number of transactions and asset size of their accounts. All fines should go into a fund for the benefit of harmed investors instead of to FINRA or the SEC.

The SEC can create specific and clear rules and regulations (like Congress). FINRA can be tasked with enforcement (like the police). Most important, there must be accountability and consequences. If a broker steals or commits fraud, they should be tried and – if guilty – go straight to jail. No more settlements without admitting or denying guilt. Chief Executives, Chief Compliance Officers, and Chief Supervisory officers must be held accountable. The Industry's system of blaming the little guy has to stop. If there are consequences at the top, there will be change. I can't recall the last time a broker-dealer, bank, or insurance company CEO was held accountable or sentenced to jail for a financial violation.

Hell, if James, "Jamie" Dimon, the current President, Chairman, and Chief Executive Officer of J.P. Morgan Chase keeps writing billion dollar checks for securities law violations, he might soon be President of the United

States. While the violations he's settled have been massive, his popularity with Wall Street only seems to grow. There is something wrong here.

Finally, I do need to throw a bone to my former broker and advisor colleagues and friends. Investing does involve risk. We're a litigious society. While there are far too many unscrupulous financial predators who take advantage of unsuspecting investors, there are also investors who are scammers. I've seen clients who knew exactly what they were doing. They deliberately took risks and hoped for the best. When things didn't work out and they incurred a loss, they were quick to sue their broker.

I'd propose that, if a broker sells an appropriate product to an appropriate investor with all appropriate representations and communication, there should be a safe harbor for the broker against frivolous claims. Investments don't always work out. Markets sometimes crash. Governments change. World crises occur. There will be losses.

If a broker did something wrong, they should pay. However, if and when a loss occurs because of a wholesale industry or market problem that's way outside the control and scope of any individual broker or advisor's conduct, there must be recognition, understanding, and exemption from personal and professional liability.

Individual brokers didn't create the tech bubble, the housing crises, or manufacture fraudulent mortgage backed securities with swaps and derivatives. The Industry and certain firms did. The Industry must be accountable. Certain firms and certain individuals at these firms must be accountable. There's a difference between general broker misconduct, specific acts by rogue brokers and fraudsters, and deliberate acts by Industry firms and executives. There must be honesty, accountability, and enforcement that protects investors against these various levels of misconduct.

Clearly-defined rules, systematic supervision, and no financial conflicts can start to fix the "Fix."

Top Ways to Protect Yourself

Until the Industry fixes the "Fix," here are some suggestions to help you protect yourself:

1. Do some research
   a. Check out the individual's credentials, experience, references
      i. Brokercheck for registered reps,
      ii. IAPD for advisors,
      iii. State insurance commission for planners/life insurance agents

   If you want help looking up your broker or advisor, visit www.investorprotector.com

   b. Check out the individual's firm (use above, plus):
      i. Years in business
      ii. Background and tenure of current management

2. Ask your broker/advisor these questions:
   a. How are you paid: commissions, fees, or both?
   b. How much do you get paid?
   c. Are the products you recommend appropriate for my goals and my objectives?
   d. Can I access my funds?
   e. Are there charges, fees, or penalties for any withdrawals?
   f. Can I lose money? How much?
   g. Who is the custodian for my funds?
   h. Who prepares my account statement?
      i. Is this statement prepared by a reputable custodian?
      ii. How often will I get a statement?

3. Request proposals in writing, via mail or email.

4. Read everything. Ask questions.

5. Get a second opinion.

6. Never sign blank forms.

7. Only make checks payable or wire funds to a well-known established institution.

    a. Never make payment to a business/corporate entity.

8. Get Read and Review Statements and Confirms.

    a. Ask for explanations of any significant changes in account value (up or down).

    b. Ask for explanations of any transactions.

        i. Was there a gain or loss – and how much?

9. Track performance against personal benchmarks and general market averages.

10. Independently monitor and review your accounts and investments, to detect and protect yourself from:

    a. Fraud

    b. Excessive fees

    c. Unnecessary transactions

    d. Hidden product costs

    e. Bad investments

    f. Unsuitable asset allocations

    g. Concentrated positions

    h. Low balances/overdraft/account fees

    i. High balances that exceed available account insurance

    j. Investment mismanagement

    k. Rogue brokers

    l. Bad firms

    m. No planning

n. Bad planning

o. Missed anniversary dates

p. Investment maturity dates

q. Undetected changes in value

With InvestorProtector™, you can connect virtually any account and protect your investments with independent monitoring and automated change alerts.

Taking control over your financial well-being and protecting your investments has never been easier.

Try www.investorprotector.com for free.

If you can't connect an account to www.investorprotector.com, it could be a red flag.

Protection from The Coming Storms

1. Rising interest rates:

Interest rates have steadily declined from an all-time high of 20%, in May of 1981, to 0.25% in December of 2008. Interest rates in the United States and around the world are at record lows.

At the same time, massive government stimulus has been underway across the globe. The housing bubble in the US almost collapsed financial systems here and abroad. The adoption of a common Euro currency without common Euro monetary and fiscal policies created and then revealed massive economic imbalances between Euro countries. Some countries have required massive bailouts while other defaulted on Sovereign debt. Multiple governments, including the US, have pursued expansionary monetary policies to keep rates low to support faltering economies and sustain unsustainable debt levels. A massive amount of liquidity has been pumped into the global economy in the hope that a rising tide of money will lift economic recovery. In short, many countries have tried to solve excessive borrowing with even more loans. Other countries have tried to solve weak economies by printing more money. Instead of creating more jobs by investing in infrastructure and education, central banks have tried to wash away problems with excessive liquidity.

There will be a price to pay for all the stimulus. Economies will recover. All the liquidity that was pumped into the global system will need to be absorbed. Rates may stay low for a while. Eventually, higher prices and higher interest rates will emerge, to soak up massive debts. For those with cash, higher rates will bring higher returns. For those with debt, higher rates will bring crushing payments.

The seeds have been sown for the next cycle of boom and bust. What should investors do? Call a financial advisor who can help you:

a. Invest in short-term bonds which have less risk from rising rates than long-term bonds.

b. Buy individual bonds which have a specific maturity date at which principal will be returned, instead of Mutual Funds or Exchange Traded Funds, which don't have any maturity date for the return of principal.

c. Consider high yield bonds, which add a premium for credit risk that can work to help offset the negative impact of rising rates on bond prices.

d. Invest in stocks that pay dividends

Historically, rising rates haven't always been bad. They generally indicate that the economy is robust, which means businesses can earn more and stock prices can rise.

2. Aging population & Longer Life expectancy:

The baby boomers are retiring in record numbers. With better medicine and healthier lifestyles, people are living longer. Longer lives mean more time in retirement. Those retirement years need to be sustained and enjoyed. This takes money. The longer someone is retired, the more money they'll need. Retirement income and living expenses must be provided by investment earnings, asset depletion, or government payments. Yes, this is an entitlements discussion.

For all the years individuals have paid into Social Security and Medicare, there is an expectation of receiving the promised benefits. Longer life spans mean longer payment demands from Social Security. Healthier lives don't mean lower medical payments – in fact, demands on Medicare may be higher, since longevity often means more health issues for longer periods of time. At present, Medicare is expected to run out of funds by 2026 and Social Security will be broke by 2033. Something must be done.

We've seen what happens in other countries with unsustainable government entitlement programs: the elderly and sick simply see income payments and medical reimbursements cut. The cuts are severe. Like many cancer treatments, the potential cure can also kill the patient. Early diagnosis is key; but preventative care is critical. There are more prospective solutions today than there will be tomorrow. The medicine will be bitter, either way; but today there may be a cure – tomorrow there will be hospice. That's the unfortunate reality.

What can be done? First, the government needs to stop waste and fraud: you can't pay people who actually *can* work to not work. A lifetime of not working in return for a lifetime of government payments is unsustainable: especially for individuals who physically and mentally can work or be of service or volunteer in some capacity. In short, the definition of a physical or mental disability must be more narrowly defined. Second, a system that rewards people for not working and having more children is fundamentally flawed. Pardon any perceived lack of social, moral, religious, racial, or political sensitivity, but a system that provides higher payments to not work or to have more kids is simply wrong. For those who legitimately need, there should be a safety net. For those who simply take, there should not be a welcome mat.

To our government that administers these entitlement programs, there must be better administration that more clearly defines and helps those who really need versus those who simply want. This is not a social experiment. I'm not a politician looking for votes. I'm addressing a fiscal reality. Better administration can reduce waste and fraud.

Next, when Government promises are kept and waste and fraud are eliminated, there should be tax incentives to help the government entitlement programs. To put it simply, the government should provide current and future income tax credits for those who don't use their promised benefits. In addition, there should also be significant incentives for those who make supplemental contributions to Social Security or Medicare. If the wealthy don't need the money, give them a tax credit for *not* taking Social Security or Medicare payments. In addition, just like there are current and future tax deductions for charitable contributions, make supplemental contributions to Social Security and Medicare tax deductible. Create a real incentive for the wealthy to contribute into the "system" and then see how this country can solve its own problem.

Stop waste and fraud; improve administration to reduce the social, racial, religious, political overtones; create economic incentives for those who don't use entitlements; and provide even greater incentives for those who make supplemental contributions into the entitlement system. I believe this country can help repair its own social system. Until the government gets its act together and does its part, here's what *you* can do, to protect yourself from longevity and health risk:

a. Life insurance enables you to ensure adequate funds will be available for the living, housing, and education needs of your dependents and beneficiaries.

b. Disability insurance enables you to protect your income from a health risk that impairs your ability to generate income.

c. Long-term care insurance on yourself or your parents can provide coverage for and protect assets from depletion from medical expenses.

d. Annuities can turn limited funds into a lifetime income stream which can protect you from running out of money if you live a long healthy life – but the income payments may be fixed and inflexible.

I don't sell insurance. I used to. I know why it's bought, versus why it's sold. Simply put, it's much cheaper and effective to share the collective risk of many than it is to take on the entire individual risk of death, disability, or extended health care costs.

That said, either you believe in insurance or you don't. I'm not here to convince you. However, if someone is pitching all the extra benefits of life insurance or annuities – such as tax-free retirement income, or the best way to save, or showing how you can turn your IRA into ten times its current value – you might want to enjoy the free meal and run like hell....

3. The Right Way to Invest: Modern Portfolio Theory and Globalization.

In the early part of my career, the latest and greatest investment strategy was a Nobel Prize-Winning approach called Modern Portfolio Theory. A landmark study that analyzed the performance differences between large pools of invested funds identified the statistical determinants of performance. In plain English, the study sought to explain why some investors had better performance than others. The conclusion was elegantly simple: asset allocation was the single greatest determinant of performance. If you owned a lot of stocks that went up, you had good performance.

Yep, a Nobel Prize was awarded for that.

In actuality, the *real* work was more sophisticated. Since these investors allocated to several asset classes, such as different types of stocks (large cap growth, small cap value, emerging markets, etc.) and different types of bonds (government, corporate, high yield, international debt, etc.), the study identified performance relationships between these different asset classes. The study went deeper than simply concluding that stocks perform differently than bonds. The groundbreaking conclusion was that not all stocks went up or down at the same time and not all bonds went up or down at the same time.

In studying the long-term behavior of different types of stocks and bonds, a long-term performance relationship could be calculated between various asset classes. Consequently, if you could calculate the historical relationship between Large Cap Growth Stocks and Small Cap Value stocks, you could theoretically calculate the expected performance of different asset allocations (combinations) of these asset classes. With data and supercomputers, humans could now calculate expected performance and volatility (risk). A well-studied financial professional, with the help of a computer and some equations, could take all the historical data for dozens of different asset classes and calculate the expected returns of different portfolio strategies. If an investor needed to achieve a certain rate of return, Modern Portfolio Theory could calculate the asset allocation that could theoretically achieve that return – with the lowest risk.

Investing was now a science. Until it wasn't.

So – what happened? It's simple: the road ahead changed. Using historical data is inherently flawed – unless history repeats exactly. You cannot drive on a windy road by looking in the rear view mirror. The historical relationships between asset classes were known for prior periods. It *cannot* be known for future periods. Modern Portfolio Theory was not a crystal ball. It was a better mousetrap to create an educated guess that a certain asset allocation *might* deliver a certain result *if* all things going forward were comparable to all things prior. While historical events tend to repeat, the combinations of geo-political, economic, social, and climate events – just to name a few – are never the same across the globe. Modern Portfolio Theory wasn't wrong. It was misapplied going forward to a changing world.

Globalization of travel, trade, economic integration, social integration, and the World Wide Web have changed the relationships between financial markets and economies. In the past, an economic catastrophe in Hong Kong or India barely affected the US. Today, a shock over there causes immediate impact here – and vice versa. The current relationship between asset classes is much more related than it was, way back in 1974 through 1983, when the groundbreaking Nobel Prize Winning analysis of investment returns was studied. If anyone thinks the world today is the same as it was almost 40 years ago, then please stop reading.

Financial markets and world economies are much more connected today than ever before. The relationships between asset classes today are much different than it was 10 years ago – let alone 20, or 30, or 40 years ago. Using Modern Portfolio Theory is like picking the ultimate buy-and-hold strategy and hoping relationships are the same (they aren't) and also hoping that history will repeat (it won't, not exactly). So – that's what happened to Modern Portfolio Theory. It stopped being so modern.

Today, asset allocation and diversification still matter; in fact, they're critical components to any portfolio strategy. Passive management (indexing) versus active management are both viable. I believe it's harder to consistently add value with active management of large stocks where almost all information is well known and widely disseminated. Niche markets, specific sectors, certain foreign economies, special situations, private transactions, etc. create better opportunities for an active manager or broker to add value. These investments also tend to carry more risk. Tactical management – where an equity manager can go to cash during volatile times or during periods of perceived risk – has become more common in modern times.

What does this all mean for you? For every investor, a periodic portfolio review is a necessity. For most, a portfolio strategy update may be in order. Times have changed. Markets are different. The same investments that worked well before may carry different potential risks and returns going forward. There are many credible sources offering complimentary portfolio reviews. Don't be afraid to get a second opinion. Or a third. Ask questions, seek information, contemplate a change.

You may not need or want to do anything, but you also might be able to lower fees, reduce risk, or improve potential return. It might be time to rebalance your portfolio, to take some gains or harvest losses, to offset taxable events. Markets have advanced lately; it might be time to reduce equity exposure or lower your interest risk by shortening fixed income investments and maturities.

You worked hard for your money. Protect it and make it work for you.

4. Frankenstein

You have many more choices today than ever before. Full service large brand name firms, bank and brokerage powerhouses, do-it-yourself discount brokers, registered representatives (brokers), registered investment advisors (advisors), certified financial planners, independent brokers, insurance agents, and more. Forget the names. The investment products tend to be the same. The rules and regulations are the same. The services are different. A fee-only advisor will avoid certain products. A broker can only sell commissionable products. A Web-based asset manager may be great for money management, while a discount broker might be great for low-cost transaction execution, but both might completely ignore your total financial well-being (taxes, insurance, budgeting, planning, college funding, retirement planning, etc.).

Over time, over many years, over various stages of your life, your needs will change. Your professional advisors will change, too. This is a process. Like a plane that takes off from New York and flies to California, the route and flight plan is known, but there are thousands of adjustments along the way. The airline has the advantage, however. It sold tickets to a scheduled flight that has to take off on time. Individuals procrastinate. Most spend more time planning a vacation than they do their financial future.

Time and time again, I've seen investors avoid dedicating time to their finances. Life is busy. Schedules are hectic. The result can be catastrophic. After waiting too long, the burden of playing catch-up can be too great. Jumping in wholeheartedly can lead to rash decisions at one moment in time that might not work out too well going forward.

Even worse is the common haphazard approach to personal finance: "I saw something interesting on TV, heard something good at work, read a great article, bought this, opened that account, responded to this offer or that..." I call it the Frankenstein portfolio. Bits and pieces assembled together to hopefully make something better than a walking corpse with "abbey normal's" brain. I've worked with far too many investors who had multiple accounts, investments, and policies at multiple institutions. They acquired or assembled bits and pieces of a plan and were hoping for the best.

You don't have to be afraid of monsters. You can take control – but only if you put in a little time and effort. Spending time to organize and develop a plan for your current and future financial situation can be immensely worthwhile. It doesn't mean you can retire early and buy a vineyard. You might be able to buy the dream car but not the boat. But planning, knowing, and doing are keys to success.

You can do it yourself. You can do it with guidance. You can completely turn it over for "professional" management. Just do it.

At www.investorprotector.com, we've created easy-to-use systems that will help you organize your financial life. We provide independent monitoring, to help you protect yourself from yourself or others. You can use interactive and robust budgeting and planning tools, to develop strategies for your present and for your future. You can point and click to see the potential impact of various strategies on your financial situation. You can use our 1-click Solutions Center to request analysis, guidance, and proposals – on a confidential basis – without any sales pressure or solicitation.

We can make all the tools available to you. It's up to you to use them. It's time to turn Frankenstein into the Statue of David. Convert your financial monster into your personal masterpiece.

Good luck.

www.investorprotector.com

With InvestorProtector™, you can connect virtually any account and protect your investments with independent monitoring and automated change alerts.

Taking control over your financial well-being and protecting your investments has never been easier.

Try www.investorprotector.com for free.

About the Author

David Levine earned his B.A degree in Economics & English from The University of Pennsylvania and his M.B.A degree in Finance from New York University's Stern School of Business.

He began his professional career at Chase Manhattan Bank and worked at Bankers Trust Company – The Private Bank. David worked at Zweig/Avatar Capital Management, an SEC Registered Investment Advisor with more than $5 billion in assets under management, and he helped set up the Investment Advisory division of Nathan & Lewis Securities, an independent broker-dealer that was successfully sold to New England Financial – a division of MetLife.

David has been licensed as a general securities representative, a registered principal, investment advisor, and insurance agent for Life, Health, Variable, Fixed, and Equity Indexed Annuities. David also successfully developed and licensed Retirement Planning software to a top 10 Mutual Fund Company.

Prior to founding InvestorProtector, David was the National Sales Manager for one of the financial services industry's fastest growing independent broker-dealers which, at its peak, had over 1,000 registered representatives and generated over $150 million in annual revenue. Most recently, David was the Director of Business Development for the broker-dealer and registered investment advisor divisions of a publicly traded financial services firm. David  left the financial services industry behind to help protect investors going forward.

As a former financial services executive who has seen more products, transactions, and investment strategies than most investors will see in a lifetime, David launched www.investorprotector.com™. His vision is to combine leading technology with proprietary services, to help investors protect their investments and life savings.

InvestorProtector
Get Connected. Be Protected.